Franny Singer was born in Leicester and attended University College, London, where she gained her degree in English. Her jobs have included waitress, ice-cream seller, assistant to a Hollywood film director – and professional cook. For this, her first cook book, she has researched and tested all the major makes of slow crock and, of course, tried them out in her kitchen.

Franny Singer's interests are languages, writing, photography and food, and she likes to keep physically and mentally fit by exercise and natural eating. She lives in North-West London.

Franny Singer

The Slow Crock Cook Book

MAYFLOWER
GRANADA PUBLISHING
London Toronto Sydney New York

Published by Granada Publishing Limited
in Mayflower Books 1978

ISBN 0 583 13040 2

A Mayflower Original
Copyright © Franny Singer 1978

Granada Publishing Limited
Frogmore, St Albans, Herts AL2 2NF
and
3 Upper James Street, London W1R 4BP
1221 Avenue of the Americas, New York, NY 10020, USA
117 York Street, Sydney, NSW 2000, Australia
100 Skyway Avenue, Toronto, Ontario, Canada M9W 3A6
Trio City, Coventry Street, Johannesburg 2001, South Africa
CML Centre, Queen & Wyndham, Auckland 1, New Zealand

Made and printed in Great Britain by
Cox & Wyman Ltd,
London, Reading and Fakenham
Set in Monotype Times Roman

Dedicated to
Stiv Zinga

Acknowledgements

Many thanks to Monica Slinn for her help with research and testing.

Contents

Introduction

We are becoming much more sensible about the way in which we cook. The electric casserole, the slow crock, the electric hay-box, the crockery chef, call it what you will, is a clever up-dating of one of the oldest and simplest means of cooking – slow simmering. Not only are you able to reduce your fuel bills by using much less electricity to cook food but slow simmering makes possible the adoption of raw ingredients that would be useless for any of the faster means of cooking. Buy a slow crock and you will use your oven less, your fuel bills will go down and your cooking improve dramatically.

This book is for those who are thinking of buying a slow crock, for those who have just bought one and wish to go a few steps beyond the advice given in the manufacturer's leaflet, and for those who are adventurous in their tastes and want to investigate how much the appliance can do. I am proposing to refer throughout to 'slow crocks' as this is the name that seems to have caught on with the public, though in fact I have tried out every appliance currently available in this country and each one seems to have been given a different name by the manufacturer. You can use this book with all types of appliance available. Many of the cooking methods and recipes can be used in ordinary casserole cooking, but there are subtle differences, so please read all of the book before lifting out some of the ideas and trying them in your (non-electric) casserole. In any case, any casserole dish will be cheaper to prepare with an electric casserole than with the conventional sort that you set on a rack in an oven or above a low heat on top of your range . . .

The slow crock first appeared in the United States in the early 1970s, but gradually people in other countries decided that this was a gimmick that not only made sense, but would last. A conventional earthenware casserole is surrounded with a low-power electric element and the whole thing encased in insulation. As a result, you have very controlled heating, with no more 'juice' going into the machine than is necessary to cook the food tenderly. When Americans started using their slow crocks they discovered all over again the supreme virtues of very slow cooking – meat doesn't become stringy and harden, juices remain where they should, in the food – and the long cooking times could be turned into a virtue. By just the simplest of calculations you can either start a meal off in the morning so as to have it ready when you return in the evening, or you can leave something cooking overnight, having prepared it just before you go to bed. Either way, you aren't faced with a last-minute panic of food preparation shortly before you want to eat! The great thing about very controlled slow cooking is that you can easily leave things to simmer gently on for a few hours beyond the allotted time and know that the food will not spoil.

I became hooked on slow crocks soon after they arrived in Britain. I can heartily urge them on any cook, however well-equipped the kitchen. More importantly, the slow crock means that you can almost make do without a conventional oven – the only limits are the size of the individual dish and the fact that very high heats (as you must have in certain sorts of baking) are impossible. Thus, for young single people in bedsits the slow crock is marvellous – it takes little space, is cheap to run, and doesn't put out unwanted cooking smells. The same reasons too make it ideal for old age pensioners – plus the fact that the slow crock is very safe and easy to use. Perhaps the nicest thing for me has been discovering a whole new type of cooking which I found fitted in easily with the rest of my life. In some cases it meant digging up half-forgotten methods and recipes, and in others I have tried to adapt and reinterpret favourite dishes, giving them a new twist as well as greater convenience and ease in preparation.

I began cooking fairly young. I loved inventing mysterious dishes I called 'combinations'. I would spend my free time in the kitchen mixing together any ingredients I could lay my hands on, just to see what sort of taste would happen. Today I produce (usually) far more palatable results, but you'll find some of the recipes here fairly unusual – they are there partly because friends have said nice things about them but also because I want you to believe that the slow crock has many, many possibilities!

1 HOW THE SLOW CROCK WORKS

The basic idea is that of a casserole, usually made of earthenware, surrounded by an element similar to that of an electric fire which heats up when electric current is passed through it. The element itself is completely enclosed

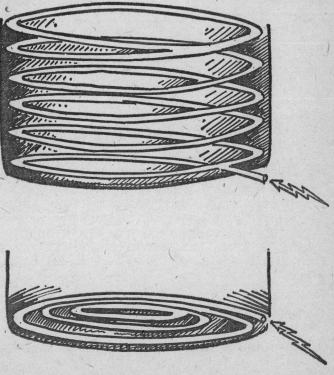

The heat in a slow crock comes from electric elements that are either wound round the side or placed on the base.

in a case which is usually made of a tough, resilient plastic, though it may at first sight (on some models) look like crockery. The outer casing should be insulated not only for electricity, so that you don't get a shock, but also for heat so that the heat of the element goes inside, to the food, and not outside, to the room. Insulation is almost as important a part of the construction of a good crockpot as anything else. For this reason, the construction of the lid, which is usually made of earthenware (though sometimes of heat-proof glass or even plastic), is important too. Not only should the lid fit fairly closely to prevent too much moisture in the form of steam from escaping, but it should also help to keep the heat in. Remember, hot air rises . . .

TYPES OF SLOW CROCK

All slow crocks work on this principle, but there are two different types on the market. With one sort you can actually lift out the earthenware casserole and separate it from the heating element and casing. With the other sort, you can't. The advantages of the 'lift-out' variety are not as great as may at first seem. In the first place, they need more electricity to keep them going and secondly there is no reason why a combined casserole and casing model should look unattractive on the table when you come to serve. But the 'lift-out' casserole can sometimes be placed under a grill to brown the topping. The integral model usually cannot. However, it is really a matter of preference and the other features that are offered.

SETTINGS AND TEMPERATURES

All slow crocks have a switch for LOW and HIGH heats. On the low setting a model that has casserole and casing com-bined would use about 70 watts. A 60-watt light bulb is the sort of power you would put in a lamp for a side-table. On

A removable slow crock can be taken from its heating case and washed separately.

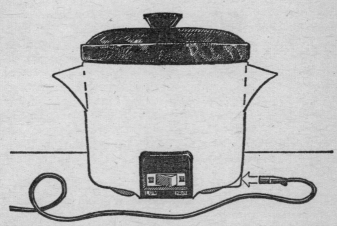

A typical non-removable slow crock – an all-in-one pot where the crockery liner is permanently attached to the heating case. In this model, notice that the cord is detachable and there are indicator lights to show that electricity is flowing.

the high setting you would be using between 120 and 150 watts (which corresponds to the size of bulb you'd put in a dark hall or a large room). On a 'lift-out' type the respective wattages will be almost twice these figures – say 100 watts or over on LOW and 200 watts or so on HIGH. A conventional electric oven may use something like 2500 watts or even more when set high, so you can see the difference. If the slow crock is pre-heated on HIGH for half an hour, the temperature of the air within the crock will reach 63°C (140°F) approximately. When food is added and the crock heated for a further half hour, the temperature reaches approximately 80°C (175°F). After 5–6 hours at the same HIGH setting the temperature reached will be approximately 98°C (200°F) – about the temperature of an electric oven on its lowest setting, and less than Gas Regulo ¼. But different makes of slow crock vary in power so you can check the temperature on your model by a simple test. Pour ½ litre (1 pt) cold water into the slow crock and heat on HIGH, testing the temperature after half an hour, one hour and 6 hours (an average cooking time). After 6 hours the water should be just simmering – just below the boil. Water boils at 100°C (212°F) so if your crock is a higher temperature on its HIGH setting the water will be boiling. Some electric cookers have a setting as low as 70°C (150°F), and some gas cookers a setting below ¼ which is simply called LOW; at these settings the ovens will be closer to the LOW setting of the slow crock which is around 82°C (175°F). Remember that the food in the crock will not be at these temperatures for it will take some time for the heat to penetrate the food, and this time will vary according to the nature of the food being cooked.

Do be careful about underpowered appliances – the difference of 10 or 20 watts heating power will make hardly any further dent in your electricity bills, but they may make all the difference to safety and speed. A temperature of 60°C (140°F) maintained for half an hour kills most bacteria but some bacteria can survive higher temperatures and longer cooling times. Some foods, particularly pork, must be thoroughly cooked if all the dangerous micro-organisms in the raw food are certain to be killed off. Some of the early American models gave their users stomach upsets because they were underpowered, and at least one British manufacturer, rather than run a similar risk, uprated one of their models after it had been on the market a short while. Nearly all models have a little indicator light to tell you that the appliance is on. If your model doesn't, you can tell by putting your hand on the outside casing after ten minutes or so, at which time it should be slightly warm. If you wish, you can always use one of those plugs with a built-in light or get a friendly do-it-yourselfer to put you a very low power neon indicator light on the connector cord. (If you do, the lamp should be connected in series on the N side of the cord – if you connect in parallel it merely tells you electricity is flowing from the plug and doesn't guarantee that it is also warming up the element.)

The comparative merits of the HIGH and LOW settings remain the only real mystery about the slow crock (and some manufacturers aren't all that helpful in their instruction books), so perhaps now is the time to explain. The simple answer is that it takes longer to reach the maximum (simmering) temperature on LOW than it does on HIGH. The way this can be applied practically is that one setting can be used instead of the other to increase or decrease cooking times respectively. LOW is approximately twice as long as HIGH.

However, there is another important difference and that is the effect of the setting on the food itself. For instance, you will find that meat cooks equally well on LOW as HIGH but that there is a difference, which is due to the temperature at which the meat is cooked, and you will notice the distinction between roasting and casseroling in the final taste and texture.

Is it safe to cook food at LOW temperatures? Some manufacturers recommend a pre-heating period on HIGH to boost the temperature of the slow crock as quickly as possible through the LOW temperature zone and other slow crocks have a higher wattage that reaches the 'safe cooking' temperature within a couple of hours. The so-called 'safe cooking' temperature is a safeguard against food that is slightly off in some way and it is really the responsibility of the cook to use fresh and wholesome food whenever cooking with whatever utensils – it is a universal rule of hygiene.

What difference does pre-heating make? Some manufacturers make specific recommendations as to when and how to pre-heat and these should always be followed. Pre-heating the slow crock means that you are warming up your machine, usually while doing the preparations for your dish and it is much the same as turning on the oven.

WHAT THE SLOW CROCK CAN DO

The slow crock can be used in four different ways:

To *simmer* soups and stews, using for the most part the LOW setting.

To *pot-roast*, placing a small amount of liquid in the bottom of the crock and then placing in it a joint of meat or poultry. You can use either the LOW or HIGH setting, depending on the type of meat and the speed at which you want the dish to be ready.

To *roast*, in which case you will cook the joint, poultry or meat loaf without liquid, preferably placing it on a rack or trivet so that the natural fats that seep out during cooking don't settle as a greasy ooze on the bottom of the joint. You'll probably have to help the process along by lightly oiling the interior of the crock so that the end result is not too dry. Again, you may use either HIGH or LOW settings.

To *steam*, using the crock as a boiler for making puddings, *pâtés*, cakes and bread. You'll have to use the HIGH setting here.

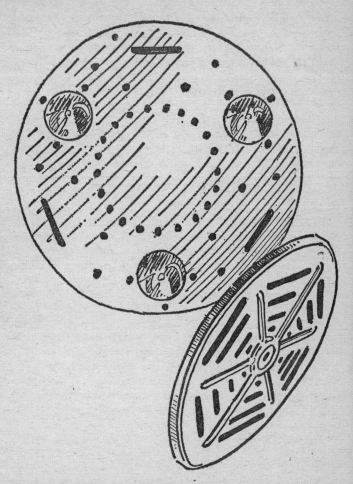

Trivets – originally made for pressure cookers but well-suited for slow crocks. They rest on the base and can be used to keep meat out of the fat and cooking juices, or to help baked apples keep their shape.

FOODS SUITABLE FOR SLOW CROCK COOKING

What foods cook best in the slow crock? Foods that bene-
fit from gentle sustained heat which include meat, poultry
and game, and also food, such as fish and fruit, that benefits from cooking in flavoursome liquids or sauces .

Which foods require special attention? Root and starchy
vegetables should be parboiled for 5–10 minutes depending
on whether they are cut small or left whole. They are difficult
to soften otherwise at these low temperatures and unless you
are using them to flavour a stew or soup this method of cooking is not ideal for them. Green vegetables and onions
should be *sautéed* to bring out their flavour, but again they
should be used for the flavour they impart to the dish and
not as the *raison d'être* of the dish. Dried beans and other
pulse foods require soaking as with any other method, and
should be cooked on HIGH for the best results.

Are there any nutritional benefits? Some nutrients such
as Vitamin C are destroyed by even low temperatures, and
others – Vitamin B, for example – are water soluble so
dissolve into the cooking liquid whatever the cooking
method. With slow crock cooking there is very little nutrient
loss. Slow crock your meat and steam your vegetables is my
advice to retain maximum nutritional value.

Most slow crocks travel well, but if you are going to a
foreign country make sure that the *voltage* of the local
power supply is the same as on the plate on your model. A
240 volt British model will work well enough on 220-volt
electric current, but would be dangerous in North America,
where the current is 110 to 120 volts. On no account should
you try to use a 240-volt mains model on a 12-volt car or
boat battery system. You can't take a slow crock with you in
your caravan unless you can provide the right voltage.

2 HOW TO CHOOSE AND USE YOUR SLOW CROCK

HOW TO CHOOSE YOUR SLOW CROCK

Whatever the shape and size all slow crocks work on the same principle – that is, cooking food at a low gentle temperature. When buying a slow crock you will find that there is quite a variety to choose from. This section will clarify the different features that you encounter when deciding which one is most suited to your needs.

SIZE

What size do you want? The small size slow crock has a working capacity of about 1½ litre (3 pint) to 2 litre (4 pint) and will adequately provide meals for up to 4 people. The large size slow crock is between 2½–3 litre (5–6 pint) and will obviously cater for larger quantities if you want to cook for the freezer or entertaining. They are not much more expensive, so it's worth the extra investment.

Do you want a removable or non-removable crockery liner? Both types of slow crock can be used at the table. If you choose a removable slow crock you will be able to treat it like any casserole and use it in the oven, under the grill or in the dishwasher. Never store any model in the fridge as the stress caused by temperature change could permanently damage the crockery liner due to thermal shock. If you choose a removable crock always check that the wattage on the LOW setting is adequate to compensate for the heat loss between the case and the crock. The combination of a low wattage with a removable crock will mean a machine that operates at temperatures too cool for attaining the safe level required for cooking food. In this case you will find yourself having to use the HIGH setting for many dishes which will result in a higher fuel consumption. Underpowered crocks are a false economy. With a non-removable crockery liner the cleaning rules are different (see p. 29) because the heating case must never be immersed in water as the electric elements will be damaged and become dangerous.

SHAPE

What shape do you want your slow crock? Once you have decided on the size you will then find that each slow crock will have varying dimensions which is important when considering the types of food you will want to cook in them. For instance, among the small models currently available, one is wide and shallow while another is deeper and less wide. These considerations will mean that when buying food to cook, its shape and bulk will be affected by this factor. All slow crocks get narrower by about $1\frac{1}{4}$ cm ($\frac{1}{2}''$) at the base of the inner crock.

SAFETY FEATURES

What safety features should you look for? The handles on the heating case, and on the crockery liner itself if removable, should be adequate to grip easily. When moving a full crock from its cooking place to the table for serving it's important to be able to hold such a hot and heavy object easily.

Models with BEAB* approval have a heating element that's sheathed, and parts that could become live are earthed. BEAB approval guarantees a higher standard of quality and safety all round.

Look especially carefully at the lid. Some of the models I have seen let themselves down badly because heat can escape

* British Electrotechnical Approvals Board

too easily. A transparent lid is not always an advantage – it usually steams up pretty promptly!

Once you have checked all of these points, by all means go by appearance, one of the great advantages of the crock being that you can serve directly from it.

Some manufacturers do not advise one to cook whole joints in their appliance and this will be a decisive factor for those who enjoy pot-roast or boiled joints.

What other features of design are important? The HIGH or LOW setting is selected on a switch or dial, and there may be an OFF position too. These should be well-marked, and simple to operate and it should be obvious whether the machine is on or not by a series of fool-proof double checks, ie:

The cord on a slow crock is either detachable or permanently attached. Is there an indicator light to show that the electricity supply is flowing? If not, is this because the cord is permanently attached? If there is no indicator light and the cord is detachable you will always have to double check that it is properly inserted in the machine and that after ten minutes or so the pot is noticeably warmer. If there is a switch or dial with an OFF position you must always check that it is set on LOW or HIGH once you have switched on the supply from the mains.

Cleaning is another consideration. How easy will it be to clean? Food never sticks or burns on hard because the temperatures are not sufficiently high to produce the same burnt black lines that you get in an oven casserole. However, if the cord is not detachable from the non-removable crock you must always be careful when cleaning that these parts of the machine are kept from being splashed with water. See more detailed discussion of this in the next chapter (p. 29).

It will also help if you read the manufacturer's description of *timings* in order to decide finally which model to buy. This will indicate the kind of machine it is and whether there are any hidden flaws not at first apparent about its heating capacity. The important facts to note are how the settings are used and the kinds of food, quantities and bulk you can cook. For instance, check that you can cook whole joints of meat if that's the kind of thing you'll feel like doing. If you unwittingly end up with a model that doesn't suit your convenience you'll assume quite wrongly that slow crocks are no good when in fact it is entirely the defect of that particular model's design. So remember that with a little application of your detection and logic, a small amount of arithmetic, a careful eye for detail like reading the small print (particularly the 'how to use' section), plus the help of this book, you should be able to find the machine that suits your purposes and has been responsibly researched by the people making it.

Do you need any extra equipment? Maybe you don't, but there are a couple of items that many cooks already have that should prove useful. The first is a rack or trivet that will fit inside the pot. When roasting meat quite a bit of fat melts and collects at the bottom of the pot, soaking into the bottom of the joint. The way to avoid this is to lift the joint off the bottom with a small rack. The aluminium trivets used in pressure cookers (see illustration on p. 19) are almost ideal for the purpose. A circular wire rack, of the sort used for cooling cakes and made from stainless steel, is even better. At the time of writing the crockpot manufacturers don't supply purpose-made racks but a bit of hunting in the kitchen departments of large stores should come up with the answer. The other item worth keeping around is a nylon scouring pad. This is just about the best thing to use for cleaning, being effective both in removing stubborn marks and in avoiding damage to the earthenware.

How to Use Your Slow Crock
Here is a brief outline of step-by-step procedure for preparing and cooking food in the slow crock. It covers all methods without going into the detail that you'll find in each chapter:
 1. Check the manufacturer's instructions for pre-heating rules, if there are any, or if recipe requires it (eg steaming).

2. For cooking, always place the slow crock on a flat, level surface that's moisture-free. Stand it on a mat or wooden board if the surface is cold (eg Formica, metal).

3. Do not let the slow crock stand in a draught when cooking (eg near open windows and doors, or outside) as this reduces the optimum simmering temperature.

4. Prepare food as directed and place it in the slow crock.

5. Add liquid as directed, either hot or cold, the quantity depending on the type of recipe. If you are adapting a recipe to the slow crock reduce liquid quantities by half as there is little liquid loss in this method of cooking.

6. Replace lid, making sure that it fits properly, for any escape of heat would seriously hinder if not prevent proper cooking.

7. Switch to selected setting. Make sure that the machine is heating, feeling the lid or outer casing after 5 minutes. There will be a noticeable temperature change, however mild.

8. Leave the slow crock to cook for the required time. Do not lift the lid, there is no need to stir food. If you want the meal earlier than required, you can always switch to the HIGH setting for the last few hours, or, if you have little time, use HIGH at the beginning. This is one of the many ways you can juggle with the settings in order to suit the timing to your needs. Of course, the simplest way by far is just to leave it for as long as possible, but there will always be those times when you need to make adjustments. By incorporating an automatic timer into the plug you can leave short cooking dishes to switch on by themselves, although this is not usually necessary except for fish or fruit, as a few extra hours of cooking will not harm the quality of most dishes.

9. To serve, skim the fat if necessary, adjust thickening for gravy or sauce and check seasoning.

10. The outer casing is made of tough, heat-resistant metal or plastic which gets warm but not too hot to touch over the long cooking periods. If the inner crock is

removable it should be handled with oven gloves or a cloth if taking it out of the case when hot.

11. Tinned or convenience food should be added in the final hour.

12. Food can be kept hot on LOW for second helpings or latecomers but once you've switched it off, all food should be removed from the slow crock and stored.

13. Food should not be reheated in the slow crock but in another container such as a saucepan, on the cooker. The only exceptions are fruit or Xmas puddings that can be boiled up within a few hours, and alcoholic punches which often improve by standing until cooked then being reheated. See individual chapters for more detail.

You may still have some questions about the use of the slow crock, such as: how long or short a time can I cook for? There are roughly 3 cooking periods into which all foods fit and the chart below gives some examples of the categories. However, as I've mentioned before, there are some cases where you can determine the timing by using a different setting.

WHOLE DAY (LOW) (HIGH)	most meat; most soup; root and starch vegetables; beans	ROAST – HIGH for whole or part of day, depends on size and kind.
PART DAY (LOW) (HIGH)	under 3 hours: sauce; fondue; hot drinks; some fish. under 6 hours: mince; fish; fruit; sausage; *pâté*; pudding, cake and bread	
OVERNIGHT (LOW)	tongue; stock (except fish); porridge; brisket	

Will the food be ready in time? Slow crock cooking requires planning ahead and you must give yourself plenty of time for the best results, an extra hour or two will do no harm whatsoever to the dish unless there are very clear instructions about exact timing. If you find that you want to eat sooner than the dish will be ready on LOW, use HIGH and vice versa.

When do I season and thicken? Seasoning and thickening can be done at the beginning or end, depending on the recipe, and it is advisable to check both before serving.

Are there any extra items I can use with a slow crock? Yes. A trivet helps to keep the shape of a meat loaf or piece of fish, and can also be used with meat if it is fatty. (See page 19.) Greaseproof paper dampened a little and placed over a joint of meat helps preserve the colour and moisture when using little or no liquid. In some cases rashers of bacon will do exactly the same job as well as adding extra flavour. Metal foil placed under the rim will speed up cooking times slightly by reflecting heat back into the food.

What kind of cook does the slow crock suit? The slow crock suits almost any kind of cook although you should be well-organized, able to plan ahead, and prepared to be adventurous and imaginative. I've tried to give a variety of recipes to cope with the different approaches cooks will make. Some will want to assemble a dish as quickly as possible with as little preparation as is necessary then place the ingredients in the crock, replace the lid, switch on and leave it until cooked – this is a simplistic approach and the results will reflect this.

There are those who always spend time preparing food carefully by browning, etc, and this again will give the dish a different appearance and the gravy or sauce a better flavour. The attention to detail is ultimately up to you. I have written my recipes with a clear description of what to expect if you do it my way, explaining as simply as possible the skills and tricks of using it, and at the same time giving the experienced cook a chance to experiment fully with the sophisticated results the crock can offer. It is after all a new machine designed to work not only as a companion to an oven or pressure cooker, but also as an alternative when the occasion, time, convenience or routine demands it. You will certainly realize the economy of using the slow crock instead of the oven, without compromising on the versatility. And whereas the pressure cooker is excellent for cooking vegetables instantly before a meal, the slow crock complements its relative speed by its own slow and gentle cooking of meat. The cook who masters the skills of using it will be able to adapt it conveniently in almost any situation.

3 CARE, SAFETY AND MAINTENANCE

CARE

CLEANING

The low slow cooking temperatures make the slow crock easy to clean because food doesn't stick or burn on and the inside is easily soaked in warm water after use without the need for excessive elbow grease or harsh detergents. You shouldn't use abrasive compounds such as household cleaners or steel wool pads.

Crockery liners that can be removed from the outer casing should be dishwasher safe – but always check your manufacturer's instructions and if you're not sure don't take the risk.

1. *Before cleaning* always disconnect the slow crock from the electric mains supply.
2. *For the first time* clean the inside of the slow crock before use to remove any residue of manufacturing oils.
3. If you wash the slow crock soon after use, fill it with *warm* water and add detergent and swish lightly round with cloth or sponge to clean. If you wash it a long time after (ie when it is cold), soak it in *cold* water and detergent, then rinse and clean.

N.B. Food should be served from the slow crock and kept hot for second helpings or latecomers, but never leave food to get cold in it. Always transfer food as soon as possible to another container for storage.

4. *Never immerse the outer casing* in water, this is dangerous and will damage the electric heating element inside. To clean the outer casing, wipe it gently with a damp cloth.

5. Do not scratch the crockery glaze with other kitchen utensils (eg to remove stubborn food) – soak for a longer period.
6. If a white residue or dull ring appears round the inside of the crockery, clean as above and rub vegetable oil onto the glaze to restore its shine.

CROCKERY CARE

It is not a good idea to subject the crockery to extreme changes of temperature, so as a guide:

> If the pot is hot do not fill it with cold water.
> If the pot is cold do not fill it with hot water.
> Do not put frozen food into a hot slow crock.

This avoids undue stress on the crockery and reduces the dangers of thermal shock and weakening of the lining.

Sharp blows or knocks could crack the pot or lid, so try to avoid hitting it against a tap or sink, or dropping it.

STORAGE

Dry the pot and lid thoroughly before storing. Store the slow crock on a wide, level shelf or table, allowing plenty of room for the outer case to stand with all feet on the ground and for the cord and plug to fit at the side coiled up.

SAFETY

The slow crock is a safe appliance to use but normal precautions for electric appliances must be observed.

In models with BEAB approval the heating element is sheathed to comply with British Safety Standards so there is no danger of electric shock should the crock crack, and any parts which could potentially become live are earthed.

1. To switch the appliance ON:

   either – place plug in the wall socket, select setting and switch on (ie if the cord is permanently attached to the machine)

   or – if the cord is detachable from the machine push the lead *firmly* into the socket on the machine, plug other end into the wall socket, select setting, switch on.

2. To switch the appliance OFF:

   either – switch off the wall socket and remove plug (if the cord is permanently attached)

   or – (if cord is detachable from machine) switch off the wall socket and remove plug, then detach lead from machine and coil up.

N.B. Even if the slow crock has an 'OFF' position on the dial or setting switch, all plugs must be removed from mains for washing purposes.

3. Do not store uncooked food in the slow crock for any length of time (because of the risk of bacteria growth).
4. Unless your slow crock has a removable inner pot, do not use it in the oven, or under the grill.
5. If your slow crock has a removable inner pot do not use the heating case for any other purposes besides slow cooking with the pot itself (ie you cannot fry eggs and bacon on the outer casing's inner metal surface – it would be highly dangerous).

MAINTENANCE

If your slow crock:
a) has a frayed or damaged cord or plug
b) is malfunctioning (ie indicator light not working, pot not heating)
c) has been dropped and cracked

d) is in any other way damaged
- Do not use it.
- Return it for repair and servicing to the address recommended by the manufacturer.

4 STOCKS AND SOUPS

The simplest kind of stock is what's left over when you've boiled vegetables such as potatoes or cooked a chicken or other meat in water. This forms the all-important basis for a good-tasting soup. Then with the addition of other vegetables or meat (herbs, seasoning, spices) and some thickening agent you can produce a variety of textures and tastes ranging from a clear consommé to a thick cream soup.

Clear soup can be an alternative to tea or coffee when you need a reviving or stimulating drink. Soup can also be a liquid meal, easily digested, but, instead of a meal with lots of separate components on one plate, soup is a unified dish of many ingredients.

If you have a refrigerator and you like soup, never throw away the water you cook your vegetables in as it will keep for up to 24 hours in cool storage. Meat stock keeps longer, and will add to the quality of the soup. To make a stock in the slow crock is an overnight job as the timing is quite long. The ingredients cook on LOW for 10–12 hours. The stock is then strained, the slow crock rinsed out and the soup can be started next morning to be ready in the evening. To make a stock followed by a soup in the slow crock is a day and a half job, but the preparation in which you're involved is a matter of 10 minutes at the beginning, middle and end.

Depending on the ingredients, the soup itself takes an average of a day to cook on LOW. If you're using cooked or instant (tinned, packet, etc) ingredients it will take less time and you'll be using the slow crock not so much for its slow cooking as its slow heating. This may be useful if you want a tasty soup at midday, after only half a day's timing. The only soups that require a HIGH setting are those that use beans or pulses. The timing in these cases will still be about a day.

I have included details of how to make the various types

of stock from scratch (white stock, brown stock, fish stock, meat stock), but you can in fact use a stock cube dissolved in hot water, or meat or yeast extract.

STOCK

Basic Recipe for Stock

Meat or chicken stock:
raw or cooked bones, skin and gristle of meat, poultry giblets
cold water to cover
onion, carrot, celery
bay leaf and other herbs
peppercorns

Fish stock:
fish and fish trimmings, fish shells
cold water to cover
onion, carrot, celery
bay leaf, fennel and other herbs
peppercorns

Vegetable stock:
vegetables and vegetable peelings and skins
dry or faded outer leaves from cabbage, cauliflower, etc
rice
cold water to cover
bay leaf, peppercorns, various herbs

Method for Brown or White Stock

To make a brown stock the onions and meat (where used) should be fried in oil until brown and then added to the slow crock with the other ingredients. A white stock is usually made without browning the ingredients.

If using bones, ask the butcher to chop them into suitable pieces, and to crack them so that the marrow oozes out during cooking.

All vegetables should be washed, peeled and cut. Use the peel and skin if wished as this adds to the colour of the stock.

Meat should be trimmed of excess fat and browned if wished for a brown stock.

Fish stock is best using white fish, as dark-skinned fish discolour the final soup. Oily fish should be avoided (eg mackerel, salmon and herring).

After the initial preparation of ingredients, add everything to the slow crock and pour cold water in (see below for proportion of water used to solid ingredients). A little vinegar may be added when using bones.

Salt should only be added at the soup stage (1 tsp salt per litre (2 pt)).

Replace lid and cook on LOW overnight or 10–12 hours. Then skim and strain if using right away or strain and allow to cool and gel. Do not skim fat off if storing as this acts as a preserving layer and the stock will keep longer.

For freezing purposes omit all vegetables and use more meat.

HOW MUCH WATER TO USE FOR THE STOCK

Meat stock	1 litre (2 pt) water to 1 kg (2 lb) meat
Fresh bone stock	1 litre (2 pt) water to 1 kg (2 lb) bones
Starchy vegetables	1 litre (2 pt) water to 1 kg (2 lb) vegetables
Green vegetables	1 litre (2 pt) water to 1 kg (2 lb) vegetables
Chicken stock	1 litre (2 pt) water to 1 kg (2 lb) white meat, bones, giblets
Fish stock	1 litre (2 pt) water to 1 kg (2 lb) fish, trimmings, bones

HOW TO CLARIFY A MEAT OR CHICKEN STOCK

Immediately after cooking, strain stock into a separate bowl and using warm water rinse out slow crock. Pour stock back into crock and switch to HIGH. Replace the lid and allow to simmer for 15 minutes.

For every litre (2 pt) of stock you need one slightly beaten egg white, and one crushed egg shell.

Take the lid off and, if boiling, allow the stock to cool down until the surface is barely moving, add egg white and crushed shell. Stir and leave with the lid off for about 10 minutes.

Switch off the machine and strain the stock through a fine sieve or muslin while still hot. Cool and refrigerate or use straight away.

Chicken or White Stock   10–12 hours LOW

1 kg (2 lb) white meat (chicken) and scraps and bones (wing, neck, giblets), 120 g (4 oz) bacon – optional, 1 onion stuck with a clove, 1 carrot, celery stalk, bay leaf, thyme and parsley, 1 litre (2 pt) water.

This method can be used for any white meat. If using a chicken, it can be cooked whole, although there are more explicit recipes further on dealing with this (Cock-a-leekie).

Wash and chop ingredients. Leave meat whole or in joints. For a real white stock the onion should be sliced and cooked in fat until transparent but not brown.

Add all ingredients to slow crock. Replace lid and cook on LOW for 10–12 hours or overnight.

If resulting broth is to be used for soup skim the fat off and adjust seasoning. For freezer storage omit all vegetables. Strain the stock and allow to cool before refrigerating. Let the layer of fat serve as a lid to preserve the stock if it is to be stored.

White or Brown Vegetable Stock   **10–12 hours LOW**

Vegetable scraps (peel, outer skins, leaves); 1 kg (2 lb) green or starchy vegetables – onion, celery, turnip (not too much), carrots (for sweetness), cabbage, cauliflower, 1 litre (2 pt) cold water, herbs, 1 tbs each oil and sugar (for brown stock only), optional – a small piece of ginger root to add an oriental flavour to the stock.

Wash and chop vegetables. For a *brown* stock fry the onion in oil and sprinkle on sugar. Place all ingredients in base of slow crock and add water. Replace lid and cook on LOW for 10–12 hours or overnight.

Then, strain and store. Use within 24 hours.

Concentrated Fish Stock (Fumet)   **6 hours LOW**

1 kg (2 lb) fish trimmings, head and bones of various fish (whiting, sole, haddock, plaice): avoid the oily fish (mackerel, salmon, herring), 1 onion, carrot and leek, a squeeze of lemon juice, 1 bay leaf, sprig of thyme, ½ litre (1 pt) each of water and red or white wine, optional – mushroom stalks and parings.

Clean and wash fish. Peel and chop vegetables. Place all ingredients in slow crock with herbs and water and wine. Replace lid and cook on LOW for a minimum of 6 hours.

Then, strain stock and use within 24 hours.

Useful Hints for Soup Making in the Slow Crock
Once you have a stock, whether made from scratch or good quality stock cubes, you can start making a soup. The other components are as follows:

SOLID INGREDIENTS   Vegetables, meat, poultry, game, fish,

beans are among the many ingredients to choose from. They should be prepared in the usual way and added with the stock to the slow crock. The proportions will vary but your main solid ingredients should be in the proportion of $\frac{1}{2}$ kg (1 lb) to every 1 litre (2 pt) stock. At the end of the cooking period these ingredients can be sieved or *puréed* to make a thick soup, or strained for a thin soup. Browning the ingredients first improves texture and flavour.

THICKENERS

One of the simplest ways of thickening the soup is to make a basic white sauce (a roux) at the beginning of the cooking period and stir it into the stock before cooking. Use 30 g (1 oz) flour and butter for every $\frac{1}{4}$ litre ($\frac{1}{2}$ pt) soup. Melt the butter in a small saucepan, add the flour and stir until yellow and cooked but not brown. Stir in a little of the stock and mix until a smooth paste is formed, then add to the slow crock with the other ingredients.

Grains such as barley and rice can also be used in the proportion of 1 tbs per $\frac{1}{4}$ litre ($\frac{1}{2}$ pt) stock. Rinse and drain and add at the beginning of the cooking period.

Potatoes also thicken a soup and when used in the slow crock should be parboiled first (see note below, 'Points to Watch').

Soups can be given a richer thickening with the addition of egg yolks or cream at the end of the cooking period. Just stir in one or two egg yolks, or a few tablespoons of cream before serving.

SEASONING   Always adjust seasoning at the end of the cooking period with salt and pepper. Chilli or tabasco sauce added in drops gives a hot aftertaste to the soup. Alcohol (sherry, wine, light lager or dry cider) also provides an unusual and sweeter taste.

GARNISH   Never to be forgotten as this adds colour and appeal to the soup. The most common is chopped parsley. Grated Parmesan cheese adds an extra bite to the flavour. Fried bread *croûtons* can be sprinkled on and make the soup more of a meal.

QUANTITIES   In general, soup is meant to whet the appetite for what's to come, or it can form a main part of the meal – so depending on the emphasis an average serving is about ¼ litre (½ pt).

Points to Watch

When using the slow crock for soup making you have to pre-cook some ingredients to ensure that they are tender enough at the end of a long cooking period. The ones to watch in this case are green and starchy vegetables that do not soften as easily as meat during the long timing at a low temperature. There are two ways of dealing with this:

1. Parboil your vegetable ingredients for 5–10 minutes, then drain and transfer to slow crock with other ingredients. Continue as recipe directs.
2. *Sauté* the vegetables in oil along with the other ingredients, then add the stock and heat to boiling before adding to a *pre-heated* slow crock. Continue as recipe directs.

Barley Soup   8 hours LOW

90 g (3 oz) pearl barley, 2 medium onions, 2 medium carrots, 3 celery stalks, 2–3 medium potatoes, 60 g (2 oz) mushrooms, salt and pepper, 1 bay leaf, 2 tbs chopped fresh dill or parsley, 1 litre (2 pt) meat stock, 2 tbs oil.

The ingredients here will give you a fairly thick soup. If you want a lighter or thinner soup, just halve the solid ingredients and use the same amount of liquid.

Pre-heat the slow crock. Rinse the barley and place in base of slow crock. Wash and dice or slice the vegetables. Heat oil in a frying pan and *sauté* the vegetables for 5 minutes. Then pour stock into the pan and heat contents until simmering. Transfer to slow crock. Add salt, pepper and bay leaf. Replace lid and cook on LOW for 8–10 hours.

To serve, remove bay leaf, adjust seasoning, garnish with chopped dill or parsley.

Beef and Mushroom Soup   8 hours LOW

$\frac{1}{4}$ kg ($\frac{1}{2}$ lb) lean minced meat, 125 g (4 oz) mushrooms, 15 g ($\frac{1}{2}$ oz) butter, 1 medium onion, 2 garlic cloves, 2 tbs tomato paste, 2 tbs oil, salt and pepper, 1 tbs chopped parsley, 1 litre (2 pt) beef stock, optional spices – $\frac{1}{2}$ tsp of chilli, cayenne or curry powder.

Pre-heat the slow crock. Peel and slice onion and garlic and brown in oil. Put meat and onion, garlic and other seasoning and spices into slow crock. Pour in stock. Replace lid and cook on LOW for 8 hours.

Half an hour before serving, add sliced mushrooms *sautéed* in butter. To serve, adjust seasoning, add tomato *purée* and garnish with chopped parsley.

Chinese Style Chicken Broth   **6–8 hours LOW**

1 chicken breast, 60 g (2 oz) bean sprouts, 125 g (4 oz) mushrooms, salt, 1 litre (2 pt) chicken stock.
Optional ingredients – pepper, soy sauce, 2 slices root ginger, 1 stalk scallion (spring onion), chopped.

Skin the chicken breast and cut the meat into thin slivers. Slice the mushrooms and chop the bean sprouts. Place these ingredients in the slow crock, pour the stock in and replace lid. Cook on LOW 6–8 hours. To serve, adjust seasoning with salt.

Cawl Mamgu – Welsh Mutton Broth   **8–10 hours LOW**

$\frac{1}{2}$ kg (1 lb) best end neck of mutton, $\frac{1}{4}$ kg ($\frac{1}{2}$ lb) leeks, 60 g (2 oz) swede or turnip, 1 small carrot, 2 small potatoes, 40–60 g ($1\frac{1}{2}$–2 oz) pearl barley, salt and pepper, 1 litre (2 pt) veal or chicken stock, 1 tbs chopped parsley.

Pre-heat the slow crock. Wash and dice vegetables. Wash pearl barley. Bring vegetables to boil in a separate saucepan, drain and transfer to slow crock. Add barley, meat, stock and seasoning. Replace lid and cook on LOW for 8–10 hours.
To serve, adjust seasoning and garnish with chopped parsley.

Cock-A-Leekie with Prunes   **8–10 hours LOW**

This is a variation of the traditional Scottish recipe in which prunes are a surprisingly effective addition.
1 kg (2 lb) boiling fowl, 200 g (6 oz) dried pitted prunes, 1 large leek, salt and pepper, chicken giblets, 1 litre (2 pt) beef stock.

Wash prunes and place them in the base of the slow crock.

Wash and slice leek. Clean boiling fowl and joint if necessary. Rinse giblets thoroughly. Place all ingredients in slow crock with seasoning to taste. Replace lid and cook on LOW for 8–10 hours.

To serve, skim, strain and clarify soup. Serve the meat and vegetables as a main course.

Pot-au-Feu   **8–10 hours LOW**

The ingredients I give here are on a small scale. It should really be made in larger quantities. The proportion of meat to water remains constant – ½ kg (1 lb) meat to 1 litre (2 pt) water.

½ kg (1 lb) beef shin, 1 beef marrowbone cracked, chicken giblets, 1 carrot, ½ turnip, 1 leek, 1 celery stalk, 1 onion stuck with a clove, *bouquet garni*, salt and pepper.

Pre-heat the slow crock. Bring all the ingredients to the boil in a saucepan and then transfer to the slow crock. Replace lid and cook on LOW for 8–10 hours.

To serve, remove the meat and serve as a separate dish with salad or vegetables. Discard bone, *bouquet garni* and giblets. Skim fat off surface of soup. Adjust seasoning.

Tomato Soup with Herbs   **6–8 hours LOW**

1 kg (2 lb) tomatoes, 1 large onion, 3 garlic cloves, 1 litre (2 pt) chicken stock, salt and pepper, 1–2 tbs fresh chopped parsley and basil or marjoram, either 2 tbs each of flour and butter or ⅛ litre cream, 1 tbs oil, garnish – 2 tbs chopped chives.

Pre-heat the slow crock. Peel and slice onions and garlic. Brown in oil. Wash and chop tomatoes roughly. Add all ingredients except thickening agents to slow crock. Replace lid and cook on LOW for 6–8 hours.

To serve, *purée* the mixture with a sieve or blender. Return to slow crock. Stir in cream or flour kneaded in butter. Adjust seasoning. Garnish with chopped chives. Serve. For a thinner soup use milk instead of cream.

Tomato Soup with Rice   6–8 hours LOW

1 kg (2 lb) tomatoes, 1 large onion, 1 celery stalk, 1 garlic clove, 4 peppercorns, 1 tsp each salt, oregano, basil, 1 tbs brown sugar, 125 g (4 oz) patna rice, 2 tbs oil, 1 litre (2 pt) vegetable or chicken stock.

Pre-heat the slow crock. Wash and chop tomatoes roughly, then blend or mash to a pulp. Place in slow crock. Heat oil in frying pan. Brown sliced vegetables and rice, washed and drained. Add all ingredients to slow crock. Replace lid and cook on LOW for 6–8 hours.

To serve, adjust seasoning.

Cream of Celery Soup   6 hours LOW

8 celery stalks or ¼ kg (½ lb) celeriac, 1 small onion and potato, 60 g (2 oz) each of flour and butter, salt and pepper, 1 bay leaf, 1 tsp chopped fennel or dill, 1 litre (2 pt) chicken stock, 1 egg yolk, 1 carton of single cream or evaporated milk.

Pre-heat the slow crock. Peel and dice onion and potato. Finely chop the celery. Melt butter in a frying pan and *sauté* these vegetables for 10 minutes. Add the flour and stir-fry for a short time until the flour turns yellow. Stir in the stock, herbs and seasoning and when simmering transfer to the slow crock. Replace lid and cook for 6 hours.

To serve, liquidize or blend the soup. Return it to the slow crock and stir in egg yolk beaten lightly with cream or milk. Adjust seasoning.

Leek and Spinach (or Sorrel) Soup   6–8 hours LOW

2 medium leeks, ½ kg (1 lb) spinach or sorrel, 1 small onion, potato, parsnip and turnip, 1 litre (2 pt) chicken or beef stock, 1 tsp dill and chopped chives, salt and pepper, 1 tsp paprika, 1 carton of single cream or evaporated milk, 4 tbs butter or margarine, *garnish* – lemon and hard-boiled egg slices.

Pre-heat the slow crock. Use white part of leeks only, wash and slice finely. Wash and chop spinach. Peel and dice remaining vegetables. Melt butter in a frying pan and *sauté* these vegetables for 10 minutes. Add stock, herbs and seasoning and when simmering transfer to the slow crock. Replace lid and cook on LOW for 6–8 hours. To serve, *purée* the soup and return it to slow crock. Stir in cream and adjust seasoning. Garnish with lemon slices and hard-boiled egg slices.

Quick Carrot Soup   2 hours LOW

½ kg (1 lb) carrots, 1 tbs soft brown sugar, ½ litre (1 pt) water, ¼ litre (½ pt) milk, salt and pepper, 1 tbs chopped fresh mint or 1 tsp dried mint.

Pre-heat slow crock on HIGH during preparations. Peel or scrape carrots and boil them in the water with the sugar until soft. Strain and reserve cooking liquid.

Liquidize carrots with milk and add *purée* to slow crock. Pour in reserved cooking liquid, salt and pepper to taste, and add mint. Stir well. Replace lid and cook for two hours on LOW. To serve, adjust seasoning, adding more milk for a thinner soup, cream for a thicker soup.

Onion Soup   **2 hours LOW**

$\frac{1}{2}$ kg (1 lb) onions, 60 g (2 oz) each of flour and butter, 1 litre (2 pt) milk, salt and pepper.

Pre-heat slow crock on HIGH during preparations. Peel and slice onions and brown in butter until soft. Stir in flour, cook until yellow and resembling breadcrumbs, then add milk and stir it until thick or alternatively, thicken at end with a *beurre manié*. Add seasoning.

Transfer ingredients to slow crock and switch to LOW. Replace lid and cook for a further 2 hours. Garnish with parsley or Parmesan cheese.

Split Pea Soup   **6–8 hours HIGH**

200 g (6 oz) split peas, $\frac{1}{4}$ kg ($\frac{1}{2}$ lb) salt pork or bacon joint, 2 tbs oil, 1 small celeriac (celery root), 1 small onion, 1 carrot, 1–2 spicy sausages, 1 bay leaf, salt and pepper, dash of Worcestershire sauce, 1 litre (2 pt) chicken stock, optional spices – 1 tsp ground cumin, pinch of cayenne pepper, 1 tsp sage, 2 garlic cloves.

Soak split peas overnight in cold water, then rinse and drain. Pre-heat slow crock on HIGH during preparations. Wash, peel and dice vegetables. Cut up bacon joint and sausage into chunks, melt oil in a frying pan and *sauté* the vegetables, then the bacon joint and sausage. Pour chicken stock into the pan and bring to the boil and transfer to slow crock. Add split peas and remaining herbs, spices, seasoning. Replace lid and cook on HIGH for 6–8 hours until peas are tender.

To serve, remove bay leaf and adjust seasoning.

Lentil Soup **6 hours HIGH**

¼ kg (½ lb) lentils, 1 large onion, 125 g (4 oz) bacon scraps, 60 g (2 oz) celeriac or 1 celery stalk, 1 carrot, 2 cloves, salt and pepper, 1 bay leaf, 1 litre (2 pt) vegetable, veal or chicken stock, optional ingredient – 2 tbs tahini*.

Pre-heat the slow crock. Wash and drain lentils, place in slow crock. Wash, peel and slice vegetables. Heat bacon in frying pan until fat runs out then brown the vegetables. Transfer to slow crock. Add remaining ingredients. Replace lid and cook on HIGH for 6 hours.

To serve, remove bay leaf and cloves. Sieve or blend soup if wished. Adjust seasoning. Serve.

Simple Sweet Corn Soup **4 hours LOW**

¼ kg (½ lb) packet or tin of sweet corn, 3 eggs, 1 litre (2 pt) strong chicken stock, 2 tbs cornflour, 1 tbs sherry, 2 tsp salt, 1 slice of cooked ham.

Place sweet corn in slow crock and pour in most of stock. Make a paste with the cornflour and a few tablespoons of stock and stir it into the slow crock. Replace lid and cook on LOW for 4 hours. To serve, beat the eggs and pour them very slowly into the soup so that they form streaks. Allow them to cook and meanwhile adjust seasoning with salt and sherry. Stir soup. Serve garnished with chopped ham.

Pea and Chicken Soup **6–8 hours LOW**

1 chicken breast, 10 lettuce leaves and 10 spinach leaves, 1 sprig of parsley, ¼ kg (½ lb) shelled peas, 3 egg yolks, 1

* Tahini is a sauce made from sesame seeds so it adds a nutty flavour to the soup.

carton of single cream, ½ tsp salt, 1 small onion, 4 tbs butter, 2 tsp sugar, 1 litre (2 pt) chicken stock.

Optional – a sprig of fresh chervil.

Pre-heat the slow crock. Skin the chicken breast and cut the meat into thin slivers. Peel and mince the onion. Wash the lettuce and spinach thoroughly then chop or shred it. Melt butter in a pan and *sauté* the lettuce and spinach for 5–10 minutes. Then transfer to slow crock.

Add chicken, onion and peas. Pour stock in. Add salt, sugar, and fresh herbs. Replace lid and cook on LOW 6–8 hours. To serve, mix egg yolks with cream and stir into soup. Adjust seasoning.

Alternatively blend or *purée* the soup when it is ready, return it to slow crock and then add the eggs and cream.

Avgo Lemono   1–2 hours HIGH/3–4 hours LOW

Greek lemon soup with a subtle taste of chicken. If possible, make a chicken stock overnight in the slow crock with a 1½ kg (3 lb) boiling fowl and 1 litre (2 pt) of water, then use it as the basis of this soup (method for stock see page 36).

1 small onion, 60 g (2 oz) patna rice, 3 eggs, 1 large lemon, salt and pepper, pinch of cayenne, 1 bay leaf, 1 litre (2 pt) strong chicken stock.

Peel and chop onion, wash rice and parboil both for 5 minutes. Drain and transfer to slow crock. Add stock and bay leaf. Replace lid, and cook on HIGH for 1–1½ hours, or LOW for 3–4 hours until rice and onion are cooked. Then, beat the eggs in a bowl and add the juice of a lemon, stirring them together. Take a ladle, and add a small drop of stock to the egg mixture stirring all the time until about ¼ litre (½ pt) of stock has been transferred to the egg mix. Then pour the diluted egg into the main body of the soup and stir until it has a thick, creamy consistency. Do not allow soup to boil or it will curdle. Adjust seasoning and serve soup at once, sprinkled with a little cayenne.

Bortsch   10 hours LOW

3 large beetroots, 1 cooking apple, 2 medium carrots, 2 medium tomatoes, juice of 2 lemons, 2 tbs brown sugar, 1 bay leaf, salt and pepper, 1 litre (2 pt) beef stock, 1 carton of sour cream, 2 egg yolks, 1 small whole boiled potato per person, 1 tsp vinegar, 1 medium onion, optional – 1 tsp allspice, small piece of parsnip, 1 garlic clove.
Garnish – chopped chives.

This soup can be very special indeed and one way is to make a strong beef stock overnight in the slow crock, and clarify it the next day ready for use with the beetroot, etc, in the morning (see meat stock recipe, page 34).
Pre-heat the slow crock. Peel and grate the beetroot, apple, carrot and bring to the boil with the meat stock in a separate saucepan and transfer to the slow crock. Add chopped tomatoes, sugar, lemon juice, sliced onion, seasoning and bay leaf, plus any optional ingredients. Mix all together, replace lid and cook on LOW for 10 hours.
To serve, blend or *purée* the soup, rinse out slow crock and return soup for reheating. Adjust seasoning. Beat two egg yolks and add to soup, stirring them in well and allowing them to cook for about 5 minutes. Serve the soup in individual bowls with a boiled potato in the middle of each covered with sour cream. If wished a garnish of chopped chives can also be added.

Oxtail Soup   10 hours LOW

1 kg (2 lb) oxtail cut in joints, ¼ kg (½ lb) bacon or ham joint, 1 onion, ½ turnip, 2 celery stalks, salt and pepper, 1 bay leaf, 10 peppercorns, 3 cloves, 2 carrots, 1 tbs mushroom ketchup,

2 tbs cornflour, 1 litre (2 pt) beef or vegetable stock; optional – glass of sherry, 1 tsp sugar.

Wash, clean and trim oxtail joints. Peel and dice vegetables. Place meat, vegetables, stock, herbs and seasoning in slow crock. Replace lid and cook on LOW for a minimum of 10 hours, until the meat is coming away from the oxtail joints. Then, strain soup, rinse out crock with hot water, return soup and skim fat off. Cut meat from oxtail, add to soup. Make a cornflour paste and stir it into the soup. Add mushroom ketchup and adjust seasoning. Cook 10 mins. If wished, burn the sugar in a clean frying pan and add it to the soup for a golden colour. Pour sherry in if wished at the end.

Bean Soup   **6–8 hours HIGH**

¼ kg (½ lb) haricot beans, 1 onion, 1 carrot, 1 celery stalk, 2 leeks, ¼ kg (½ lb) cracked ham or veal bone, 1 fresh green chilli, 1 garlic clove, 1 sprig of rosemary, salt and pepper, 2 tbs oil, 1 litre (2 pt) stock or water.
Garnish – Parmesan cheese.

Soak haricot beans overnight in cold water, then rinse and drain. Pre-heat slow crock on HIGH during preparations. Wash, peel and slice the vegetables. De-seed the chilli pepper. Heat oil in a frying pan and *sauté* vegetables for 5 minutes then add stock and heat until boiling. Transfer to slow crock and add beans, seasoning, bones and herbs. Replace lid and cook on HIGH for 6–8 hours until beans are tender.

To serve, remove bones, pepper, bay leaf and rosemary. Adjust seasoning. Garnish with Parmesan cheese.

Alternatively, you can sieve or *purée* the soup, return it to the slow crock to heat up and then serve.

Chilli Soup   **8 hours LOW**

¼ kg (½ lb) lean minced beef, 3 small sweet carrots, 1 small
celery stalk, 2 garlic cloves, 200 g (6 oz) potatoes, 60 g (2 oz)
each of sweet corn and green peas, 1 small onion, salt and
pepper, ½–2 tbs chilli powder, 1 bay leaf, 120 ml (¼ pt) oil,
juice of 1 lemon, 1 litre (2 pt) beef stock.

Pre-heat the slow crock. Peel and dice potatoes, celery and
carrot and parboil for 2–3 minutes. Drain and add to slow
crock. Place meat on top and sprinkle on sweet corn, herbs,
peas and seasoning. Add beef stock. Replace lid and cook
on LOW for 8 hours.

Before serving, heat oil in a frying pan and fry the chopped
onion and garlic. Use chilli according to taste, although it's
supposed to be a very hot soup. Mix chilli powder with an
equal amount of water and stir into frying pan with onion
and cook together. The chilli should colour the oil but
not emulsify with it. Keep hot, and hand this hot sauce
separately.

Adjust seasoning of soup. Add lemon juice. Remove bay
leaf.

Gulyas   **8–10 hours LOW**

Gulyas is the Irish Stew of Eastern Europe – a traditional
soup-stew made with beef or veal cooked with onions and
spiced with paprika.

½ kg (1 lb) shin of beef or veal, ¼ kg (½ lb) onions, 30 g (1 oz)
each of fat and flour, 2 potatoes, 2 tomatoes, 1 green pepper,
1 garlic clove, *bouquet garni*, salt and pepper, 2 tbs paprika,
6 coriander seeds and 3 whole allspice, 1 litre (2 pt) water.
Optional – 1 glass of red wine (white wine if veal is used).

Pre-heat the slow crock. Peel and slice onions and brown
in fat. Meanwhile, cut the meat into small cubes, removing

any excess fat or gristle. Pound the coriander and allspice seeds and mix them with the paprika, garlic and salt. Roll the meat first in the spice mixture, then in the flour and fry it for a few minutes. Cut up the green pepper, tomatoes and potatoes and add them to the pan. Pour the wine on and let it reduce a little, then add the stock. Bring to the boil and transfer to the slow crock. Add *bouquet garni*. Replace lid and cook on LOW for 8–10 hours. To serve, adjust seasoning.

Mulligatawny   8–10 hours LOW

½ kg (1 lb) diced lean veal, 2 medium onions, 1 garlic clove, 2 small sweet apples, 1 bay leaf, salt and pepper, 1 litre (2 pt) chicken or vegetable stock, 2 tbs each of fat and cornflour; optional ingredients – 1 tbs *garam masala**, 125 ml (¼ pt) coconut milk, lemon slices.

Pre-heat the slow crock. Peel and slice onions and apples, crush garlic in salt. Heat fat in a frying pan and brown the meat and vegetables. Sprinkle on flour and *garam masala*. Stir-fry a little. Add some of the stock slowly, enough to make a smooth paste, heat a little then transfer to slow crock. Add remaining stock to slow crock, with salt, pepper and bay leaf. Replace lid and cook on LOW for 8–10 hours.

Add coconut milk (an infusion of coconut flakes and hot water, strained) towards the end of the cooking period – 10 or 15 minutes.

To serve adjust seasoning and accompany with rice. Garnish with lemon slices.

Vegetarian Mulligatawny   6 hours HIGH

¼ kg (½ lb) red lentils instead of meat, 1 litre (2 pt) vegetable stock instead of chicken stock, all other ingredients the same as above.

* A mixture of Indian spices, parched (roasted) and ground.

Same method as above. Wash lentils before adding to slow crock – but no need to soak them. Cook on HIGH for 6 hours.

North Sea Chowder   5 hours LOW

½ kg (1 lb) fresh or frozen white fish fillets (cod, haddock, plaice), 125 g (¼ lb) salt pork or bacon, 1 medium onion, 2 medium potatoes, ½ litre (1 pt) each of water and creamy milk, salt and pepper, 1 bay leaf, dash of Worcestershire sauce, pinch of tarragon; optional – 2 tsp horseradish sauce.

Pre-heat the slow crock. Cut salt pork into cubes and heat in a frying pan until the fat melts. Drain and transfer to slow crock. Peel and dice onion and potato and parboil for 10 minutes.
Cut fish into chunks. Add fish, onion, potato, seasoning, herbs and liquid to slow crock. Replace lid and cook on LOW for 5 hours. To serve, remove bay leaf, add a dash of Worcestershire sauce and stir in the horseradish if wished. Adjust seasoning.

Soupe à la Bonne Femme   4–6 hours LOW

¼ kg (½ lb) spinach or sorrel, 2 egg yolks, 125 g (4 oz) butter, 125 ml (¼ pt) single cream, salt, 1 litre (2 pt) chicken stock.

Pre-heat the slow crock. Cut spinach or sorrel into ribbons and then chop slantwise. Wash thoroughly. Melt the butter in a pan, add a little salt and *sauté* the spinach or sorrel for about 3–5 minutes. Then add the stock and heat to boiling before adding to a slow crock. Replace lid and cook on LOW for 4–6 hours until the spinach is soft. Then, mix the egg yolks with a little stock, stir and pour mixture into the slow crock, and keep stirring. When you have a smooth consistency pour in the cream, adjust seasoning and serve with hot French bread.

Soupe aux Poissons 5 hours LOW

60 g (2 oz) crab meat, 2 pilchards, a 125 g (4 oz) piece of cod and haddock, ½ a herring and mackerel, 2 tbs oil, 1 bay leaf, a sprig of thyme and parsley, 1 clove, 1 tomato, 1 leek, salt and pepper, 1 garlic clove, a pinch of saffron or turmeric, 3 tbs dry white wine, 1 litre (2 pt) water, 1 tbs vermicelli, garnish – mild grated cheese.

Pre-heat the slow crock. Clean the fish and vegetables, and chop up. Heat oil in a pan and *sauté* the fish and vegetables. Pour on wine, then stock and bring to boiling point before transferring to the slow crock. Add herbs, spices and seasoning. Replace lid and cook on LOW for 5 hours. Half an hour before serving, remove herbs, sieve the soup and return it to the slow crock, add the crab meat and the vermicelli which should be parboiled for 5 minutes first in boiling water. To serve, adjust seasoning and garnish with a mild cheese.

5 FISH AND SEAFOOD

Fish takes a very short time to cook in the slow crock, as little as 2 hours if you use the HIGH setting. So I have not emphasized the benefits of long slow cooking because there are none for fish, in fact it doesn't improve it at all and should be avoided. What I have done is to concentrate on sauces and stuffings that accompany fish because the other feature of the slow crock is that it preserves and enhances taste and flavour and it is this characteristic that makes slow crock fish cooking very worth while.

The cooking of fish depends on its fat content. In the slow crock this rule is slightly modified as there are only a few variations to choose from, namely:

With liquid to cover the base, plus optional use of trivet – for a steamed effect.

Up to ¼ litre (½ pt) stock or wine for stews, casseroles, braises.

A lightly greased slow crock with no liquid – for a baked effect.

Up to 1 litre (2 pt) hot stock/water for poached/'boiled' effect.

Lean fish are best for cooking in liquid, eg cod, flounder, haddock, pike, sea bass, perch and carp. They remain firm.

The oily fish should be 'baked' or 'steamed'. The types of fish suited to this are salmon, mackerel, trout and herring.

FROZEN FISH

After thawing, cook exactly as fresh fish. Frozen fish should be 'hard' when bought. Never re-freeze fish after it thaws.

BUYING FISH

A good fishmonger's or market will display the fish packed on ice. Fresh fish is very perishable and should be carefully handled and kept at a low temperature from the moment it is caught. Fresh fish has a characteristic smell which is pleasant and easy to detect with just a little experience. Fresh fish has a firm and elastic flesh that leaves no impress to the touch of fingers. The gills should be red, and the eyes bright and bulging, with the scales closely adhering to the flesh. Fish can be bought either dressed or drawn. Drawn (whole) fish have only their scales and entrails removed. Dressed fish have scales, head, fins, tail and entrails removed.

HOW MUCH TO BUY

A drawn or whole fish weighing $\frac{1}{2}$ kg (1 lb) will serve two people; $\frac{1}{2}$ kg (1 lb) steaks will serve three; $\frac{1}{2}$ kg (1 lb) fillets will serve four.

STORING FISH

If storing in the refrigerator fish should not be allowed to pervade other food with its smell and should either be kept in a covered glass bowl or wrapped in greaseproof paper. Clean it before storing if it is not being used for a day or two. Unless purchased frozen, fresh fish bought from fishmongers should be cooked the same day, as it is already 12–24 hours old.

TINNED FISH

Like any other tinned food, tinned fish can be easily heated up in the slow crock and become part of a very pleasant casserole and the brine or oil from the tin can help to make the basis of a good sauce.

PREPARATION OF FISH

Many fishmongers will obligingly prepare and clean a fish for you if asked. However, there will be some occasions when you'll have to do it yourself.

Scaling To remove the scales from a fish hold the tail and scrape a blunt-edged knife over the fish from tail to head. Hold knife at a slant to prevent scales from flying. It is less messy if you do this with the fish held under water in a large bowl.

Skinning Cut out the fins with scissors. Cut away a narrow strip of skin along the entire length of the back. Cut and loosen skin at the gills and pull skin off towards the tail, following closely with a knife to avoid tearing the flesh. Skin the other side in the same way.

Dressing Make a slit in the stomach and remove entrails and any clots of blood. Remove head and tail unless fish is very small. Wash thoroughly and wipe with a dry cloth.

Boning Use a very sharp pointed knife. Begin at the tail end and slip the knife between the flesh and the backbone and cut the entire length of each side of fish, keeping knife as close as possible to backbone. On a large fish, do not cut all the way through the back but keep the two sides together for stuffing. Smaller fish are cut into separate fillets.

FISH RECIPES

Basic Recipe for Baked Fish Fillets or Steaks
                                                        4–6 hours LOW

1–1½ kg (2–3 lb) fish (bass, haddock, halibut, perch, pike, trout, salmon, tuna, flounder).

Cut fillets or steaks about 1–2 cm ($\frac{1}{2}$–1″) thick. Dip in salted milk then roll in breadcrumbs and place in the base of the greased slow crock. Replace lid and cook on LOW for 4–6 hours until fish is flaky. Serve with a hot sauce.

Baked Stuffed Fillets or Steaks   **4–6 hours LOW**

Grease the base of the slow crock lightly. Spread a layer of fish then a layer of stuffing alternately until the ingredients are used up. Season each layer with salt, pepper and lemon juice. Sprinkle surface with buttered breadcrumbs or *sautéed* vegetable slices such as green pepper or onion. Replace lid and cook on LOW for 4–6 hours until fish is flaky. Serve plain or with a sauce or lemon butter.

Baked Spiced Fish   **4–6 hours LOW**

1 fish about 1–1$\frac{1}{2}$ kg (2–3 lb) grey mullet, bream, sea bass, etc, 2 tsp each of cumin and curry powder, 2 tsp oregano, 2–3 large tomatoes, 2 garlic cloves, 1 large lemon, salt and pepper, oil, 60 ml (2 fl oz) wine or sherry.

Gut fish and chop head off. Chop garlic and place inside the fish. Sprinkle spices, herbs and seasoning over the fish. Slice lemon and tomatoes and place half on the base of the slow crock. Lay fish on top. Pour on wine, then place the remaining lemon and tomatoes on top. Replace lid and cook on LOW for a minimum of 4 hours until fish is tender. To serve, lift fish out, and place on warm serving dish with tomatoes and lemons around it. Adjust the seasoning of the juices and hand round separately. Accompany with boiled potatoes.

Baked Cod with Beer Sauce   **4–6 hours LOW**

1 kg (2 lb) cutlet of cod, 125 g (4 oz) mushrooms, 60 g (2 oz) streaky bacon, 1 tsp vinegar and brown sugar, 2 tbs minced onion, 1 garlic clove, 1 bay leaf, 2 cloves, ½ grated apple, salt and pepper, pinch of nutmeg, ¼ litre (½ pt) lager or light ale, 30 g (1 oz) each of butter and cornflour.

Rub the fish with salt and pepper and let it stand while the other ingredients are prepared. Cut the bacon into small pieces, peel and slice the mushrooms and place both in the base of the slow crock. Add the bay leaf, minced onion, crushed garlic, cloves, apple, nutmeg and vinegar mixed with sugar. Place fish on top. Pour in the lager. Replace lid and cook on LOW for 4–6 hours until fish is flaky.

When cooked, remove fish and keep warm. Knead the cornflour with the butter and stir it into the cooking liquid in little pieces, allowing it to cook for at least 5 minutes. Stir well and adjust seasoning.

Baked Stuffed Mackerel   **6 hours LOW**

4 small–medium mackerel. *Stuffing*: 60 g (2 oz) cooked rice, 1 small onion, 125 g (4 oz) mushrooms, 2 tsp chopped fennel or parsley, salt and pepper, 60 g (2 oz) butter. *Sauce* – 4 tbs each of wine vinegar and water, 1 tsp allspice, 3 bay leaves, 1 tbs orange juice.

Clean fish, removing backbones, heads and tails. Mix together the rice with the chopped onion and mushrooms, herbs and seasoning. Bind with melted butter. Stuff each fish with the mixture and then place in base of slow crock. Mix wine vinegar, water and orange juice and pour into slow crock, then add allspice and bay leaves. Replace lid and cook on LOW 6 hours until fish is cooked. To serve, remove fish and place on a warm serving dish. Strain the cooking liquid and pour it over the fish or hand separately.

Basic Recipe for Steamed Stuffed Whole Fish
                                    4–6 hours LOW

Choose a fish that will fit your slow crock, weighing between
1½–2½ kg (3–5 lb). Remove head and tail if wished. Bone if
wished. Slit and clean the fish and then rub the inside with
salt. Stuff. Fasten edges together with toothpicks, cocktail
sticks or thread.

Place either on the base of the slow crock or on a trivet.
Brush with melted butter, sprinkle with salt and lemon
juice. Add a few tablespoons of water to cover the base of
the slow crock. Replace lid and cook on LOW for 4–6 hours
until fish is flaky and a white liquid drains from fish. Serve
hot with a sauce.

Poached or Boiled Fish   **3–4 hours LOW**

Pre-heat the slow crock. Use lean fish, whole, fillets,
steaks or slices. Wrap or tie fish in cheesecloth and place in
slow crock. Cover with hot water. Add 1 tbs lemon juice or
vinegar to each litre (2 pt) of water. Add chopped celery,
parsley, onion and bay leaf. Replace lid and cook on LOW
3–4 hours. To serve, drain fish and remove cheesecloth,
serve with a hot sauce. Use the liquid as a basis for soups or
a sauce for the fish.

Poached Fish with Egg Sauce   **4–6 hours LOW**

1 kg (2 lb) white fish fillets, 1 celery stalk, 1 onion, 4 tbs
butter, 3 tsp salt, *bouquet garni* – 6 peppercorns, strip of
lemon peel, 1–2 bay leaves, fennel stalk, tarragon.
Sauce – 2 egg yolks, 2 tbs ground almonds, 1 tbs milk.
Water, juice of 1 lemon, 1 small sprig parsley.

Pre-heat the slow crock. Peel and slice onion, chop celery
and *sauté* them in butter. Transfer to slow crock. Place fish

fillets on top, add seasoning and *bouquet garni*. Pour in juice
of lemon and water to a depth of 1·5 cm ($\frac{1}{2}$"). Replace lid and
cook on LOW for 4–6 hours.

Then make sauce: Beat egg yolks with milk until light, and
add almonds. Add tablespoon of cooking liquid at a time,
stirring continuously. When you have about 125 ml ($\frac{1}{4}$ pt)
of sauce, pour it back over the fish, allow the sauce to cook
for 5–10 minutes. Adjust seasoning, remove *bouquet garni*,
serve.

Poached Fish with Tomato Sauce   **4–6 hours LOW**

1 kg (2 lb) whole or filleted white fish, 1 onion, 1 carrot, 1
celery stalk, $\frac{1}{4}$ kg ($\frac{1}{2}$ lb) fresh or tinned tomatoes, 125 ml
($\frac{1}{4}$ pt) single cream, 2 tbs butter, salt and pepper, 1 tsp
cinnamon, 1 tsp marjoram, white wine.

Pre-heat the slow crock. Clean and dry fish. Salt it inside
and out and let it stand during remaining preparations. Peel
and slice onion, carrot and celery and parboil in boiling
water for 3 minutes. Drain and transfer to slow crock. Skin
tomatoes if fresh by plunging into boiling water. Then chop.
Stir them into the vegetables already in the slow crock and
sprinkle on cinnamon and marjoram. Melt butter in a frying
pan and *sauté* the fish very lightly, then pour on white wine
and let the fish soak in it a few minutes. Transfer to slow
crock and make sure that the wine comes to a depth of
about 1·5 cm ($\frac{1}{2}$"). Replace lid and cook on LOW for 4–6
hours. To serve, mix cream with an equal amount of cooking
liquid (added gradually), and then pour mixture back over
the fish and allow it to heat up. Adjust seasoning. Serve.

Poached Salmon Steaks   **4–6 hours LOW**

1 kg (2 lb) salmon steaks, $\frac{1}{2}$ tsp salt, 1 tsp pickling spices,
1 tbs each of chopped parsley and chives, 1 green pepper and

small onion, juice of 1 lemon, 1 tbs oil, hot water, optional – chilli sauce.

Pre-heat slow crock during preparations. De-seed and slice pepper, peel and slice onion and *sauté* in oil. Transfer to slow crock. Pour hot water into the base of the slow crock (about 1·5 cm, $\frac{1}{2}''$) and add spices, seasoning and lemon juice. Wrap the fish up in cheesecloth and tie securely or place on a trivet in the slow crock. Replace lid and cook on LOW 4–6 hours until fish is cooked. To serve, remove steaks, drain and keep warm, garnish with the vegetables, adjust the seasoning of the sauce, adding chilli sauce if wished, and then pour it over the fish.

Basic Recipe for Braised or Stewed Fish   4–6 hours LOW

1–1$\frac{1}{2}$ kg (2–3 lb) lean fish, $\frac{1}{4}$ litre ($\frac{1}{2}$ pt) stock or wine, 2 tbs butter and flour, salt and pepper, 2 medium onions and tomatoes, 1 tbs chopped parsley and fennel.

Peel and chop onions and tomatoes. *Sauté* onions lightly in butter and transfer to slow crock with tomatoes. Toss fish in seasoned flour and brown lightly in butter. Place on top of vegetables, pour on stock. Replace lid and cook on LOW 4–6 hours until fish is flaky. To serve, adjust seasoning and garnish with fresh chopped herbs.

Sweet Curried Fish   4–6 hours LOW

1 kg (2 lb) filleted white fish, 2 medium onions, 2 garlic cloves, 1 sweet apple, 60 g (2 oz) mushrooms, 1 tbs Madras curry powder, juice of 1 lemon, grated rind of $\frac{1}{2}$ lemon, salt and pepper, 1 bay leaf, 1 tbs wine vinegar, 2 tbs each of butter and cornflour, 90 ml (3 fl oz) fish or chicken stock, garnish – chopped parsley, toasted almonds.

Cut fish into small pieces and place in base of slow crock. Peel and chop apple and vegetables. Mix cornflour with crushed garlic, spices, lemon juice and vinegar to make a paste. Melt butter in a frying pan and *sauté* the apple and vegetables lightly, then add paste and *sauté* for another minute or so. Add the stock, stir thoroughly and pour it over the fish. Add bay leaf and remaining seasoning. Replace lid and cook on LOW for 4–6 hours until fish is flaky. To serve, adjust seasoning. Garnish with chopped parsley and toasted almonds.

Spiced Fish Steaks   **4–6 hours LOW**

1 kg (2 lb) mullet, carp or bass steaks, 125 g (4 oz) mushrooms, 2 tsp salt and pepper, 2 tsp coriander seeds, 4 cardamom pods, $\frac{1}{2}$ tsp ground cloves, 1 tsp ground ginger, 4 small tomatoes, 125 ml ($\frac{1}{4}$ pt) dry white wine, 2 tbs minced onion, 3 tbs flour and butter.

Pound all the spices and seasonings together and sprinkle this mixture over the cleaned and dried fish. Let it stand for about an hour or so. Wash and slice mushrooms and tomatoes and place in base of slow crock, mixed with minced onion. Place steaks on top, and pour wine over them. Replace lid and cook on LOW for 4–6 hours. To serve, remove fish and keep warm. Knead butter with flour and stir it into cooking liquid. Allow to cook and thicken. Adjust seasoning and pour the sauce over the fish.

Spiced White Fish Casserole   **4–6 hours LOW**

1 kg (2 lb) white fish, 1 small onion, 1 celery stalk, 125 g (4 oz) frozen green beans, 4 tomatoes, 1 tsp salt and pepper, 2 tbs chopped parsley, $\frac{1}{2}$ tsp saffron or turmeric, $\frac{1}{2}$ tsp each of ground ginger and cumin, $\frac{1}{4}$ tsp cayenne, 125 ml ($\frac{1}{4}$ pt) sour cream, 6 tbs vinegar.

Peel and mince the onion and mix it with the herbs, seasoning and spices. Spread this mixture over the cleaned and sliced fish and let it stand for about an hour or so. Wash and dice the celery, beans and tomatoes and place in base of slow crock. Place fish on top. Pour vinegar over this. Replace lid and cook on LOW for 4–6 hours. To serve, pour in sour cream and stir well. Re-heat and adjust seasoning.

Mustard Herring   4–6 hours LOW

4 large herrings, 1 tbs ready mixed mustard, 125 ml ($\frac{1}{4}$ pt) dry cider, 1 tsp paprika, 1 bay leaf, 3 peppercorns, 1 carton of sour cream.

Scrape each herring from tail to head with a knife to remove scales. Slit fish along underside to tail and remove roe and blood vessels. Open each fish out and place cut side down on a flat (wooden) surface. Press firmly along centre backbone to flatten fish. Turn over and remove backbone. Trim tails and fins then pat dry with kitchen paper. Season with salt and pepper.

Mix the mustard with paprika and spread evenly over each herring. Then roll each one up and secure with a cocktail stick if necessary. Place in slow crock. Pour cider into slow crock and add peppercorns and bay leaf. Replace lid and cook on LOW 4–6 hours until fish is cooked. Then remove, allow to cool and serve with salad and sour cream.

Fish and Gooseberry Sauce   4–6 hours LOW

4 small mackerel, $\frac{1}{4}$ kg each (8 oz) green gooseberries, juice and rind of 1 lemon, 1 tsp sugar, 1 tsp ground ginger or nutmeg, 1 egg, salt and white pepper, water.

Optional – sprig of rosemary, 125 g (4 oz) mushrooms, 2 tbs butter.

Top and tail gooseberries, wash and place in base of slow crock. Sprinkle them with sugar, spice, grated lemon rind and juice. Add water to cover fruit. Clean and prepare mackerel. If wished, stuff with optional ingredients: wash and slice mushrooms and *sauté* in butter. Then stuff the fish with the mushrooms and crushed rosemary. Place on top of gooseberries. Replace lid and cook on LOW for 4–6 hours. To serve, remove fish and keep warm. Mix egg yolk with a little cooking juice and stir into gooseberries. Mash the whole mixture and adjust seasoning. Serve.

This recipe could also be used for mullet and herring.

Halibut with Cucumber Herb Sauce   4–6 hours LOW

4 halibut steaks, 1 whole cucumber, 2 sprigs fresh tarragon, 60 g (2 oz) lean cooked ham, small piece of celery, salt and pepper, pinch of ground mace, 2 tbs chopped parsley or chives, 125 ml (¼ pt) white wine, 4 tbs water, 2 egg yolks, 125 ml (¼ pt) single cream, 2 tbs butter, lemon juice.
Optional garnish – lemon slices.

Sprinkle fish with salt and pepper and a little lemon juice and let it stand during the other preparations. Peel and slice cucumber then *sauté* it in butter for a few minutes and transfer to base of slow crock. Place chopped ham and celery on top. Sprinkle with seasoning, herbs and spice. Place fish on top and add wine and water. Replace lid and cook on LOW 4–6 hours until fish is cooked.

Then, remove fish and keep warm. *Purée* or sieve the cucumber mixture and return it to slow crock. Mix egg yolks with cream and stir this into sauce. Allow it to heat up, adjust seasoning and pour it over the fish. Garnish with thin lemon slices if wished.

Stuffed Haddock in Rich Fish Sauce   4–6 hours LOW

4 fillets of fresh haddock (approx. ¼ kg (½ lb) each).

Stuffing – 200 g (6 oz) oatmeal, 125 g (4 oz) shelled walnuts, 2 tsp dried fennel, 60 g (2 oz) minced onion *or* 2 tbs chopped chives, salt and pepper, pinch of nutmeg, 2 egg yolks, 60 g (2 oz) butter, milk to moisten if necessary, 2–3 sprigs of rosemary.

Sauce – 1 tbs vinegar or lemon juice, 4 tbs tomato paste, ¼ litre (½ pt) fish stock, 3 chopped anchovies or a few drops of anchovy essence, 1 tbs each of butter and cornflour, 125 ml (¼ pt) single cream, optional – 3–4 tbs sherry.

To make the stuffing mince the onion and chop the walnuts. Melt 60 g (2 oz) butter and cook the onion and walnuts for a few minutes then add the finely chopped rosemary, fennel and oatmeal. Cook. Transfer the mixture to a bowl and add the beaten egg yolks to bind. Moisten with a little milk if necessary. Add seasoning and spice. Divide the stuffing equally between the fillets and either roll each one up, or lay two fillets together with the stuffing in between.

Then, mix the tomato paste with the vinegar and add it to the slow crock with the fish stock. Add chopped anchovy or essence. Place the fish on a trivet or on a piece of metal foil and add to slow crock. Replace lid and cook on LOW 4–6 hours until fish and stuffing are cooked.

To serve, remove fish carefully and keep warm. Also take out trivet or foil. Knead together the cornflour and butter and add gradually to the cooking liquid. Stir well and allow to cook for 5 minutes. Then thicken the sauce with the cream, and add sherry if wished. Stir, adjust seasoning and serve with the fish.

Eel Casserole   4–6 hours LOW

1 kg (2 lb) eel pieces, ¼ kg (½ lb) prunes, 125 g (4 oz) mushrooms, ¼ litre (½ pt) white wine, juice of 1 lemon, salt and

T–C

pepper, 2 tbs each of butter and cornflour, *bouquet garni* –
strip of lemon peel, sprig of tarragon and parsley, 1 bay leaf,
1 fennel stalk.
Optional for a richer sauce – 1 egg yolk, 2 tbs cream or top
of the milk.

Wash prunes and place them in the base of the slow crock.
Wash and dry eel pieces and sprinkle with lemon juice then
place on top of prunes. Wash and slice mushrooms and
spread them around the eel. Add *bouquet garni*, seasoning
and wine. Replace lid and cook on LOW 4–6 hours until eel
is cooked.

To serve, knead butter with cornflour and stir gradually
into casserole. Allow to cook for 5 minutes. Stir well. Adjust
seasoning. Remove *bouquet garni*. For a richer sauce mix
egg yolk with cream and stir into slow crock, allowing it to
heat up before serving.

Fish Diavolo   **4–6 hours LOW**

¾ kg (1½ lb) filleted white fish, 2 medium onions, 1 tsp
turmeric or saffron, 1 tsp grated nutmeg, salt and pepper,
2 egg yolks, 60 ml (2 fl oz) milk, ¼ kg (½ lb) tomatoes, 1 tsp
chilli powder, 1–2 tbs wine vinegar, oil.

Rub fish with turmeric and nutmeg and set aside. Chop
tomatoes and mix in chilli powder and vinegar. Add salt and
pepper to taste, then place in base of slow crock. Peel and
chop onions and *sauté* lightly in oil and transfer to slow
crock. Place fish on top. Replace lid and cook on LOW for
4–6 hours until fish is tender and flaky. To serve, beat egg
yolks with milk and stir into dish. Adjust seasoning, serve.

Matelote of Fish   **4–6 hours LOW**

1 kg (2 lb) assorted fish pieces, 125 g (4 oz) streaky bacon,
$\frac{1}{4}$ kg ($\frac{1}{2}$ lb) small onions, salt and pepper, 3 tbs fresh mint
leaves, 3–4 garlic cloves, $\frac{1}{4}$ litre ($\frac{1}{2}$ pt) red wine, 2 tbs brandy
(optional), 30 g (1 oz) each of butter and cornflour, garnish –
croûtons of fried bread and watercress.

Cut the fish into pieces about 5 cm (2″) long. Parboil the
peeled onions for 5 minutes. Chop the mint and crush the
garlic. Brown the bacon in its own fat and chop it up. Add
all these ingredients to the slow crock, sprinkle on seasoning
to taste and add wine. Replace lid and cook on LOW for 4–6
hours until fish and onions are cooked.

To serve, pour in the brandy if wished. Thicken the stew
with a *beurre manié*. Stir and allow it to cook 5 minutes.
Adjust seasoning, garnish with *croûtons* and watercress.

Gefillte Fish   **4 hours LOW or 2 hours HIGH**

Jewish fish balls poached in a rich fish stock, served chil-
led with horseradish.

1 kg (2 lb) mixed freshwater fish fillets (pike, carp), 1
medium onion, salt and pepper, 2 eggs, $\frac{1}{4}$ tsp sugar, 2 tbs
matzo meal, 1 litre (2 pt) hot fish stock (see page 37), 2
bay leaves, 2 cooked sliced carrots (garnish), horseradish.

During preparation of fish balls pre-heat slow crock on
HIGH and add HOT stock.

Peel and chop onion and pound it with the fish fillets to a
smooth mixture. In a large bowl mix it with eggs, matzo
meal, sugar and 1 tsp salt, $\frac{1}{4}$ tsp pepper. Moisten with water
if necessary. Then, moisten hands and shape the mixture
into balls. Carefully drop them into the fish stock. Replace
lid and cook on LOW 4 hours or HIGH 2 hours.

Then, remove the fish balls to a large dish and allow to cool. Adjust the seasoning of the stock and strain $\frac{1}{4}$ litre ($\frac{1}{2}$ pt) over the fish balls when cool. Garnish the dish with 2 cooked, sliced carrots. Chill. Serve with horseradish.

6 | MEAT

Since most of us do our own catering we are used to following through the chain of events from choosing a piece of meat at the butcher's or in a supermarket to the preparation and cooking of the dish. The process is rather like that of an artist painting a portrait. Our instinct, usually guided by knowledge of a traditional recipe, will help to bring out the inherent character of the meat and with the addition of spices, herbs and seasoning, our equivalent to the artist's palette of colours, will enhance that basic quality. Yet given the same ingredients each interpretation will vary with each cook or artist. Good meat cooking depends on the interpretation of the following principles: that ingredients should taste of what they are. Cooking should preserve, not destroy, the identity of the main ingredients, and additional ingredients should complement this essential aim, which leads to the principle – think simple. The simplest formulas are often the most successful. And this is the way the slow crock cooks best – simply.

Cooking meat in the slow crock is a simple affair because slow cooking brings out the full flavour of even the most basic ingredients. You choose the meat, and remember: meat will be succulent, and tender because there's been hardly any evaporation during the cooking period, and food retains its moisture. It is a two-sided coin because if you're disappointed that you can't get a crisp roast, you'll be more than pleasantly surprised by the flavour of the sauce or gravy that is all the more intense.

It is true that the more preparation you put into a dish the more the slow crock displays its full potential and brings beautiful and memorable results that rate equally with dishes cooked by conventional means. (And after all the slow crock is based on a traditional method.) On the other hand, even the simplest and quickest preparation of a pot-roast can bring an equally justified conclusion that the slow crock does it all for you.

To show just how versatile is the slow crock I have included a separate chapter, '"Cordon Bleu" made easy in the slow crock', where the recipes involve more preparation and contain unusual ingredients, but not necessarily more expensive cuts of meat; plus a variety of dishes for the adventurous palate.

In this chapter, too, I have indicated the ways in which additional processes can be used with the slow crock – for example, making a sauce at the end of the cooking period. Generally I have assumed that, like me, you enjoy or are in the habit of doing a certain amount of preparation. For instance, browning meat improves the appearance of a dish as well as enhancing the flavour. Also, browning produces a better sauce at the end. In the slow crock it will reduce overall cooking time, but, perhaps the main reason I do not consistently advise browning is because I regard the slow crock as a convenience machine that reduces in every way the need for certain time-consuming kitchen traditions. There are exceptions to this which I shall mention when they occur.

I have included some detailed recipes on the use of convenience or short-cut food for no other reason than that I accept the need for some people to be able to compose a dish as quickly as possible, then rush off to work or out on business and expect a decent-tasting meal when they return. The slow crock will also prove itself here, particularly if this kind of food is combined with some fresh meat, as I have usually specified.

TIMING

Day
Most meat cooked on a LOW setting takes a day, that is *6–8 hours minimum* (eg lamb and pork chops, stewing lamb, pork). This will vary with the quality of the meat. Cheap or

tough stewing beef or brisket will take longer (10–12 hours) while expensive or tender beef will take less (8–10 hours).

Half-day
Pre-cooking meat such as mince for moussaka or meat balls will reduce cooking to about half a day, approximately 4–6 hours.

Overnight
In some cases it is a good idea if a meat dish is cooked overnight, as in the case of tongue. This gives flexibility to the length of cooking needed which can be between 12 and 16 hours, and the dish itself will be ready for the next stage of preparation by the morning, leaving the slow crock free for other uses.

Overcooking
Rarely will a meat dish suffer from overcooking if you are a few hours late – this is one of the attributes that makes the slow crock an adaptable machine to use.

Speeding up
If you want to speed up your meat cooking use HIGH and cut timing by approximately half. Or you can bring all your ingredients to the boil in a separate container and then transfer them to a *pre-heated* slow crock. (NB Never add pre-heated ingredients to a cold slow crock.) This can reduce timing by approximately a third. But again this depends on the type of meat being used (see page 70, *Day*). The pre-heating method is most suited to stews where there is plenty of liquid in the recipe.

ONE-POT MEALS

The slow crock provides the option of cooking an entire meal in one container. Traditional dishes such as Irish Stew, Lancashire Hot Pot and more unusual ones such as Chilli Con Carne are among the simplest.

Always remember that when using ingredients that cook on different settings, such as beans (HIGH) and beef (LOW), use the higher setting.

LIQUID

Food contains a substantial amount of moisture so it is wise to be conservative in the amount of liquid used, even for a stew. You will find that the stock may be as much as twice the volume you started with by the end of the cooking period. This is particularly true when using vegetable ingredients as well as meat.

METHODS OF COOKING MEAT

There are two ways of cooking meat in a slow crock: either with a little liquid which produces a pot-roast, roast or braise, or using lots of liquid which gives a stew or casserole, or a 'boiled' dish. For the sake of convention and also to make myself and the slow crock more easily understood I have used the familiar names to describe the different effects one can achieve in the slow crock, and so that you can see for yourself what to expect in terms of traditional dishes that you know. There is a table opposite to explain the various methods used with the two choices offered by the slow crock.

When cooking with the minimum amount of liquid it is often useful to cover the joint with a piece of greaseproof paper, dampened a little, which helps preserve the colour without affecting the cooking time. You can use metal foil but this tends to speed things up. Greaseproof paper is particularly useful when cooking a joint of brisket overnight for example.

It is advisable to parboil starchy vegetables, such as carrots, parsnips, turnips, swedes, potatoes, for 5–10 minutes, as the temperature is rather low for starchy and root vegetables to soften easily.

Sautéing is more applicable to onions, leeks and green vegetables – and it also brings out their flavour.

METHODS OF COOKING MEAT

METHOD/LIQUID	a little liquid 250 ml (½ pt) or under	lots of liquid 250 ml (½ pt) or over
Pot-Roast or Roast	Whole joints. Small – up to 1½ kg (3 lb) Large – up to 2½ kg (5 lb)	
Braise	Small pieces of meat – chops, slices, cubes, mince, or whole piece	
Casserole or Stew		Small pieces of meat – chops, slices, cubes, mince
'Boil' (simmer)		Whole joints. Small – up to 1½ kg (3 lb) Large – up to 2½ kg (5 lb)

SETTING/LIQUID	a little liquid 250 ml (½ pt) or under	lots of liquid 250 ml (½ pt) or over
HIGH	ROAST	
LOW	POT-ROAST BRAISE	STEW OR CASSEROLE 'BOIL' (simmer)

Quantities are for four, which means that if you have a large size slow crock that you want to use to full capacity you should double the recipe. Joints of meat vary in size and shape and your choice will depend on which will fit in your slow crock. A general guideline is that a small slow crock can cook a joint weighing up to 1½ kg (3 lb) and a large slow crock can cook a joint of up to 2½ kg (5 lb), but check your manufacturer's instructions first. At time of writing one manufacturer does not recommend cooking whole joints of meat, poultry or game, in which case take note and always joint the poultry and game or chop the meat. (Kenwood's model.)

POT-ROAST AND ROAST

1. Choose a joint that will fit your slow crock. Small – up to 1½ kg (3 lb), large – up to 2½ kg (5 lb). If the meat is fatty you can cook it on a trivet.
2. Season the meat and brown it if wished. Vegetables such as onions or tomatoes used for flavouring should be washed, sliced and placed on the base of the slow crock, or at the side if a trivet is used.
3. Place the meat in the slow crock – directly on the base, on top of the vegetables or on the trivet. For a pot-roast add a small amount of flavoursome liquid (beer, wine or rich stock), not more than 125 ml (¼ pt), replace lid and cook on LOW for 8–10 hours. For a roast, grease the inside of slow crock with oil or fat, if wished add a tbs of wine, replace lid and cook on HIGH for about 6 hours.
4. When cooked, transfer the joint and any vegetables to another container and keep warm. Remove trivet, if used. Skim fat off cooking juices then pour gravy over meat or thicken with flour or cornflour to make a sauce.

BRAISE

1. Decide what proportion of meat and vegetables or other ingredients you will use. Per serving: 200 g (6 oz) boneless

meat or $\frac{1}{4}$ kg ($\frac{1}{2}$ lb) meat with bone. A small capacity slow crock will take up to 1$\frac{1}{2}$ kg (3 lb) meat, a larger capacity up to 2$\frac{1}{2}$ kg (5 lb), plus one or two fruits and vegetables for flavour.

2. Vegetables should be washed, sliced, *sautéed*, or par-boiled, and placed on the base of the slow crock; the depth of this layer will depend on the balance of ingredients that you want. Fruit should be washed and sliced (or placed whole if small enough – grapes, dried fruit) on the base of the slow crock. Liquid is added until it nearly covers the layer. Don't add more than 125 ml ($\frac{1}{4}$ pt).

3. Trim any excess fat from the meat, then toss it in seasoned flour and brown if wished. Alternatively, place the meat in the slow crock and thicken the sauce with flour or eggs, etc, at the end of the cooking period. The preparation of the meat will depend on the kind of dish you want to create just as the choice of vegetables will alter the flavour. A traditional vegetable accompaniment will include slices of onion, carrot, celery, turnip, tomato or swede. If you want the dish to have a special flavour select one or two distinctive vegetables, for example, aubergine or leek.

4. Place meat in slow crock. Replace lid and cook on LOW for 6–8 or 8–10 hours depending on the meat (see Timing, page 70). When cooked, either serve meat separately with vegetables mashed into the gravy or, if there are enough, serve vegetables as an accompaniment or garnish, and hand gravy separately.

STEWS AND CASSEROLES

Traditionally there are two types of stew – white and brown. In a white stew, sometimes called a *fricassée*, the meat is not browned but blanched. The liquid is usually thickened at the end of the cooking period unless, as in an Irish Stew, ingredients such as potatoes cause the thickening.

In a brown stew, sometimes called a *ragoût*, meat is browned with or without vegetables, and a little flour is stirred in after the browning.

Stews are known by many different names that describe their ingredients or the traditions behind them. Here are a few of the better known:

Blanquette	A white *ragoût* of lamb, veal, chicken or rabbit. The sauce is made with egg yolks and cream, traditionally garnished with small onions and mushrooms.
Cacciatore or *Chasseur*	The Italian and French name respectively for a hunter's stew. A brown stew with meat or chicken cooked in wine or stock, accompanied by herbs, mushrooms and shallots.
Carbonnade	Stew with beer.
Cassoulet	A haricot bean stew with pork and mutton, goose or duck. Traditional flavouring includes garlic, an onion stuck with cloves, a carrot and a *bouquet garni*.
Daube	Stew with wine.
Fricassée	A white stew with meat, poultry or fish, made with a white stock and served with a white sauce.
Marengo	Name given to Napoleon's victory feast after a battle with the Austrians in 1800. The shell-shocked cook found a few scraps and combined them into a dish that has since become famous. They included chicken, egg, tomato, crayfish, garlic, bread, oil and brandy.
Navarin	A French stew in existence long before the battle that changed its name took place (Navarino), consisting of mutton or lamb cooked with root vegetables or small onions and potatoes.
Ragoût	Pieces of meat, poultry or fish lightly browned then slowly cooked in stock with vegetables.
Salmis	A brown *ragoût* usually made with game or poultry, cooked in a rich brown sauce.

And there are many others which have connotations with

their places of origin, eg *Provençale, Niçoise, Bourguignonne*.

All these classic differences are liberally interpreted in this chapter, as you will see.

Casserole takes its name from the utensil in which a stew is traditionally cooked and is no different in principle from a stew. For some there is a strong link between stews, war, rationing and school meals and so while these associations linger people prefer to use an alternative name.

Basic Method for a Brown or White Stew

1. The thickening for the stew can be made by a basic *roux* sauce – 1 or 2 tbs of flour cooked in butter to which a small amount of stock is then added, then poured into the stew in the slow crock at the beginning. Alternatively the thickening may be provided by the ingredients themselves (potatoes, tomato *purée*). Or, the thickening process can take place at the end of the cooking period with the addition of cream, sour cream, egg yolks, or a *beurre manié* (equal quantities of flour and butter kneaded together and added bit by bit at the end and stirred until cooked). An alternative thickening agent to flour is cornflour, often used in Oriental cooking; it gives a lighter texture and is quicker in cooking.
2. Vegetables should be washed, peeled, de-seeded, sliced, diced or chopped. Boneless meat should be cut into small cubes or pieces about 5 cm (2″) square. Meat with bone or joints should be divided into larger pieces although this is usually done by the butcher if you ask.
3. For a white stew the meat can be *blanched* (veal, rabbit, chicken), and the vegetables too. A thickening can be made by the roux method or at some other stage in the cooking (see point 1).

For a brown stew toss meat in (seasoned) flour then fry in fat until brown. *Sauté* the vegetables.
4. Transfer all ingredients to slow crock, add stock, season-ing and herbs. Replace lid and cook on LOW for 6–8, 8–10 or 10–12 hours depending on the ingredients and the amount

of pre-cooking you have done. (The less pre-cooking the longer the cooking period in the slow crock; the tougher the meat the longer the cooking.) At the end, thicken the gravy (see point 1) and then adjust seasoning.

5. The amount of liquid used will depend on the quantity of meat. Remember also that the slow crock will not lose moisture but retain it so you will always have more than you started with. Generally, cover $\frac{2}{3}$ of the ingredients with stock.

Simple Slow Crock Stew

Buy enough meat to fill the slow crock (between $1\frac{1}{2}$–$2\frac{1}{2}$ kg, 3–5 lb) depending on size of slow crock. Trim off any excess fat. Place meat in slow crock. Add seasoning, herbs and stock. Mix all ingredients together. Replace lid and cook on LOW 8–10 hours, minimum. To serve, add thickening, adjust seasoning.

'Boiling' or Slow Simmer

This method is suited to whole joints of fresh meat, game and poultry, eg breast of lamb or veal, chicken; or salt meat (bacon, ham, pork, beef) and tongue. Smaller pieces lose flavour to the liquid unless this is done for a specific purpose such as enhancing a soup. Well-known boiled dishes are Scotch Broth, Pot-au-Feu, Boiled Beef and Dumplings and Cock-a-Leekie. The boiled meat is served as one course together with the vegetables cooked in the same stock, and the liquid is served as a soup. Consequently you will find some of these dishes in the soup chapter (see Chapter 4, pages 41–2).

Choose a joint that will fit comfortably into the slow crock with some room to spare. Salt meat should be soaked for a few hours or overnight, and the seasoning should be reduced in the cooking liquid.

Place joint in the slow crock, add sliced or chopped vegetables, seasoning and herbs including an onion stuck with one or two cloves. Add water to cover $\frac{2}{3}$ of the joint and cover it with a piece of damp greaseproof paper if wished. Replace lid and cook on LOW for 10–12 hours minimum or overnight.

When cooked remove joint from liquid and either refrigerate or keep warm depending on whether a hot or cold dish is wanted. To make soup strain off vegetables and use them either as accompaniment to meat or as a *purée* for the soup. Skim fat from stock and clarify (see Chapter 4, page 36). Reheat on HIGH if necessary, and stir in vegetable *purée* if wished.

Dumplings can be added in the last hour of cooking.

Short-Cut or Convenience Food
Tinned, dried or dehydrated ingredients can be added to the slow crock and cooked on LOW for up to 6 hours until they are thoroughly heated. Follow the instructions on the packets that give liquid quantities needed to reconstitute ingredients.

MARINADES

A marinade is a highly seasoned liquid in which meat, fish, poultry, and game may be soaked prior to cooking. The idea is to let the ingredients soak from 4 to 48 hours in a flavoured liquid to imbue it with its aroma and help to tenderize it.

The amount of liquid used varies, but usually it does not cover the meat entirely so that the meat can be turned once or twice during marination. The contents of a marinade vary greatly and here you can put your imagination to work. The basic liquid should ideally be slightly acid to help soften the fibres. The meat is then placed in a large bowl with the marinade and stored in a cool place or refrigerator throughout the process. The marinade is strained and later used as part of the cooking liquid. Once removed from the marinade the meat should be wiped dry, ready for use in the preparation of the dish.

LIQUIDS between 125–250 ml ($\frac{1}{4}$–$\frac{1}{2}$ pt) vinegar, beer, wine, brandy, cider, sherry, lemon juice and oil in smaller quantities.

SPICES peppercorns, dry mustard, cayenne, garlic, curry powder.

HERBS bay leaf, juniper berries, thyme, bruised parsley stalks, marjoram, rosemary, mixed herbs, *bouquet garni.*

VEGETABLES chopped onions, carrots and shallots.

PRESERVES redcurrant jelly, marmalade.

FRUIT orange rind, lemon rind.

ACCOMPANIMENTS FOR MEAT DISHES

Dumplings

125 g (4 oz) suet shredded or finely chopped, $\frac{1}{4}$ kg ($\frac{1}{2}$ lb) self-raising flour, or plain flour plus 1 tsp baking powder, pinch of salt, approx. 1 cup of cold water.

Sift flour, add salt and suet, mix well. Moisten with water to make a light dough. Divide mixture into small prune-size pieces or larger if wished, and roll into balls. Add these to a slow crock dish one hour before the end if LOW setting used, or $\frac{1}{2}$ hour if HIGH setting used. When cooked, remove from liquid with a perforated spoon.

Variations:
Herb dumplings: add 1 tbs or more of chopped mixed herbs
   to mixture.
Potato dumplings: halve the quantity of suet and add 2 raw
   grated potatoes
   or replace suet with $\frac{1}{4}$ kg ($\frac{1}{2}$ lb) cooked mashed potato.

Basic Bread Stuffing

125 g (4 oz) stale breadcrumbs, salt and pepper to taste, $\frac{1}{4}$ tsp thyme or marjoram, 60 g (2 oz) each of melted fat and chopped onion, 1 egg.

Combine bread, seasoning, herb and onion. Add fat and bind with an egg.

N.B. Stuffing swells on cooking so it should always be loosely packed.

Variations:
Celery stuffing: add 60 g (2 oz) finely chopped celery.
Chestnut stuffing: add 30 g (1 oz) finely chopped celery and $\frac{1}{2}$ kg (1 lb) boiled chopped chestnuts.
Mushroom stuffing: *Sauté* 60 g (2 oz) sliced mushrooms in the fat and add to ingredients.
Parsley stuffing: add 2–3 tbs chopped fresh parsley.
Prune stuffing: Omit herbs and prepare a half quantity of the bread stuffing. Cook and stone 125 g (4 oz) prunes and add them chopped to the mixture, with 60 g (2 oz) grated apple.
Raisin stuffing: Add 60 g (2 oz) seedless raisins.
Sage stuffing: Omit herbs and add 1 tbs crumbled or chopped sage leaves.

BEEF RECIPES

Pot-Roast Ordinaire   **8–12 hours LOW**

Beef rump, chuck, topside or brisket rolled in a round joint, 90 ml (3 fl oz) red wine, $\frac{1}{2}$ tsp each of basil and paprika, salt and pepper, 2 tbs chopped chives, fat or oil.

Season joint, melt fat in a frying pan and brown joint all over. Place in slow crock. Pour on the wine. Sprinkle on the herbs. Replace lid and cook on LOW for at least 8 hours until tender.

To serve, remove joint and keep warm. Skim fat from surface of gravy. Use *beurre manié** to thicken gravy if wished. Adjust seasoning.

Variations: Use tomato juice spiked with a dash of Worcestershire sauce and lemon juice instead of red wine. Or, add 3 tbs mixture of finely chopped carrot, onion and celery instead of chives.

Pot-Roast Creole   8–12 hours LOW

Beef rump, topside, chuck or brisket rolled in a round joint, 4 slices of streaky bacon, 2–3 green chilli peppers and tomatoes, 1 onion, 2–3 cloves of garlic, salt and pepper, *bouquet garni*, pinch of allspice, 2 tbs vinegar.

Wash and slice vegetables and place in bottom of slow crock. Spike the joint with pieces of garlic and lay the bacon rashers across it. Then place on top of vegetables. Sprinkle on remaining ingredients. Replace lid and cook on LOW for at least 8 hours until tender.

To serve, remove joint and keep warm. Skim fat from surface of gravy. Use *beurre manié* to thicken gravy, if wished. Adjust seasoning. Remove peppers.

European Pot-Roast   8–10 hours LOW

Beef rump or sirloin, 8 dried figs, prunes or apricots, 125 ml (¼ pt) white wine, ½ tsp ginger, salt and pepper, oil.

Wash dried fruit, drain and place on bottom of slow crock. Heat oil in a frying pan. Season the meat then brown it on all sides. Place in slow crock. Add ginger. Pour on white

* See page 77.

wine. Replace lid and cook on LOW for at least 8 hours until tender. Skim and thicken gravy as above.

American Pot-Roast   8–10 hours LOW

Beef joint for pot-roasting, 1 green pepper, 1 small onion and courgette, 125 g (4 oz) mushrooms, 90 ml (3 fl oz) each of red wine and tomato juice, 2 cloves garlic, salt, pepper and paprika to taste, 2 tbs butter.

Wash and slice vegetables then *sauté* in butter, and place on base of slow crock. Spike the meat with pieces of garlic and place in slow crock. Pour on liquid and sprinkle joint with seasoning and spice to taste. Replace lid and cook on LOW for at least 8 hours until joint is tender.

Braised Ribs of Beef   8 hours LOW

1½–2 kg (3–4 lb) lean short ribs of beef, 125 ml (¼ pt) red wine, 1 tsp rosemary, a bay leaf, 2 cloves of garlic, 1 onion stuck with 4 cloves, 1 carrot, flour, salt and pepper, 4 tbs fat or oil.

Toss ribs in seasoned flour and then brown them well in the fat. Place sliced carrot, herbs, garlic, onion stuck with cloves in slow crock and place browned ribs on top. Pour on the wine. Replace lid and cook on LOW for approximately 8 hours until the meat is easily taken from the bone. To serve, adjust seasoning.

Variations: For a braise with more vegetable ingredients, use less meat and add the following – 4 medium potatoes sliced, 125 g (4 oz) runner beans sliced, 3 extra carrots sliced.

Brisket and Barley   **12 hours LOW**

Brisket rolled and boned, 2 medium onions, 2 medium carrots, 125 g (4 oz) pearl barley, 1 tsp ready mixed mustard, 1 bay leaf, ½ tsp thyme, 250 ml (½ pt) beef stock or brown ale, optional – ½ tsp celery seed.

Wash barley, drain and place on base of slow crock. Slice vegetables and place at side. Place brisket on the barley. Add liquid, herbs, seasoning and spice. Replace lid and cook on LOW for about 12 hours until tender.

To serve, remove meat and keep warm in a separate container. Strain off the vegetable and barley mixture and place around meat. Make a gravy from the remaining liquid and hand round separately.

Cider Brisket with Sausage   **12 hours LOW**

Brisket rolled and boned, ¼ kg (½ lb) each of garlic sausage and salt pork, 1 carrot, 1 stalk celery, 1 bay leaf, 6 peppercorns, salt and pepper to taste, 250 ml (½ pt) cider.

Place joint in slow crock. Chop up garlic sausage and salt pork, carrot and celery and place around the joint. Add cider, seasoning and herbs. Replace lid and cook on LOW for about 12 hours until tender.

To serve, remove meat and keep warm in a separate container, and surround it with the chopped ingredients. Make gravy from the remaining liquid.

Alternatively, the brisket can be first marinaded overnight in the cider and then cooked as above.

Beer Braise   **8 hours LOW**

1–1½ kg (2–3 lb) slice of topside, 125 ml (¼ pt) beer or ale, 1 large onion, a stalk of celery, a sprig each of thyme and parsley, 1 bay leaf, 2 cloves of garlic, salt and pepper to taste, 2 tbs each of flour and butter or margarine.

Slice the onion, celery and garlic and *sauté* quickly in the butter. Transfer to slow crock.

Rub meat with seasoned flour and then brown gently in the butter. Place in slow crock. Pour beer over the ingredients. Add the herbs. Replace lid and cook on LOW for 8 hours or so until the meat is tender. To serve, remove herbs.

Silver Braise   8 hours LOW

1–1½ kg (2–3 lb) slice of silverside, 2 leeks, ¼ kg (½ lb) fresh or tinned tomatoes, 1 onion and carrot, 4 rashers of bacon, salt and pepper, *bouquet garni*, 2 tbs red wine vinegar, 2 tbs tomato paste or *purée*.

Trim, wash and slice the vegetables. Arrange them on the base of the slow crock. Add *bouquet garni*. Place meat on top and layer with bacon rashers. Season with salt, pepper and vinegar. Replace lid and cook on LOW for 8 hours or until meat is tender. To serve, arrange meat on a serving dish with vegetables around. Remove *bouquet garni* from stock. To serve, stir tomato *purée* into gravy and adjust seasoning.

Chinese Style Braised Beef   8 hours LOW

1 kg (2 lb) rump steak, ¼ kg (½ lb) mushrooms, 1 medium onion, 2 tbs soy sauce, 4 tbs olive oil, 1 tbs cornflour, 2 tbs dry white wine, salt and black pepper.

Peel and chop onion roughly and place in base of slow crock. Wash and slice mushrooms and place on top. Slice meat thinly across the grain and place in slow crock. Mix soy sauce, oil, cornflour and wine and pour over the meat and vegetables. Season to taste with a little salt and plenty of black pepper. Replace lid and cook on LOW for 6–8 hours until the meat is tender.

Spicy Beef Casserole   10 hours LOW

1 kg (2 lb) cubed stewing steak, ¼ kg (½ lb) onions, 1 tbs French mustard, 1 tbs tomato *purée*, ½ tsp carraway seeds, 1 tbs red wine vinegar, 250 ml (½ pt) brown stock, salt and pepper, 1 tbs each of oil and flour.

Peel and slice onions, heat oil and *sauté* them lightly. Sprinkle on flour and allow to cook. Transfer to slow crock and place meat on top. Mix remaining ingredients and add to slow crock. Replace lid and cook on LOW for 10 hours.
To serve, adjust seasoning.

Sweet and Sour Casserole   10 hours LOW

1 kg (2 lb) cubed stewing steak, ¼ kg (½ lb) fresh or tinned tomatoes, 1 onion, 1 tbs each of ready mixed English mustard and honey, 1 clove garlic, salt and pepper to taste, optional – 1 tbs each of blackcurrant jam and sweet chutney. 125 ml (¼ pt) beef stock, garnish – pineapple chunks, ground ginger. 1 tbs cornflour and butter (optional).

Peel and chop vegetables and place in base of slow crock, put meat on top. Mix the rest of the ingredients and pour into the dish. Replace lid and cook on LOW for 10 hours until meat is tender. To serve, adjust sweetening. Add a dash of ginger for a piquant effect. Garnish with pineapple chunks if wished. Mix thoroughly before dishing out.
If wished, add *beurre manié** at end to thicken.

* See page 77.

Steak and Kidney Casserole   **8–10 hours LOW**

1 kg (2 lb) stewing steak, ¼ kg (½ lb) ox kidney, vegetables, either 1 parsnip, carrot and onion or ¼ kg (½ lb) mushrooms, *bouquet garni* including a bay leaf, pinch of dry mustard, dash of Worcestershire sauce, salt and pepper to taste, 250 ml (½ pt) brown ale, Guinness or stock, 1 tbs flour and oil.

Peel and slice vegetables and *sauté* in oil. Transfer to slow crock. Trim excess fat from meat, skin and slice kidneys. Chop meat. Then toss meat and kidneys in seasoned flour and brown gently in oil. Place in slow crock. Add remaining ingredients and replace lid. Cook on LOW for 8–10 hours until meat is tender. To serve, mix all ingredients thoroughly and adjust seasoning.

Variation: If using mushrooms as the vegetable ingredient, you can also add a small tin of oysters, stirred in during the last hour of cooking.

Red Wine Casserole   **8 hours LOW**

¾ kg (1½ lb) lean chuck or rump steak cut into cubes or slices, ¼ kg (½ lb) shallots, ¼ kg (½ lb) carrots, 1 bay leaf, ½ tsp each of sweet basil and oregano, 1 garlic clove, scant 125 ml (¼ pt) red wine, 1 tbs each of flour and oil, salt and pepper to taste, optional – 90 ml (3 fl oz) sherry, 3 tsp sugar, 2 tbs butter.

Peel and slice vegetables and *sauté* lightly in oil, then transfer to slow crock. Brown meat on all sides, sprinkle on flour and stir, then place on top of vegetables in slow crock. Pour on wine and add seasoning.

Replace lid and cook on LOW for 8 hours until meat is tender. Before serving, melt butter and stir in sugar until dissolved. Add this and the sherry to the casserole and stir in. Adjust seasoning, remove bay leaf. Serve.

Orange Beef Casserole   **10 hours LOW**

1 kg (2 lb) cubed stewing beef, 2 medium onions, a small tin
of mandarin oranges, 1 carrot, 125 ml ($\frac{1}{4}$ pt) cider, 1 clove
garlic, $\frac{1}{2}$ tsp each of oregano and marjoram, beef stock cube,
salt and pepper, 1 tbs oil and flour.

Peel and slice vegetables and *sauté* in oil. Then place in
slow crock with meat on top. Mix remaining ingredients except the mandarin oranges and pour on. Replace lid and
cook on LOW for 10 hours until meat is tender. Pour on the
mandarin oranges with their juice for the last hour of
cooking. Thicken the sauce with a *beurre manié** if wished.
To serve, adjust seasoning.

Cider Stew   **8–10 hours LOW**

1 kg (2 lb) cubed stewing beef, 2 potatoes, 2 onions, 1 stalk
celery, 1 apple, 1 carrot, 250 ml ($\frac{1}{2}$ pt) cider, salt and pepper
to taste, thyme.

Peel and chop vegetables and fruit. Parboil the potatoes
then place in bottom of slow crock with fruit and other
vegetables. Trim excess fat off meat and place on top of
other ingredients. Add seasoning, herbs, and cider. Replace
lid and cook on LOW for about 8 hours until meat and
potatoes are tender.
Optional – marinate meat overnight in cider.

Olive Stew   **8–10 hours LOW**

1 kg (2 lb) cubed beef chuck, 1 onion, 1 stalk celery, 2 cloves
garlic, $\frac{1}{4}$ kg ($\frac{1}{2}$ lb) tomatoes, 125 g (4 oz) green stuffed olives,
125 ml ($\frac{1}{4}$ pt) each of beef stock and tomato juice, juice of 1

* See page 77.

lemon, 1 tsp Worcestershire sauce, salt and pepper, $\frac{1}{2}$ tsp paprika, 1 tbs each of cornflour and butter.

Peel and chop vegetables, mince garlic and place in bottom of slow crock. Place meat on top, trimmed of excess fat. Add seasoning and liquid. Replace lid and cook on LOW for about 8 hours until meat is tender. Half an hour before serving, stir in the green olives. Add *beurre manié* to thicken. Adjust seasoning. Serve.

American Stew   **8 hours LOW**

$\frac{3}{4}$ kg (1$\frac{1}{2}$ lb) cubed stewing steak, 4 small courgettes, $\frac{1}{4}$ kg ($\frac{1}{2}$ lb) packet or tin of sweet corn, salt and pepper to taste, $\frac{1}{2}$ tsp paprika, 125 ml ($\frac{1}{4}$ pt) each of brown stock and brown ale, 1 tbs each of flour and oil. Optional – 1 carton of cream.

Wash and slice courgettes then *sauté* lightly in oil and place in bottom of slow crock. Toss meat in seasoned flour and brown in oil. Transfer to slow crock. Pour stock and beer into slow crock. Replace lid and cook on LOW for about 8 hours. An hour before serving, stir in sweet corn. Just before serving, stir in cream if wished, and adjust seasoning.

Beef and Chilli Casserole   **8 hours LOW**

$\frac{3}{4}$ kg (1$\frac{1}{2}$ lb) cubed round steak, 1 onion, 2 garlic cloves, 4 fresh green chillies, 4 green tomatoes, $\frac{1}{2}$ tsp oregano, 1 tbs each of fat and flour, 125 ml ($\frac{1}{4}$ pt) vegetable stock, garnish – chopped coriander.

Peel and slice onion. Mince garlic. Dust meat with flour. Melt fat in frying pan and brown onions, then meat and garlic. Place in slow crock. Wash and chop the remaining ingredients and add to slow crock. Pour stock and herbs over dish. Replace lid and cook on LOW for 8 hours until meat is tender. To serve, garnish with coriander.

Basic Meat Loaf Braise   6 hours LOW

1 kg (2 lb) minced beef, 1 egg to bind, salt and pepper, mixed herbs, dash of Worcestershire sauce, pinch of cayenne and turmeric, 1 clove minced garlic, oil, a few tbs of flavoursome liquid (stock, wine, ale).

Combine all ingredients and shape into a loaf. Brown loaf lightly on all sides and place on trivet in slow crock. Cover with a piece of damp greaseproof paper. Pour a little flavoursome liquid into base of slow crock. Replace lid and cook on LOW for 6 hours. To serve, remove loaf and keep warm. Remove trivet. Skim fat from gravy and adjust seasoning, then pour it over the meat loaf.

Meat Loaf Braise with Spicy Sauce   6 hours LOW

1 kg (2 lb) minced beef, 1 egg, 1 minced onion, 125 g (4 oz) breadcrumbs (optional), salt and pepper to taste, mixed herbs, pinch of paprika and garam masala.

Sauce: 125 ml ($\frac{1}{4}$ pt) chilli sauce, 3 tbs tomato ketchup, 1 tsp Worcestershire sauce, $\frac{1}{2}$ tsp dry mustard.

Make meat loaf as above and place on trivet in slow crock. Pour spicy sauce ingredients over the meat. Replace lid and cook on LOW for 6 hours.

Meat Loaf Roast – Basic Method   6 hours LOW

Ingredients as for meat loaf braise, oil.

Grease slow crock lightly with oil. Combine all ingredients and shape into a loaf. Brown if wished. Place in slow crock. Cover with a piece of damp greaseproof paper. Replace lid and cook on LOW for 6 hours.

Steam-Bake Meat Loaf – Basic Method   4 hours HIGH

Ingredients as for meat loaf braise (see page 90).

Choose a tin that will fit your slow crock and grease it. Switch slow crock to HIGH during preparations. Combine all ingredients and place in tin. Cover with metal foil and place in slow crock. Pour boiling water around until it reaches half-way up the side. Replace lid and cook on HIGH for 4 hours or until the meat is firm and cooked.
Variation: Lay bacon rashers over the meat loaf.

Meat Ball Stew – Basic Method   6 hours LOW

Ingredients as for meat loaf braise (page 90) plus stock or sauce (see individual recipes below), flour, oil.

Combine all ingredients and shape into balls. Toss in seasoned flour and brown lightly in oil. Transfer to slow crock. Pour sauce over. Replace lid and cook on LOW for 6 hours. To serve, skim fat and adjust seasoning.

Meat Ball Stew   6 hours LOW

1 kg (2 lb) minced beef, 2 eggs, 125 g (4 oz) breadcrumbs, 1 packet onion soup mix, flour and oil.
Sauce 1 – 125 ml ($\frac{1}{4}$ pt) strong beef stock, 3 tbs tomato paste, pinch each of dry mustard, ground cumin and coriander, squeeze of lemon juice, dash of soy sauce, optional – 1 tbs peanut butter or tahini sauce.

Sauce 2 – 90 ml (3 fl oz) each of chilli sauce and water, 90 g (3 oz) brown sugar, 1 medium size tin each of sauerkraut and cranberry sauce.

Make meat balls as above (page 91) and place in slow crock. Mix ingredients for one of the sauces and pour over the stew. Replace lid and cook on LOW for 6 hours. To serve, adjust seasoning.

Welsh Meat Balls   4–6 hours LOW

1 kg (2 lb) leeks, ½ kg (1 lb) minced beef, 60 g (2 oz) bread-crumbs, 2–3 eggs, juice of 2 lemons, salt and black pepper, oil, butter, 2–3 tbs sherry or green ginger wine.

Wash leeks and remove tough outer leaves. Trim both ends. Boil in slightly salted water until tender. Drain and mince or chop finely.

Mix meat, leeks, breadcrumbs and eggs, seasoning, to a smooth paste. Shape into small balls and brown lightly in oil and butter.

Place meat balls in base of slow crock. Sprinkle on lemon juice and sherry so that base of crock is covered with liquid. Replace lid and cook on LOW for 4–6 hours.
Variation: Use spinach instead of leeks.

Easy Chilli Con Carne   4–6 hours LOW

200 g (6 oz) cooked or tinned red kidney beans, ¼ kg (½ lb) minced beef, 1 onion and green pepper, 1 garlic clove, small tin of tomato *purée*, 3 tsp chilli powder, ¼ litre (½ pt) stock, a pinch of cayenne, a pinch of cumin, ½ tsp celery salt, pepper, oil.

Drain beans and place in bottom of slow crock. Chop vegetables and *sauté* lightly in oil, then add minced meat, seasoning and spices and cook until red colour of meat changes to brown. Mix all ingredients thoroughly together in slow crock and pour in stock. Replace lid and cook on LOW for 4 hours until thoroughly cooked. Adjust seasoning before serving.

Variations: For a hotter chilli increase chilli powder to 2 tbs and add some crushed dried red pepper. ¼ tsp powdered cloves adds a different tang to the dish.

Chilli Con Carne   **6–8 hours HIGH**

375 g (¾ lb) lean beef, 375 g (¾ lb) boneless pork, ¼ kg (½ lb) red kidney beans, 1 medium onion, 3 garlic cloves, salt and pepper, ½ litre (1 pt) rich beef stock, ½–3 tbs chilli powder, 1 bay leaf, ½ tsp each of oregano and ground cumin, 1 tbs bacon fat and flour, pinch of bicarbonate of soda.

Soak beans overnight in cold water, rinse and drain and place in slow crock.

Trim excess fat from meat and cut into cubes. Melt bacon fat in frying pan and brown meat, peeled and chopped onion and garlic. Drain and transfer to slow crock. Blend chilli powder and flour with the remaining fat and juices in the frying pan and add to slow crock with remaining herbs and seasoning. Pour stock into dish. Replace lid and cook on HIGH for 6–8 hours until the beans are tender. To serve, mix ingredients together thoroughly and adjust seasoning. Accompany with rice.

Angloburgers   **6 hours LOW**

¼ kg (½ lb) each of bulk pork sausage and minced cooked ham, ½ kg (1 lb) minced beef, 1 small green pepper and onion, ½ tsp marjoram, 125 g (4 oz) breadcrumbs, 1 small tin condensed tomato soup, oil, 1 egg, pinch of nutmeg.

Brown sausage lightly in oil, then drain and transfer to a mixing bowl. Chop the green pepper and onion finely and add to bowl with the remaining solid ingredients. Mix thoroughly and bind with an egg. Shape into 8 patties, brown lightly in oil and place in slow crock. Pour half the soup over, replace lid and cook on LOW for 6 hours. Serve with mustard sauce if liked (see below).

Variation with mustard sauce: Remainder of condensed soup, 2 tbs each of ready mixed mustard and water, 1 tbs each of vinegar and sugar, 1 tbs butter or margarine.

Cook and stir these ingredients until thick and bubbly then pour over burgers before serving, if wished.

Moussaka   **4 hours LOW**

$\frac{3}{4}$ kg (1$\frac{1}{2}$ lb) minced beef, 2–3 medium size aubergines, 1 medium size onion, 1 tomato, 2 tbs tomato paste, $\frac{1}{2}$ tsp allspice or 1 tsp cinnamon, salt and pepper to taste, oil, 2 tbs minced parsley, $\frac{1}{4}$ litre ($\frac{1}{2}$ pt) *Béchamel* sauce (see page 95), 3 tbs red wine (optional), garnish – grated Cheddar cheese.

Peel and slice aubergines thinly, or slice them unpeeled. Salt them and allow to drain for an hour or so to allow bitter juices out. Rinse and dry. Then *sauté* the aubergine slices in oil and set aside.

Peel and slice onion and fry until golden. Add minced beef, seasoning, spice and herbs. Stir and *sauté* until well browned. Then add peeled and chopped tomato, tomato paste, parsley and red wine. Simmer until meat is cooked and liquid is absorbed.

In base of slow crock place a layer of aubergines alternated with layers of meat and onion, until all ingredients are used up. Begin and end with an aubergine layer.

Prepare *Béchamel* sauce (see page 95) and pour over the dish. Replace lid and cook on LOW for 4 hours until layers have blended. Half an hour before serving sprinkle grated cheese on top of moussaka.

Variations: A layer of mashed potato can be spread over the top, and in some cases, the other ingredients will have to be reduced slightly to accommodate this addition.

Courgettes can be used instead of or in addition to aubergines. A richer moussaka can be made by sprinkling each layer with Parmesan cheese or slices of Gruyère.

Béchamel sauce for moussaka:
2 tbs each of flour and butter or margarine, $\frac{1}{4}$ litre ($\frac{1}{2}$ pt) hot milk, pinch of grated nutmeg, 1 egg yolk, 1 bay leaf, 4 peppercorns, salt and pepper.

Heat milk for 5 minutes with bay leaf and peppercorns: this is known as infusion. Melt butter in a saucepan and add flour away from heat. Stir until well blended. Cook for a minute or so on LOW, pour on strained milk slightly cooled, stirring gradually until it boils. Be careful to avoid forming lumps by adding milk gradually. Season to taste, and add a pinch of nutmeg. Simmer until sauce thickens. Beat the egg yolk and stir in a little of the sauce. Beat well. Pour back into the pan slowly, stirring continuously. Do not allow the sauce to boil again.

Goulash   **8–10 hours LOW**

1 kg (2 lb) stewing beef or veal cut into cubes, 1 onion, 1 carrot, 1 green pepper, 2 tsp paprika, $\frac{1}{2}$ tsp dry mustard, 1 bay leaf, salt and pepper to taste, 125 ml ($\frac{1}{4}$ pt) red wine, 2 tbs tomato *purée*, 1 carton of sour cream.
Optional: 4 pitted prunes, 2 cloves garlic, $\frac{1}{2}$ tsp carraway seeds. Oil.

Peel and slice vegetables and *sauté* in oil. Add to slow crock (also prunes if used). Brown meat and place in slow crock. Crush garlic in salt, combine with herbs, spice and seasoning, tomato *purée* and red wine, pour over meat.

Replace lid and cook on LOW for 8–10 hours until meat is tender. Before serving, stir in the cream and adjust seasoning.

Beef and Beans   6–8 hours HIGH

¾ kg (1½ lb) chuck steak, 200 g (6 oz) haricot beans, 1 onion, 1–2 garlic cloves, 1 tomato, 2 tbs tomato *purée*, ½ tsp chervil, salt and pepper, pinch of bicarbonate of soda (optional), water.

Soak beans overnight in cold water, then rinse and drain and place in bottom of slow crock. Peel and chop vegetables and mix them in with the beans. Trim excess fat off meat and cut into small cubes and place in slow crock. Do not add salt at this stage, but a pinch of bicarbonate of soda instead. Add remaining seasoning and water to cover beans. Replace lid and cook on HIGH for 6–8 hours until beans are tender. Adjust seasoning with salt before serving, and mix ingredients together.

Variation: For a spicy version include 3–4 tsp chilli powder and 1 chopped green pepper.

Beef (or Veal) Olives   8–10 hours LOW

¾ kg (1½ lb) beef or veal fillet, ¼ kg (½ lb) thinly sliced bacon, 200 g (6 oz) breadcrumbs, 3 tbs chopped parsley, 1 egg yolk, grated peel of ½ lemon, salt and pepper to taste, a pinch of nutmeg, 60 g (2 oz) fat or dripping, 125 ml (¼ pt) brown stock, 1 tbs each of flour and butter.

Cut meat into thin strips (7 cm × 10 cm or 3″ × 4″) and lay each on a strip of bacon. Brush egg yolk over the meat. Mix together the breadcrumbs, parsley and lemon peel and bind with some melted fat. Season to taste. Spread mixture evenly over each strip and roll up tightly, securing with a cocktail stick or toothpick. Place the olives in the slow crock and add the stock. Replace lid and cook on LOW for at least 8 hours

until the olives are tender. Thicken sauce with *beurre manié*
(see page 77) towards end of cooking period.

Stiphado   **8 hours LOW**

¾ kg (1½ lb) chuck steak, ¾ kg (1½ lb) onions, 2 garlic cloves,
4 tbs tomato *purée*, ¼ litre (½ pt) red wine, 3 tbs olive oil, salt
and pepper.

Peel and slice onions. Cut beef into thin slices and rub
with salt and pepper. Heat oil in a frying pan and fry first
onions, then meat and garlic until brown. Place onions and
garlic, then meat into slow crock.
Mix tomato *purée* with wine and pour into slow crock.
Replace lid and cook on LOW for 8 hours until meat is
tender.

Beef Ragoût with Prunes   **8 hours LOW**

¾ kg (1½ lb) cubed chuck steak, 200 g (6 oz) pitted prunes,
200 g (6 oz) salt pork or bacon, 1 large onion, 125 g (4 oz)
mushrooms, 125 ml (¼ pt) beef stock, pinch each of nutmeg,
cinnamon and ginger, salt and pepper to taste, *bouquet garni*,
1 tbs fat and flour.

Wash prunes and place them in base of slow crock. Heat
fat in a pan and brown the bacon, chopped onion and finally
the meat, tossed in flour. Transfer ingredients to slow crock.
Spread the washed and sliced mushrooms over the meat,
then add seasoning and spices, and pour on stock. Replace
lid and cook on LOW for 8 hours until the meat is tender.
Adjust seasoning before serving. Remove *bouquet garni*.

T–D

Short Ribs of Beef   **8–10 hours LOW**

1½ kg (3 lb) short ribs of beef, 1 large onion and tomato, 125 ml (¼ pt) red wine, 2 tbs horseradish, ¼ tsp each of salt, pepper and ginger, 1 tbs each of fat and flour.

Peel and chop onion and *sauté* lightly in melted fat, drain and transfer to slow crock with peeled and chopped tomato. Then brown meat and place in slow crock. Combine seasoning and add to slow crock, pour on wine. Replace lid and cook on LOW for 8–10 hours until meat is tender. Before serving thicken sauce with flour and allow to cook for a few minutes. Adjust seasoning. Serve.

Stuffed Flank Steak   **8–10 hours LOW**

1 kg (2 lb) flank steak, oil. *For stuffing* – 90 g (3 oz) breadcrumbs, 30 g (1 oz) finely chopped nuts, 2 tbs chopped parsley, 1 egg, pinch of basil, salt and pepper, pinch of nutmeg, optional – 2 tbs Parmesan cheese. *For sauce* – 125 g (4 oz) mushrooms, 1 garlic clove, 2 tbs minced onion, 2 tbs flour, 4 tbs red wine or brandy, 125 ml (¼ pt) brown stock, 2 tbs redcurrant jelly.

Score meat on both sides to facilitate rolling. Mix together ingredients for stuffing and bind with an egg. Spread stuffing over the steak, roll up carefully and fasten with skewers or string. Place in slow crock.

Wash and slice mushrooms, mince the garlic and then mix all ingredients for sauce together and pour this onto the dish. Replace lid and cook on LOW for 8–10 hours until meat is tender.

Tomato Steak   **8–10 hours LOW**

1 kg (2 lb) steak, 2 small onions, 1 stalk celery, 1 green pepper, 125 ml (¼ pt) tomato soup fresh or tinned, salt and
pepper, a pinch each of basil, marjoram and oregano,
squeeze of lemon juice, pinch of paprika.

Peel onion, de-seed pepper, then dice all the vegetables
finely. Place in slow crock. Cut steak into cubes or strips and
place on top of vegetables. Pour tomato soup on and add
the herbs and seasonings, with a squeeze of lemon juice.
Replace lid and cook on LOW for 8–10 hours until meat is
tender.

Alternative Tomato Sauce: ½ kg (1 lb) fresh or tinned
tomatoes, 2 tbs red wine, 1 minced garlic clove, pinch of
cinnamon. (Omit tomato soup in main recipe.)

If using fresh tomatoes, peel and chop and add all
ingredients to slow crock after the meat. Continue as above.

'Boiled' Beef and Dumplings   **10 hours LOW**

1½ kg (3 lb) salt silverside or topside, *bouquet garni* (bay leaf,
parsley, thyme), 6 peppercorns, 1 onion stuck with a clove,
carrot and turnip.
For rich dumplings – 125 g (4 oz) flour, 60 g (2 oz) fat or
margarine, salt and pepper, egg to bind. Cold water.

Salt meat should be soaked overnight in cold water, then
rinsed and drained and the water thrown away.
Place meat in slow crock and surround with peeled and
chopped vegetables. Add *bouquet garni* and seasoning. Pour
on water so that it covers at least ⅔ of the joint. Replace lid
and cook on LOW 10 hours or more. Make dumplings as in
the basic recipe on page 80, adding beaten egg before water,
and add to slow crock an hour before end of cooking time

or switch to HIGH half an hour before serving and drop dumplings into the liquid.

Boeuf en Daube Provençale   8–10 hours LOW

1 kg (2 lb) top rump of beef*, 300 g (6 oz) salt pork or bacon, 100 g (3 oz) pork rinds, 1 medium sized carrot, onion and tomato, 2 cloves garlic, *bouquet garni* (thyme, parsley, bay leaf and a piece of orange peel), 125 ml ($\frac{1}{4}$ pt) red wine, salt and pepper, 2 tbs oil.
Optional – 125 g (4 oz) black olives.

Cut salt pork (or bacon) into small cubes and with the rinds heat in a frying pan until the fat runs out, then drain and set aside. Peel and slice carrot and onion and *sauté* lightly in remaining pork fat, then add to slow crock and place half of pork and rinds on top. Brown meat (heating more oil if necessary) then transfer to slow crock and place remainder of pork and rinds on top. Crush the garlic in salt and add, together with the remaining seasoning and herbs, to slow crock. Pour on wine. Replace lid and cook on LOW for 8–10 hours until meat is tender.

Half an hour before serving add the black olives. To serve, remove *bouquet garni* and skim off some of the fat. Accompany with noodles or rice.

Boeuf à la Bourguignonne   8 hours LOW

1 kg (2 lb) sirloin, topside or chuck, 125 g (4 oz) salt pork or bacon, 1 large onion, *bouquet garni* (thyme, parsley, bay leaf), 1 garlic clove, 125 ml ($\frac{1}{4}$ pt) each of red wine and beef stock, 2 tbs each of oil and flour, salt and pepper, garnish – 125 g (4 oz) mushrooms, butter.

---

* In *daubes* the meat is either cut up or cooked in the piece, which will affect cooking times.

Cut meat into chunks and marinate overnight in red wine, oil, sliced onion and *bouquet garni*.

Next day, heat bacon or pork in frying pan until fat runs out. Drain and set aside. Strain marinade and reserve liquid. Dry meat and brown quickly in bacon fat. Sprinkle meat with flour and stir for a minute or two, allowing fat to absorb the flour. Place meat and bacon in slow crock and pour wine and stock on. Add a crushed garlic clove and *bouquet garni*. Replace lid and cook on LOW for at least 8 hours until meat is tender. Before serving, garnish dish with sliced mushrooms cooked in butter. Remove *bouquet garni* and adjust seasoning.

Beef Stroganoff   8–10 hours LOW

1 kg (2 lb) beef steak fillet or chuck, 2 onions, 125 g (4 oz) mushrooms, 2 tbs flour, 60 g (2 oz) butter, 3 tsp paprika and garlic salt, pepper, 125 ml ($\frac{1}{4}$ pt) sour cream, 2 tbs each of red wine and beef stock, optional vegetable ingredients: green pepper, carrot, celery, tomato. Optional spices and herbs: celery salt, onion powder, Worcestershire sauce, bay leaf, basil, oregano, rosemary.

Cut meat into strips (1 cm, $\frac{1}{2}''$) and dredge with seasoned flour. Peel and slice onions finely. Wash and slice mushrooms. Melt butter in a frying pan and fry first onions, then mushrooms, adding more butter if necessary. Place in slow crock. Fry meat for a few minutes and then transfer to slow crock. Season the dish generously. Add the liquid. Replace lid and cook on LOW for 8–10 hours until meat is tender. Stir in the sour cream about ten–fifteen minutes before serving.

If using optional vegetable ingredients clean and dice them finely then *sauté* quickly in butter and add to the slow crock with the onions, etc.

Estofat de Boeuf   **8–10 hours LOW**

1–1½ kg (2–3 lb) rolled topside or top rump of beef, 1 pig's trotter, ¼ kg (½ lb) salt pork or bacon, 1 large onion, 2 carrots, 2 garlic cloves, *bouquet garni* of bay leaf, thyme and parsley, pork dripping or oil, salt, ¼ litre (½ pt) red wine, horseradish or sauce tartare.

Peel and slice vegetables and cook in melted fat in a frying pan until onions look clear, then drain and transfer to slow crock. Brown joint all over then place in slow crock. Add salt pork and the trotter (split). Pour on wine, add *bouquet garni* and a little salt. Replace lid and cook on LOW 8–10 hours.

To counteract the fatty sauce at the end, accompany with either boiled potatoes or rice. This dish is very good served cold, in which case the vegetables should be strained off while hot, and the fat removed when the sauce has cooled and set. Remove pig's trotter and serve as a separate dish coated with butter and breadcrumbs and grilled.
Variation: The meat can be marinaded overnight in the wine.

Boeuf en Daube Creole   **8–10 hours LOW**

1 kg (2 lb) topside or round of beef, ¼ kg (½ lb) salt pork or bacon, 1 large onion, ¼ kg (½ lb) tomatoes, *bouquet garni* (bay leaf, parsley, thyme, basil), salt and pepper, 2 cloves garlic, 90 ml (3 fl oz) rum, oil.
Optional: 125 g (4 oz) green stuffed olives.

Cut salt pork into cubes and heat in frying pan until fat runs out, then drain and place in bottom of slow crock. Peel and slice onion and *sauté* lightly in remaining fat, then mix with the pork in the slow crock. Peel and chop tomatoes and stir into other ingredients in slow crock.

Trim any excess fat from meat and place in slow crock. Pour on rum and add remaining seasoning and herbs. Crush the garlic. Replace lid and cook on LOW until meat is tender. Half an hour before serving stir in the green olives. To serve, remove *bouquet garni*, adjust seasoning, and crush the tomatoes into the sauce.

Carbonnade de Boeuf   8–10 hours LOW

1 kg (2 lb) braising beef, 200 g (6 oz) small onions or shallots, 1 garlic clove, salt and pepper, pinch of nutmeg and sugar, dash of vinegar, ¼ litre (½ pt) brown ale, *bouquet garni*, 2 tbs each of flour and butter.

Peel and cut onions. Cut meat into slices and dredge in seasoned flour. Melt butter and brown first the onions then the meat. Transfer to slow crock, sprinkle on crushed garlic and remaining ingredients. Replace lid and cook on LOW 8–10 hours until meat is tender. To serve, adjust seasoning.

Sweet Spiced Beef and Pork   8 hours LOW

½ kg (1 lb) each of cubed beef chuck and lean pork, 2 small onions, 1–2 sweet red peppers and green chillies, 4 tomatoes, 90 g (3 oz) raisins, 90 g (3 oz) blanched almonds, 2 garlic cloves, 1 bay leaf, ½ tsp each of oregano and cumin, juice of ½ lemon, 125 ml (¼ pt) each of red wine and beef stock, salt and pepper, fat, 30 g (1 oz) each of butter and flour.

Wash and prepare vegetables: peel and chop onions and tomatoes, de-seed and chop peppers, mince garlic. Melt fat in a frying pan and *sauté* vegetables lightly then add to slow crock with raisins and almonds.

Then brown the meats gently in the fat, drain and transfer to slow crock. Add seasoning, spices, stock and wine. Replace lid and cook on LOW for 8 hours until meat is tender. Thicken with *beurre manié* (page 77). Allow to cook for a few minutes. Adjust seasoning. Serve with hot bread.

VEAL RECIPES

Veal Sofrito (see Lamb Sofrito, page 118)

Stuffed Veal (see Stuffed Mutton page 120)

Rolled Breast of Veal   **8–10 hours LOW**

1–1½ kg (2–3 lb) boned breast of veal, slice each of cooked ham and tongue, salt and pepper, 125 ml (¼ pt) wine or chicken stock, good pinch of rosemary, thyme, sage, *garnish* – chopped parsley, sliced beetroot.

Lay the meat flat on a board and beat it. Then season with salt, pepper and herbs. Lay the slice of tongue and ham on top and roll up, tie or secure. Place in slow crock and add liquid. Replace lid and cook on LOW for 8–10 hours. When meat is tender, remove from liquid and lay on board pressed down with a weight, till cold. Serve garnished with parsley and beetroot slices.

Veal Stew   **8–10 hours LOW**

1 kg (2 lb) stewing veal, 1 onion, carrot and green pepper, 4 potatoes, 2 garlic cloves, 1 tsp tarragon and thyme, 6–8 rashers of bacon, salt and pepper, 125 ml (¼ pt) white wine, carton of sour cream.
Optional: 2 tbs brandy.

Peel, slice and blanch vegetables. Heat bacon in a frying pan until the fat runs out, then drain and set aside. *Sauté* the vegetables in the bacon fat until golden brown and transfer to base of slow crock. Then *sauté* the cubes of veal and place on top of vegetables in slow crock. Sprinkle meat with herbs and seasoning and lay bacon rashers over the top. Pour wine in. Replace lid and cook on LOW for about 8 hours until the meat is tender. Before serving stir in sour cream and brandy. Adjust seasoning.

Sunflower Veal   **8–10 hours LOW**

1 kg (2 lb) stewing veal, 125 g (4 oz) mushrooms, 2 medium onions, 125 ml ($\frac{1}{4}$ pt) each of white wine and chicken stock, 2 tbs ready mixed mustard, salt and pepper, 3 tbs sunflower or sesame seeds, salt and pepper, pinch of thyme, 1 tbs each of oil and butter, 2 tbs flour.
Optional: sour cream.

Trim meat and toss in seasoned flour. Brown in a mixture of oil and butter. Drain and set aside. Peel and slice onions and *sauté* in the oil and butter. Place onions and sliced mushrooms on base of slow crock with meat on top. Add remaining seasoning and stock. Replace lid and cook on LOW for 8–10 hours until the meat is tender. Before serving stir sour cream into dish. Garnish with toasted sunflower or sesame seeds. Adjust seasoning.

Osso Buco   **8–10 hours LOW**

1 kg (2 lb) shin of veal cut into pieces, 1 onion, 2 carrots, 1 garlic clove, $\frac{1}{4}$ kg ($\frac{1}{2}$ lb) tinned or fresh tomatoes, 2 tbs tomato paste, salt and pepper, *bouquet garni*, 1 tbs chopped parsley, 125 ml ($\frac{1}{4}$ pt) each of white wine and stock (chicken or vegetable), grated rind of $\frac{1}{2}$ lemon, flour.

Peel, slice and blanch vegetables and place in slow crock. Place meat on top. Add remaining ingredients, herbs and seasoning. Pour liquid on. Replace lid and cook on LOW 8–10 hours. To serve remove *bouquet garni*. Thicken the stock with a *beurre manié* if wished. Adjust seasoning and garnish dish with parsley and lemon rind.

Veal Roll   6 hours HIGH

1 kg (2 lb) boned breast of veal, 200 g (6 oz) sausage meat, 125 g (4 oz) cooked ham or tongue, 1 onion, 60 g (2 oz) breadcrumbs, 30 g (1 oz) nuts, pinch of tarragon and thyme, salt and pepper, 2 tbs wine, cider or brandy.
Garnish: hard-boiled egg slices, chopped parsley.

Switch slow crock to HIGH while preparing the ingredients. Mince or chop meat, vegetables and nuts finely and then mash all the ingredients together in a bowl, adding seasoning to taste. Grease a bowl or tin that will fit your slow crock and press the mixture into it. Cover with metal foil and place in slow crock. Pour boiling water around until it reaches half-way up the side of the container. Replace lid and cook on HIGH 6 hours. Then remove tin and press down with weights until cool and firm in shape. To serve, garnish with hard-boiled egg slices and chopped parsley.

Jellied Veal   10 hours LOW

Prepare a day in advance.

1 kg (2 lb) lean veal from shoulder or knuckle, ½ kg (1 lb) gammon, 2 small onions, *bouquet garni* (1 celery stalk, strip of lemon rind, parsley, thyme, 1 clove), 2–3 peppercorns, 20–30 g (¾–1 oz) gelatine, 2 hard-boiled eggs, 1½ tbs chopped parsley, salt and pepper, water.

Trim and tie up veal if necessary. Remove gammon rind and place bacon in bottom of slow crock. Place meat on top. Peel and chop onion and place in slow crock, add the *bouquet garni* and other seasoning. Cover ⅔ of joint with cold water. Replace lid and cook on LOW for about 10 hours.

Transfer all the ingredients to another large container and allow to cool. Then remove meat. Taste stock and adjust seasoning. Reduce if necessary to improve flavour. Dissolve gelatine in ½ litre (1 pt) of the stock and allow to cool.

Meanwhile cut veal and gammon into small pieces and place in alternate layers with egg slices in a basin, tin or mould, adding parsley and seasoning. Then pour on the cool stock until the meat is covered by about 1 cm (½″). Leave until the following day before turning out.

Veal Collops   8–10 hours LOW

¾ kg (1½ lb) veal cut in slices from the leg, 400 g (¾ lb) rindless bacon rashers.
Stuffing: 125 g (4 oz) each of beef suet and breadcrumbs, ¼ tsp parsley, ½ tsp sweet marjoram, pinch of cayenne, nutmeg, pinch of grated lemon peel and garlic, salt and pepper to taste, 1 egg (or milk) to bind, oil, water.
Garnish: mushrooms.

Lay a rasher of bacon on each slice of veal. Mix stuffing ingredients together and bind with egg or milk. Spread mixture onto meat, roll tightly and secure with a toothpick or cocktail stick. Brush each roll with oil and brown lightly in a heated frying pan. Transfer to slow crock. Add a tablespoon or so of water, to cover base of slow crock. Replace lid and cook on LOW for 8–10 hours until meat is tender. Serve with brown gravy and mushroom garnish.
Variation: Serve with a white sauce (see page 186) flavoured with mace, lemon and chopped parsley.

Variation: with prunes – add 125–200 g (4–6 oz) dried prunes to base of slow crock.

Veal Cutlets Fricassée   8–10 hours LOW

1 kg (2 lb) veal cutlets, 2 onions, salt and pepper to taste, 1 bay leaf, 90 ml (3 fl oz) dry sherry, 125 ml (¼ pt) chicken stock, pinch of thyme, 1 tsp chopped parsley, 2 tbs flour, 1 tbs each of oil and butter.
Garnish: 90 g (3 oz) toasted almonds.
Thickening: 2 egg yolks.

Toss cutlets in seasoned flour and brown in a mixture of oil and butter. Drain and set aside. Peel and slice onions thinly and *sauté* until just golden brown, then place in bottom of slow crock with cutlets on top. Add herbs and liquid. Replace lid and cook on LOW for 8–10 hours until meat is tender. To serve, remove cutlets and keep warm. Thicken gravy with beaten egg yolks, stir in almonds and chopped parsley and pour over meat.

Veal Blanquette   8–10 hours LOW

1 kg (2 lb) veal cutlets, ¼ kg (½ lb) mushrooms, 2 onions, salt and pepper, 1 tsp marjoram, 125 ml (¼ pt) white wine, 1 carton of sour cream, 2 tbs chopped parsley, 1 tbs each flour and oil.

Peel and slice onion and *sauté* in oil until transparent; drain and transfer to slow crock. Toss meat in seasoned flour and *sauté* lightly, then place on top of onions. Wash and chop mushrooms and sprinkle into slow crock. Add herbs and wine. Replace lid and cook on LOW until meat is very tender, about 8–10 hours.
    To serve, stir in sour cream, adjust seasoning and garnish with parsley.

Veal Tomatino   **6 hours LOW**

4–6 thick veal chops, $\frac{1}{4}$ kg ($\frac{1}{2}$ lb) fresh or tinned tomatoes, 1
tsp fresh chopped rosemary, salt and pepper, juice of 1
lemon, optional – 1–2 garlic cloves minced, 1 tbs each of
flour and butter.

Peel and chop tomatoes, if necessary, and place in slow
crock with veal chops on top. Sprinkle with seasoning and
herbs. Squeeze on lemon juice. Replace lid and cook on
LOW for about 6 hours until meat is tender. To serve, adjust
seasoning. To thicken, add *beurre manié* (see page 77).

Japanese Style Veal   **8–10 hours LOW**

$\frac{3}{4}$ kg ($1\frac{1}{2}$ lb) veal fillet, 1 cucumber, 2 sweet red apples, 1
green pepper, 125 g (4 oz) mushrooms, salt and pepper, 1 red
pepper.
Sauce: 3 tbs of vinegar, 1 tbs soy sauce, 2 tbs sugar or
honey, 125 ml ($\frac{1}{4}$ pt) chicken stock, pinch of ginger, coriander, $\frac{1}{2}$ tsp turmeric, 1 tbs each of oil and flour.

De-seed and slice peppers, peel and slice remaining fruit
and vegetables. *Sauté* them all quickly in oil, add flour, cook
for a minute or two and place on base of slow crock. Place
cubed veal on top. Mix together ingredients for sauce and
pour into slow crock. Replace lid and cook on LOW for 8–10
hours until meat is tender. To serve, check seasoning. If you
want a thick syrup-sauce switch the slow crock to HIGH, mix
ingredients thoroughly and allow the liquid to reduce with
the lid off. Accompany with boiled rice or noodles.

Variation: Add a few chopped spring onions to vegetable
ingredients *or* sprinkle on a tablespoon of chopped chives.

LAMB AND MUTTON RECIPES

Pot-Roast Lamb with Lentils   6 hours HIGH

1 boned shoulder of lamb approx. 1–1½ kg (2–3 lb), 4 rashers bacon, 125–200 g (4–6 oz) red lentils, 2 small onions, salt and pepper, ½ tsp thyme, 1 tbs chopped parsley, 250 ml (½ pt) brown stock, 1 bay leaf.
Optional: ½ tsp celery seed and cumin.

Wash and drain lentils then place on bottom of slow crock. Heat bacon in a frying pan until the fat runs out, then drain and transfer to slow crock. Brown meat thoroughly and place in slow crock. Add remaining ingredients. Replace lid and cook on HIGH for 6 hours until meat is tender and lentils are soft. Adjust seasoning before serving. Remove bay leaf and mix the lentils thoroughly.

Moroccan Pot-Roast   8–10 hours LOW

1½–2½ kg (3–5 lb) of lamb cut from shoulder or leg, ¼ tsp each of saffron and cumin, plenty of salt and pepper, butter, 1–2 tbs lemon juice mixed with water.

Combine salt, saffron (or turmeric) and cumin and rub lamb with this mixture. Season to taste with black pepper. Place in base of slow crock and pour a little lemon juice and water into base. Replace lid and cook on LOW until the meat is tender, approximately 8–10 hours. To serve, remove lamb from slow crock and *sauté* in butter until golden. Accompany with rice.

Sweet and Sour Pot-Roast Lamb Shanks or Leg
                                                    8–10 hours LOW

4 lamb shanks or 1–1½ kg (2–3 lb) leg of lamb, 125 g (4 oz) raisins, 1 tsp each of cumin and cinnamon, 1 onion, 3 tbs

honey, 2 tbs lemon juice, $\frac{1}{4}$ kg ($\frac{1}{2}$ lb) tinned or fresh tomatoes, salt and pepper to taste, a little water, 1 tbs tomato paste, 1 bay leaf, pinch of marjoram and thyme.

Peel and chop tomatoes and onions and mix with tomato paste, lemon juice and washed raisins, plus a little water. Place in bottom of slow crock. Rub lamb with spices and honey and place in slow crock. Add herbs. Replace lid and cook on LOW for 8–10 hours until meat is tender. To serve, remove meat and keep warm. Skim fat from gravy and adjust seasoning. To thicken gravy add *beurre manié* if wished.

Roast Leg of Lamb   6 hours HIGH

$1\frac{1}{2}$–$2\frac{1}{2}$ kg (3–5 lb) leg of lamb or mutton, 3 tbs mint sauce or jelly, 1–2 garlic cloves, 1 tsp rosemary and basil, pinch of cayenne, salt and pepper, flour, oil.
Optional: trivet.

Grease inside of slow crock lightly with oil.
Rub joint with cut clove of garlic, salt, pepper and cayenne. Then brown thoroughly in hot oil in a frying pan. Transfer to slow crock and place on trivet if wished. Sprinkle herbs onto meat, and pour mint sauce or jelly over. Replace lid and cook on HIGH for about 6 hours. To serve, remove joint and keep warm. Skim fat from gravy and thicken with flour if necessary. Adjust seasoning.

Roast Shoulder of Lamb   6 hours HIGH

$1\frac{1}{2}$–$2\frac{1}{2}$ kg (3–5 lb) shoulder of lamb, 1–2 garlic cloves, salt and pepper, $\frac{1}{2}$ tsp paprika, 1 tsp each of oregano and rosemary, oil.
Optional: trivet.

Grease inside of slow crock lightly with oil.

Rub lamb with cut clove of garlic, salt, pepper and paprika. Then brown in hot oil in frying pan. Transfer to slow crock and place joint on trivet if wished. Sprinkle herbs onto joint. Replace lid and cook on HIGH for about 6 hours. To serve, remove joint and keep warm. Skim fat from gravy and thicken if necessary with flour. Adjust seasoning.

Baked Lamb and Potatoes   **6–8 hours LOW**

1 kg (2 lb) boneless lamb, ½ kg (1 lb) potatoes, ¼ kg (½ lb) fresh or tinned tomatoes, salt and pepper, 1 onion, 1 tsp chopped rosemary, a few tbs of white wine (optional).

Peel, chop and blanch potatoes and onions then transfer them to slow crock with peeled and chopped tomatoes. Rub seasoning into lamb and brown on all sides and place in slow crock. Sprinkle on rosemary. Replace lid and cook on LOW for 6–8 hours until meat and potatoes are tender. Adjust seasoning to serve. If wished, pour on a few tablespoons of white wine for flavour.

Smoky Roast Lamb   **6–8 hours HIGH**

1½–2½ kg (3–5 lb) loin or shoulder of lamb, 4–6 rashers of bacon, small can of anchovy fillets, 1 tsp tarragon, 2 celery stalks. Garnish – 2 pickled gherkins. *Marinade* – 4 tbs each of white wine and oil, 1 onion and carrot, 2–4 cloves, 1 garlic clove, pepper.

Peel and chop onion and carrot finely and place in a large bowl with the cloves, wine and oil. Rub the lamb with a cut clove of garlic and place it in the marinade for at least 24 hours, turning occasionally.

Next day, drain the joint and place in the bottom of the slow crock. Lay bacon rashers and anchovy fillets over the joint, and sprinkle on the tarragon with pepper to taste. Chop celery into small pieces and place around the side of the joint. Replace lid and cook on HIGH for 6–8 hours until the meat is tender. To serve, remove joint and place on a warm dish, garnish with slices of gherkin and the braised celery. Make a gravy from the cooking juices.

Herb Lamb   8 hours LOW

1 kg (2 lb) lean stewing lamb, 2 onions, $\frac{1}{4}$ kg ($\frac{1}{2}$ lb) tomatoes fresh or tinned, juice of 1 lemon, grated rind of $\frac{1}{2}$ lemon, 2 tsp marjoram, 125 ml ($\frac{1}{4}$ pt) stock, salt and pepper, fat or dripping, 1 tbs flour.

Peel and chop vegetables and place in bottom of slow crock. Toss meat in flour. Melt fat in frying pan and brown meat gently, then place in slow crock. Add remaining ingredients. Replace lid and cook on LOW for 8 hours until meat is tender. To serve, adjust seasoning and garnish with grated lemon rind.

Dilled Lamb   6–8 hours LOW

1 kg (2 lb) lamb shank, shoulder or neck, 1 celery stalk, 1 onion, 2 carrots, $\frac{1}{2}$ tsp dill seeds, 1 bay leaf, salt and pepper, 1 tbs each fat and flour, 125 ml ($\frac{1}{4}$ pt) stock or water. *Optional*: frozen artichoke hearts.

Peel, slice and blanch vegetables (except artichokes) then place in slow crock. Dredge meat in seasoned flour and brown in fat, then transfer to slow crock. Add remaining seasoning and herbs, and pour in stock. Replace lid and cook on LOW for 6–8 hours until meat is tender. If using artichoke hearts, make sure that they are thoroughly thawed

and add an hour before end of cooking time. Adjust seasoning before serving.

Lamb Curry   **6–8 hours LOW**

1 kg (2 lb) boneless lamb from leg or shoulder, 2 medium
onions, 2 garlic cloves, 1 tbs curry powder (or ½ tsp each of
ginger and turmeric, good pinch of paprika and cayenne)
salt and pepper, 1 tbs each of flour, butter and oil, 60 ml
(2 fl oz) stock or water, ¼ litre (½ pt) of yoghurt.
Optional ingredients: 1 green pepper, 2–3 tomatoes, 1–2
apples, a handful of raisins.

Trim excess fat from meat and cut into small cubes. Peel
and chop onions and garlic. Mix the spices with the flour.
Melt oil and butter in a frying pan and *sauté* first the
vegetables and then the meat lightly and transfer to slow
crock. Remove pan from heat, stir in the flour, seasoning
and spices and cook a few minutes. Then add stock gradually
to make a sauce and pour it into the slow crock. Replace lid
and cook on LOW for 6–8 hours until the lamb is tender. To
serve, stir in the yoghurt and adjust seasoning.

Lancashire Hot Pot   **6–8 hours LOW**

1 kg (2 lb) middle neck of mutton, ½ kg (1 lb) potatoes, 2
kidneys, 1 onion, 1 carrot, 60 g (2 oz) fat or dripping, 30 g
(1 oz) flour, salt and pepper, 1 tsp sugar, 1 tbs chopped
parsley, scant ½ litre (1 pt) stock.

Peel, slice and blanch vegetables and place on base of slow
crock. Place mutton on top. Melt fat in frying pan. Skin and
slice kidneys, dredge in flour and brown gently, drain and
transfer to slow crock. Add seasoning and stock. Replace
lid and cook on LOW 6–8 hours until meat and potatoes are

tender. Adjust seasoning to serve and garnish dish with chopped parsley.

Irish Stew   **8 hours LOW**

1 kg (2 lb) middle neck of lamb, 1 turnip, carrot and onion, 2–3 potatoes, salt and pepper, ½ litre (1 pt) stock or water, 1 bay leaf, pinch of cumin, ¼ tsp rosemary, pinch of savory.

Peel, slice and blanch vegetables then place in base of slow crock. Add lamb, seasoning, herbs and liquid. Replace lid and cook on LOW for at least 8 hours until meat and vegetables are tender.

Navarin of Lamb   **6–8 hours LOW**

1 kg (2 lb) boned shoulder or breast of lamb, 4 small carrots and onions, 1 small turnip, 2 medium potatoes, salt and pepper to taste, *bouquet garni*, ½ litre (1 pt) stock or water, 2 tbs tomato paste, 1 tbs flour and fat, 1 tsp sugar.
Garnish: chopped parsley.

Cut lamb into cubes and brown in fat, drain and transfer to slow crock. Stir the sugar into the fat until it browns lightly then add flour and cook until it bubbles. Remove from heat and gradually stir in stock and tomato paste. Pour this over the meat in the slow crock.

Peel and slice vegetables, blanch and place in slow crock. Then mix all the ingredients thoroughly together. Add seasoning and *bouquet garni*. Replace lid and cook on LOW for 6–8 hours until meat and vegetables are tender. To serve, adjust seasoning. Garnish with chopped parsley.

Lamb Paprikash   **6–8 hours LOW**

1–1½ kg (2–3 lb) middle or best end of neck, ¼ kg (½ lb) each
of onions and tomatoes, 1–2 tsp paprika, salt and pepper,
1 carton of sour cream or yoghurt, 1 tbs chopped parsley,
1 tbs each of flour and butter, 125 ml (¼ pt) stock.

Trim excess fat from lamb. Peel and chop vegetables and
place in slow crock with lamb on top. Add seasoning and
stock. Replace lid and cook on LOW for 6–8 hours until lamb
is tender. Add *beurre manié*, then stir in cream or yoghurt.
Adjust seasoning to taste. Serve, garnished with chopped
parsley.

Lamb, Sausage and Beans   **6–8 hours HIGH**

4 lamb shanks, 125 g (4 oz) garlic sausages, ¼ kg (½ lb)
haricot beans, 1 onion and carrot, 1 bay leaf, salt and
pepper, water.
Optional: pinch of bicarbonate of soda.

Soak beans overnight in cold water. Next day, rinse and
drain and place in bottom of slow crock, cover with water.
Peel, slice and blanch vegetables and place them with the
meat in the slow crock. Sprinkle on seasoning. Replace lid
and cook on HIGH at least 6 hours until the beans are tender.
To serve, adjust seasoning.

Lamb and Butter Beans   **6-8 hours HIGH**

¾ kg (1½ lb) middle neck of lamb, 125–200 g (4–6 oz) butter
beans, 1 carrot, leek and parsnip, salt and pepper, 1 tbs
tomato *purée*, 1–2 garlic cloves, water.
Optional: pinch of bicarbonate of soda.

Soak beans overnight in cold water. Next day, rinse and drain and place in bottom of slow crock. Add water to cover, a pinch of bicarbonate, and tomato *purée*. Peel, slice and blanch vegetables and place on top of beans, then place meat in. Sprinkle on seasoning, replace lid and cook on HIGH for approximately 6 hours until beans are tender.

Apricot Lamb   6–8 hours LOW

1 kg (2 lb) boneless lamb, ¼ kg (½ lb) dried apricots, ¼ kg (½ lb) courgettes, 1 onion and carrot, 1 tsp ground cumin, salt and pepper, 125 ml (¼ pt) white wine, 1 tbs each of fat and flour, 1 tbs fresh chopped mint.

Peel, slice and blanch vegetables, transfer to slow crock with washed apricots. Cube meat and brown in oil, sprinkle on flour and stir until cooked. Place in slow crock. Sprinkle on seasoning and spices, then pour on wine. Replace lid and cook on LOW for 6–8 hours until meat is tender. Adjust seasoning before serving.

Lamb Chop Stroganoff   6–8 hours LOW

4 thick lamb chops, ½ kg (1 lb) fresh or frozen peas, 1 tsp sugar, pinch each of nutmeg and mace, salt and pepper, 1 tbs lemon juice, 90 ml (3 fl oz) water, 60 g (2 oz) butter, 1 carton of cream, garnish – 3 tsp chopped parsley.
Optional: ¼ tsp ground cumin and tarragon.

Rub the lamb chops with seasoning and spices and place in bottom of slow crock. Sprinkle on lemon juice. Replace lid and cook on LOW 6–8 hours. Half an hour before serving cook the peas, drain and set aside. When chops are cooked, transfer them to a serving dish and keep warm. In a separate pan melt the butter, dissolve sugar in it and stir into the slow crock with the peas. Stir cream into the peas and garnish with chopped parsley, then serve around the chops.

Moroccan Lamb   **6–8 hours LOW**

1 kg (2 lb) cubed lamb, 1 aubergine, 1 tbs lemon juice and a dash of vinegar, 2 onions, 2–3 garlic cloves, $\frac{1}{2}$ tsp each of cumin, coriander and ginger, salt and pepper, oil.
Garnish: toasted almonds, hard-boiled egg slices.

Peel and slice onion and aubergine, *sauté* in oil with crushed garlic until brown and transfer to slow crock. Season lamb with spices, etc and *sauté* in oil until brown then transfer to slow crock. Sprinkle lemon and vinegar into dish. Replace lid and cook on LOW for 6–8 hours until meat is tender. Serve garnished with toasted almonds and hard-boiled egg slices. Adjust seasoning before serving. To thicken add *beurre manié* if wished.

Lamb Sofrito   **10–12 hours LOW**

This is based on a Middle Eastern method of cooking meat which is half-way between roasting and stewing, with the use of oil and very little water. It can also be used for veal. The idea is to cook the meat on LOW until it is virtually falling apart.
1–1$\frac{1}{2}$ kg (2–3 lb) joint of lamb or veal (leg or loin), 3 tbs oil, salt and pepper, juice of half a lemon, water, 1 tsp turmeric or saffron.
Optional vegetables: thinly sliced and *sautéed* or parboiled potatoes, tomatoes, onions or aubergines.

Heat oil in a frying pan and brown meat all over. Sprinkle with salt, pepper, lemon juice and turmeric (or saffron).

Cover base of slow crock with the vegetables. Transfer meat to slow crock and moisten with a tablespoon or so of water. Replace lid and cook on LOW 10–12 hours.

Stuffed Chump Chops   6–8 hours LOW

4 chump lamb chops, 4 chicken livers, 1 medium onion, 1 tbs lemon juice, salt and pepper, 4 large mushrooms, ¼ tsp curry powder, 3 tbs butter, garnish – watercress. A few tbs white wine to cover base of slow crock.

Trim fat from chops and make a slit in each. Peel and chop onion, chop liver. Melt butter in a frying pan and *sauté* liver and onion until golden brown. Mash liver and onion with lemon juice, and season to taste with salt, pepper and curry powder, then add finely chopped mushrooms. Stuff this mixture into the slit made in the chops and place in the slow crock. Add wine. Replace lid and cook on LOW 6–8 hours until the chops are tender. To serve, garnish with watercress.

Blanquette of Lamb   6–8 hours LOW

¾ kg (1½ lb) lean boneless lamb, 125 g (4 oz) onions, 1 celery stalk, 1 bay leaf, 1 tsp thyme, salt and pepper, ¼ litre (½ pt) stock or water, 3 tbs each of flour and butter, 1 egg yolk, 2 tbs cream or top of the milk, *garnish* – chopped parsley.

Peel and chop vegetables and place with diced lamb into the slow crock. Add herbs, seasoning and stock. Replace lid and cook on LOW for 6–8 hours until meat and vegetables are tender.

Then, add *beurre manié*, stirring thoroughly. Beat egg yolk and add cream and pour into the slow crock. Adjust seasoning. Serve, garnished with parsley.

Stuffed Mutton (or Veal)   **8–10 hours LOW**

1½–2½ kg (3–5 lb) boned shoulder or loin of mutton (or veal), 2 carrots and/or potatoes, 1 small onion, 1 garlic clove, salt and pepper, water.
Stuffing 1: 2 onions, ½ kg (1 lb) sausage meat, 1 tbs chopped parsley, 1 egg, pinch each of thyme, marjoram, savory, 30 g (1 oz) walnuts.
Stuffing 2: 1 cucumber, 4–6 spring onions, 200 g (6 oz) breadcrumbs, 1 garlic clove, 30 g (1 oz) fat, pinch each of dill, parsley and tarragon, 1 egg yolk, salt and pepper.

Prepare one of the stuffings: mince or chop ingredients finely, add herbs and seasoning and bind with egg. Spread the mixture inside the meat, then roll up and secure with a skewer or tie with string. Rub joint all over with a cut clove of garlic then place in base of slow crock and sprinkle with seasoning. Place peeled, chopped and blanched vegetables around the side and add enough water to cover the base of the slow crock. Replace lid and cook on LOW for at least 8 hours until the meat is tender.

PORK RECIPES

Pot-Roast Pork   **10–12 hours LOW**

1½–2½ kg (3–5 lb) of pork, ¼ kg (½ lb) fresh or tinned tomatoes, 125g–200 g (4–6 oz) raisins, 90 ml (3 fl oz) cider, wine or sherry, salt and pepper, honey, 2 tbs chopped rosemary, 1 tbs each flour and butter.

Make several deep incisions in the joint and stuff them with a mixture of raisins and rosemary leaves. Season the joint with salt and pepper and then rub honey all over it. If possible allow it to stand covered for a few hours in a cool place to absorb the flavours.

Place joint on trivet in slow crock. Place peeled and chopped tomatoes around and pour liquid over the meat. Replace lid and cook on LOW 10–12 hours until meat is very tender and succulent.

To serve, remove joint and keep warm. Take out trivet. Skim fat from the surface of the gravy and mash the tomatoes. Adjust seasoning. Thicken gravy with *beurre manié* (see page 77).

Pot-Roast Loin of Pork Provençale   10–12 hours LOW

1½–2½ kg (3–5 lb) of pork, salt and pepper, approx. 10 sage leaves, 1 tsp thyme, 1 bay leaf, 2–3 garlic cloves, 90 ml (3 fl oz) white wine, olive oil.

Make incisions in the joint and stuff a sage leaf in each. Rub joint with cut clove of garlic, salt and pepper. Sprinkle with olive oil. Allow to stand covered in a cool place for a few hours to absorb flavours.

Place joint on trivet in slow crock. Sprinkle on wine and crushed herbs. Replace lid and cook on LOW 10–12 hours until meat is very tender. To serve, remove joint and keep warm. Take out trivet. Skim excess fat from surface of gravy and adjust seasoning.

Variation: Add button onions and mushrooms to slow crock and serve as accompanying vegetables or garnish.

Piquant Pot-Roast   10–12 hours LOW

1½–2½ kg (3–5 lb) loin of pork, 125 ml (¼ pt) stock, salt and pepper, 1 tbs each of vinegar and redcurrant jelly, 4 tbs black treacle, 1 tsp dry mustard, ¼ kg (½ lb) tin pineapple chunks, 1 tbs flour.

Mix together the treacle, mustard, salt and pepper, fruit juice from pineapple tin and stock. Place meat in slow crock and pour liquid mix over. Replace lid and cook on LOW 10–12 hours until meat is tender. Turn the meat over once or twice during the last phase of cooking.

When tender, remove joint and keep warm. Skim excess fat from surface of gravy. Blend the flour, jelly and crushed pineapple chunks and add to slow crock. Switch slow crock to HIGH. Adjust seasoning. Serve immediately.

Pot-Roast Ham in Wine   10–12 hours LOW

$1\frac{1}{2}$–$2\frac{1}{2}$ kg (3–5 lb) joint of fresh ham, 1 garlic clove, 2 onions, 1 celery stalk, salt and pepper, 3 whole cloves, 125 ml ($\frac{1}{4}$ pt) white wine, 1 tbs each oil and flour.
Optional: 60 g (2 oz) raisins, 2 bay leaves.

Rub ham with cut clove of garlic, salt and pepper. Then stick cloves in the meat. Place joint in slow crock and pour on wine. Place peeled and chopped vegetables, and raisins if wished, around the ham. Sprinkle on crushed bay leaves. Replace lid and cook on LOW for 10–12 hours until meat is tender. To serve, remove joint and vegetables and keep warm. Skim fat from surface and reduce gravy to a syrup by switching to a HIGH setting or thicken gravy with a *beurre manié* (see page 77).

Roast Pork   6–8 hours HIGH

$1\frac{1}{2}$–$2\frac{1}{2}$ kg (3–5 lb) loin of pork, salt and pepper, 1 tsp thyme, 1 bay leaf, 1 tbs French or German mustard, 4 tbs soft butter or margarine, flour, 2 tbs sherry or cider.

Mix butter, mustard and crushed herbs into a smooth paste and rub into the joint. Sprinkle the joint with salt and pepper to taste. Then, if possible, allow to stand covered for a few hours in a cool place.

Place joint in slow crock. Replace lid and cook on HIGH

for 6–8 hours until the meat is tender. To serve, remove joint and keep warm. Skim fat from the surface, thicken gravy with *beurre manié* (see page 77). Add sherry or cider to flavour and adjust seasoning.

Caraway Pork Casserole   **6–8 hours LOW**

1 kg (2 lb) pork fillet, 1 onion and red pepper, 1 sweet apple, 6–8 baby carrots, 60 g (2 oz) mushrooms, butter, 1 tsp each of thyme and caraway seed, salt and pepper, 250 ml (½ pt) cider or chicken stock.

Peel, de-seed and slice vegetables and fruit. Melt butter and *sauté* them quickly then drain and transfer to slow crock. Cut pork into pieces of similar size and fry in butter until golden brown. Transfer to slow crock. Add seasoning, herbs and stock or cider. Replace lid and cook on LOW for 6–8 hours. To serve, mix all ingredients together and adjust seasoning. Thicken gravy with a *beurre manié* (see page 77).
Variation: omit apple and use 2 celery stalks instead. Stir in a carton of yoghurt at the end of the cooking period.

Pork and Pears   **6–8 hours LOW**

4 thick pork chops, ¼ kg (½ lb) tin of pears, salt and pepper, ½ tsp marjoram, squeeze of lemon juice, small packet of frozen peas and sweet corn.

Drain juice from can of pears and pour into slow crock. Squeeze on a little lemon juice. Place chops in slow crock and season with salt, pepper and marjoram. Replace lid and cook on LOW for at least 6 hours until chops are tender.
An hour before serving, slice up pears and add to slow crock with peas and sweet corn – stir them into the liquid

and place chops on top. To serve, thicken with a *beurre manié* (see page 77) and adjust seasoning.

N.B. If using *fresh* pears add them at the beginning of the cooking period and use cider instead of pear syrup as the cooking liquid. Use added sweetening.

Pineapple Ham   **6–8 hours LOW**

4 gammon slices, ¼ kg (½ lb) pineapple rings, 4 tbs fruit syrup, 125 g (4 oz) mushrooms, 1 tbs brown sugar, pinch of cinnamon, 30 g (1 oz) chopped nuts, pinch of pepper.

Place gammon on base of slow crock with pineapple rings on top. Pour on fruit syrup. Mix sugar with cinnamon and a dash of pepper and sprinkle over dish. Scatter nuts and chopped mushrooms on top. Replace lid and cook on LOW for at least 6 hours until the gammon is tender.

Variations: Use peaches instead of pineapple. Press 2 cloves into each slice of gammon. Spread gammon slices with a mixture of tomato ketchup and English mustard (to taste) then roll a banana up in each slice. Make 125 ml (¼ pt) of cheese sauce and pour over. Garnish with chopped nuts and tomatoes.

Chop Suey   **6–8 hours HIGH**

¾ kg (1½ lb) lean cubed pork, 2 celery stalks, 2 onions, 120 g (4 oz) each of mushrooms and chestnuts, 125–200 g (4–6 oz) haricot beans, 250 ml (½ pt) chicken stock, 3 tbs soy sauce, 1 tsp thyme.

Optional: ¼ kg (½ lb) bean sprouts, salt and pepper, 2 tbs each cornflour and oil.

Soak beans overnight in cold water, rinse and drain the next day and place in base of slow crock. Heat oil in frying pan and *sauté* chopped celery and onion, then drain and transfer to slow crock with mushrooms and chestnuts chopped roughly. *Sauté* cubes of meat lightly and sprinkle cornflour over, then cook until yellow. Transfer to slow crock. Add seasoning and thyme. Pour on stock and soy sauce. Replace lid and cook on HIGH 6–8 hours until beans are tender. If using bean sprouts, add to slow crock in last hour, or cook separately.

Variation: *Sauté* 2 kidneys with the meat and add to slow crock, it gives a sharper flavour to the pork.

Pork Fillet in White Wine   6–8 hours LOW

4 pork chops or 2 pork fillets approx. 400 g ($\frac{3}{4}$ lb) each, 1 large onion, 125 g (4 oz) mushrooms, $\frac{1}{4}$ kg ($\frac{1}{2}$ lb) apples, $\frac{1}{4}$ kg ($\frac{1}{2}$ lb) tomatoes, French mustard, 90 ml (3 fl oz) each of white wine and strong chicken stock, salt and pepper, *bouquet garni*, brown sugar, 2 tbs each of butter and flour. *Garnish*: chopped parsley.

Peel and slice onion then *sauté* slices in butter until transparent. Sprinkle on the flour, stir until it turns yellow and transfer to slow crock. Slice and wash the mushrooms and place on top. If using fillets, flatten and cut into four. Spread the meat with a thin layer of mustard and place it on top of the onion and mushrooms. Then place on top a layer of sliced apples sprinkled with brown sugar and finally a layer of sliced tomatoes. Add *bouquet garni*, seasoning, stock and wine.

Replace lid and cook on LOW 6–8 hours until pork is succulent and tender. To serve, remove *bouquet garni* and adjust seasoning. Garnish with chopped parsley.

Choucroute Garnie (Sausages and Sauerkraut)

4–6 hours LOW

60–125 g (2–4 ozs) sausages per person (Dutch, German, garlic, knockwurst, bockwurst, frankfurter, beef, pork, etc), 125 g (4 oz) salt pork or bacon, ¼ kg (½ lb) sliced salami or other smoked meats, ¾ kg (1½ lb) sauerkraut, 1 bay leaf, 5–6 peppercorns, 4 juniper berries (optional), 2 tbs chopped parsley, 125 ml (¼ pt) each of white wine and beef stock, oil.

Drain sauerkraut and place in base of slow crock with herbs, seasoning and liquid. In a separate frying pan, heat oil and brown the sausages if using uncooked ordinary English beef or pork variety. Otherwise, place sausages and salami on top of sauerkraut, replace lid and heat thoroughly on LOW for at least 4 hours. To serve, arrange sauerkraut in the middle of a warm serving dish and place sausages and salami around.

Ham and Chicken Casserole (see Chicken, Chapter 6, page 129)

Gingered Spare Ribs

6–8 hours LOW

1–1½ kg (2–3 lb) spare ribs, 2 tbs lemon juice, 60 ml (2 fl oz) each of soy sauce and beef stock, 2 garlic cloves, 2 tsp ground ginger, salt and pepper, 1–2 tbs honey or brown sugar, 2 tbs each cornflour and oil.

Mix flour with salt, pepper and ginger. Dredge the spare ribs in flour then brown in hot fat and place in slow crock. Melt honey, add lemon juice, stock and soy sauce and pour over meat. Add minced garlic. Replace lid and cook on LOW 6–8 hours. To serve, switch slow crock to HIGH setting and allow liquid to reduce to a syrup to coat the spare ribs, if necessary. Adjust seasoning.

POULTRY AND GAME

Poultry and game can be cooked whole* or in joints in the slow crock using the same basic methods that I have described in detail earlier in this chapter. Always make sure that the chicken or bird fits properly into the slow crock and allows the lid to rest firmly on the rim otherwise proper cooking cannot take place. Stews, casseroles and braises cook on LOW for 6–8 hours with 125 ml–½ litre (¼–1 pt) stock. Pot-roasts and roasts use a minimum amount of liquid, 125 ml (¼ pt) for 8–10 hours LOW or 6–8 hours HIGH. A slow crock with a capacity of 1½ litres (3 pt) or more will cook a whole joint or bird of 1½ kg (3 lb). One with a capacity of 2½ litres (5 pt) or more will cook a whole joint or bird of 2½ kg (5 lb). Cooking times will increase if you use a stuffing.

Basic Method for a Stew or Braise   **8 hours LOW**

4–6 joints of poultry or game, salt and pepper, *bouquet garni*, 1 or 2 vegetables for flavour (sliced onion and carrot), ¼ litre (½ pt) wine or stock, 2 tbs each of oil and flour.
Optional: cream.

Peel and slice vegetables and place in base of slow crock. Wipe the joints of poultry or game and toss in seasoned flour then brown in oil in a frying pan. Transfer to slow crock and add stock or wine and *bouquet garni*. Replace lid

---

* At present only one manufacturer does not recommend cooking whole joints of meat or whole poultry and game – in which case take note and always joint the poultry and game or chop the meat (Kenwood's model at the time of writing this book).

and cook on LOW 6–8 hours until tender. To serve, add cream if wished and adjust seasoning.

Basic Method for Pot-Roast or Roast
                    10–12 hours LOW or 6–8 hours HIGH

1½–2½ kg (3–5 lb) chicken or game depending on size of slow crock, salt and pepper, *bouquet garni*, 1 or 2 vegetables for flavour, 2 tbs each oil and flour, 125 ml (¼ pt) wine or stock (for a pot-roast) *or* oil to grease inside of slow crock (for roast).
Optional: bacon rashers, lemon juice, garlic.
Stuffing: 125 g (4 oz) per ¼ kg (½ lb) poultry or game.

If roasting, rub the inside of the slow crock lightly with oil. If bird is fatty use a trivet on which to place the bird while cooking.

Season the carcass inside and out with salt and pepper, rub with garlic and add lemon juice. Brown in oil. Stuff if wished, but do not fill too full to allow the stuffing to swell during cooking.

Place bird inside slow crock and lay bacon rashers across the bird. If pot-roasting, add wine or stock. Add herbs. Replace lid and cook on selected setting until tender. Check the dish an hour or so before serving and turn the bird over. To serve, remove bird and keep warm. Skim fat from gravy and thicken with a *beurre manié* (see page 77). Adjust seasoning.

Pot-Roast Chicken   **6–8 hours HIGH**

1½ kg (3 lb) roasting chicken, stuffing – 60 g (2 oz) black olives, 60 g (2 oz) breadcrumbs, 1 garlic clove, 2 tbs chopped parsley, 1 egg, pepper, pinch of nutmeg, 3 tbs oil.

Stone and chop the olives and mix with the breadcrumbs,

minced garlic and chopped parsley. Bind with an egg and season with pepper and nutmeg. Stuff the chicken and tie securely.

Heat the oil in a frying pan and brown the chicken well all over. Transfer to slow crock and replace lid. Cook on HIGH 6–8 hours or until the chicken is thoroughly roasted. Turn it over if wished once during the final two hours.

Variations: Place bacon rashers over the chicken while cooking.

Pound 1 tbs tarragon with a clove of garlic, salt and pepper and knead it with 2 tbs butter, rub the chicken inside and out with this mixture. Proceed as above.

Sprinkle the chicken inside and out with a mixture of 1 tbs paprika, chopped fresh rosemary and oregano, then sprinkle with lemon juice, salt and pepper.

When cooked set fire to 4 tbs brandy, cognac or whisky and pour flaming over the bird before serving.

Ham and Chicken Casserole   6–8 hours LOW

$\frac{1}{4}$ kg ($\frac{1}{2}$ lb) each of boneless chicken and salt pork or bacon, 1 large onion, 4 medium potatoes, 125 g (4 oz) mushrooms, 1 tbs chopped parsley, $\frac{1}{2}$ tsp paprika, salt and pepper, $\frac{1}{2}$ tsp tarragon, 125 ml ($\frac{1}{4}$ pt) white wine or stock, garnish – 125 g (4 oz) grated Cheddar cheese.

Peel and slice potatoes and parboil them for 5 minutes. Drain and transfer to slow crock. Peel and slice onions and mushrooms and place on top. Trim fat from the pork or bacon and cut into chunks. Dice the chicken. Add the meat to the slow crock with herbs and spices, pepper to taste, but not too much salt. Pour on liquid. Replace lid and cook on LOW for 6–8 hours until chicken and potatoes are tender.

Half an hour before serving mix the ingredients together and adjust seasoning. Sprinkle the grated cheese on top and leave it to melt. Replace lid until ready to serve.

T–E

Chicken Braised with Okra   **8 hours LOW**

4–6 chicken pieces, 2 garlic cloves, $\frac{1}{4}$ kg ($\frac{1}{2}$ lb) tomatoes, 1 green pimento, 200 g (6 oz) okra, 2 tbs chopped mint leaves, salt and pepper, olive oil and butter.

Rub the chicken pieces with cut garlic, salt, pepper and oil. Set aside. Meanwhile, chop tomatoes and pimento, leave okra whole and *sauté* in butter then place in slow crock with seasoning. Place chicken on top and sprinkle with mint. Replace lid and cook on LOW for 6–8 hours until the chicken and okra are tender. To serve, adjust seasoning and accompany with rice.

Chicken and Tomato Sauce   **10 hours LOW**

$1\frac{1}{2}$ kg (3 lb) roasting chicken, *sauce* – $\frac{1}{2}$ kg (1 lb) tin tomatoes, 1 carrot, 2 medium onions, 1 celery stalk, 2 bacon rashers, 4 tbs each of red wine and vinegar, salt and pepper, fresh chopped parsley, garlic, 1 tsp dried basil and oregano, 1 tbs each of oil and butter, flour.

Season the chicken inside and out with salt and pepper, rub with a garlic clove or two. Dice the bacon and heat in a frying pan until the fat melts. Drain and set aside. Melt the oil and butter and *sauté* the chopped onions, celery and carrot then add tomatoes and heat up with the wine and vinegar. Add remaining herbs and seasoning, stir and transfer to slow crock with bacon.

Dredge chicken in flour and brown all over. Transfer to slow crock. Replace lid and cook on LOW for 8–10 hours until tender. To serve, lift out chicken, carve and keep warm. Adjust seasoning of sauce and pour over chicken.

Variations: Before serving stir into the sauce 2–3 tbs sherry.

Garnish the dish with 125 g (4 oz) mushrooms *sautéed* in butter.

Add a packet or can of sweet corn half an hour before serving and stir it well into the sauce.

Omit carrot and tomatoes and use a small can of concentrated orange juice, thawed and mixed with the wine and vinegar.

Chicken Coriander   **8 hours LOW**

¾ kg (1½ lb) boneless chicken, 1 cooking apple, 2 carrots and onions, 125 g (4 oz) mushrooms, 3 tsp each of coriander and mild French mustard, 2 tbs flour and oil, salt and pepper, ¼ litre (½ pt) dry cider, 1 carton of sour cream.

Cut chicken into small pieces and toss in flour. Brown in oil, drain and set aside. Peel and slice fruit and vegetables and *sauté* lightly in oil and place in slow crock with chicken on top. Pour cider onto dish and then add remaining seasoning and spices. Replace lid and cook on LOW for about 6 hours until chicken is tender. To serve, stir sour cream in and adjust seasoning.

Chicken Paprikash   **8 hours LOW**

4 chicken joints, 1–2 tbs paprika, 125 ml (¼ pt) tomato juice, 1 medium onion, 1 bay leaf, sprig of tarragon, 30 g (1 oz) each of flour and butter, salt and pepper, 1–2 garlic cloves (optional), 1 carton of yoghurt.

Skin the chicken joints and dredge with seasoned flour. Peel and chop onion and fry in butter until soft. Transfer to slow crock. Brown the chicken joints and add to slow crock. Combine paprika, tomato juice and seasoning and pour over chicken. Add herbs and crushed garlic. Replace lid and cook on LOW for 6–8 hours until chicken is tender. To serve, remove chicken joints and keep warm. Stir the yoghurt into the cooking liquid and adjust seasoning, then pour the sauce over the chicken.

Curried Chicken   8 hours LOW

1–1½ kg (2–3 lb) chicken pieces, 1 medium onion, 1–2 garlic cloves, 1 tbs curry powder, 1 celery stalk, 1 green pepper, ¼ tsp each of ground ginger and turmeric, pinch of paprika and cayenne, 1 tsp sugar, 1 tbs chutney, salt to taste, juice of 1 lemon, ¼ litre (½ pt) chicken stock.
Optional: 1 small carton of double cream. 2 tbs each of flour and butter.

Remove skin from chicken pieces and place in bottom of slow crock. Mix crushed garlic with lemon juice, spices and flour to make a paste. Peel and chop vegetables. Melt butter in a frying pan and *sauté* the vegetables lightly, then add paste and fry for a further minute or two. Add a little of the chicken stock, stir thoroughly and pour into slow crock with remaining stock. Replace lid and cook on LOW for 6–8 hours until chicken is tender. To serve, stir in double cream and adjust seasoning. Accompany with rice.

Chestnut Chicken   10 hours LOW

1½ kg (3 lb) chicken, 2 dozen chestnuts, ½ litre (1 pt) chicken stock, 1 celery stalk, salt and pepper, 1 bay leaf.
Stuffing: 1 onion, 125 g (4 oz) each of sausage meat and mushrooms, 60 g (2 oz) breadcrumbs, 1 egg, 1 tsp chopped parsley, 4 tbs butter.

Pour boiling water over the chestnuts and leave for 2 minutes then drain and skin. Place in base of slow crock with chopped celery.
Sauté the chopped onion in half the butter then mix it

with the sausage meat and minced mushrooms, add seasoning and breadcrumbs and bind with an egg. Stuff the chicken, tie securely and brown the bird well on all sides in the remaining butter. Transfer to slow crock. Pour on enough chicken stock to cover the chestnuts. Replace lid and cook on LOW for 8–10 hours until the meat is tender and the stuffing firm.

To serve, remove the chicken and keep warm. Carefully remove the chestnuts and either leave them whole, placing them around the bird, or use, mashed, in the sauce. Adjust the seasoning of the stock, which will have been well-flavoured by the chestnuts, and serve it separately as a soup or with the chicken as gravy, or thicken by reducing and adding *beurre manié* and serve as a sauce.

Orange and Almond Chicken   8 hours LOW

4 chicken pieces, salt and pepper, paprika, 3 medium oranges, 3 tsp sugar or honey, 60 g (2 oz) chopped almonds, 60 g (2 oz) margarine, 1 sprig of rosemary, water.

Season the chicken with salt, pepper and paprika then *sauté* lightly in margarine, drain and transfer to slow crock. Squeeze the juice from two of the oranges, mix with an equal amount of water and pour over the chicken. Add rosemary, and replace lid, then cook on LOW 6–8 hours until chicken is tender.

Before serving, melt the sugar in the margarine then stir in the almonds and cook until brown. Stir this into the slow crock and adjust the seasoning if necessary. Remove skin and pith from remaining orange and cut into slices and arrange them over the chicken. Serve.

Redcurrant Chicken   **8 hours LOW**

4 chicken pieces, 1 tbs redcurrant jelly, ½ tsp ground ginger,
½ tsp dry mustard, few drops of tabasco sauce, 3 tbs each of
lemon juice and lime juice, salt and pepper, 2 tbs each of
butter and cornflour.

Season chicken with salt, pepper, ginger, mustard and
juices. Allow it to stand for at least 1 hour. Then place
chicken in slow crock with a little water to cover the base.
Replace lid and cook on LOW for 6–8 hours, until tender.

To serve, stir redcurrant jelly into sauce and knead butter
with cornflour, adding it bit by bit to the liquid, stirring it in
well. Allow to cook. Adjust seasoning, serve.

Chicken à la King   **6–8 hours LOW**

¾ kg (1½ lb) boneless chicken, 125 g (4 oz) mushrooms, 1
carrot, 1 onion, 3 pimentos, 125 ml (¼ pt) chicken stock, 125
ml (¼ pt) double cream, glass of sherry, 1 egg yolk, salt and
pepper, *bouquet garni,* garnish – chopped parsley.

Peel and slice carrot, then blanch for 3 minutes in boiling
water, drain and place in base of slow crock. Peel and slice
onion and mushrooms and place on top. Dice the chicken
and place in slow crock. Sprinkle on herbs, seasoning and
chopped pimento. Pour stock on. Replace lid and cook on
LOW for 6–8 hours until chicken and carrot are tender.

Fifteen minutes before serving mix all the ingredients together in the slow crock. Mix the egg yolk with the cream
and stir it into the slow crock. Adjust seasoning, then pour
on sherry if wished. Remove *bouquet garni*. Replace lid.
Serve, garnished with chopped parsley.

Chicken Divan   **6–8 hours LOW**

4 chicken breasts, 2 tbs lemon juice, 1 tsp Worcestershire
sauce, 2 bay leaves, 4 peppercorns, $\frac{1}{4}$ litre ($\frac{1}{2}$ pt) chicken
stock, salt, 1 small onion, 1 tsp grated orange rind, juice of
1 orange, 1 tsp brown sugar, 60 g (2 oz) black grapes, 30 g
(1 oz) each of cornflour and butter.

Place chicken breasts in slow crock. Add seasoning, spices,
herbs and stock. Replace lid and cook on LOW 6–8 hours
until chicken is tender.

Half an hour before serving, mince the onion. Melt the
butter in a pan and add the sugar, stir until caramelized then
add onion and cook. Sprinkle the cornflour over the onion
and stir until cooked. Remove from heat and add the
Worcestershire sauce, orange and lemon juice and orange
rind. Stir until there is a smooth sauce. Set aside.

Remove chicken from slow crock and keep warm. Strain
the stock and return it to slow crock. Add the sauce and
the black grapes (pitted) to the slow crock, stir, adjust
seasoning, replace lid and allow to heat.

Meanwhile, bone the chicken and cut it into chunks.
Immediately stir it into the slow crock sauce, allow all the
ingredients to heat up. Serve.

Alternative method: Cut and bone chicken before cooking.

Jamaica Chicken   **8 hours LOW**

4 chicken joints, 1 cooking apple, 125 g (4 oz) raisins, 1 green
pepper, 1 onion, 1 tbs chutney, 2 tbs black treacle or
molasses, salt and pepper, 4 cardamom pods, $\frac{1}{2}$ tsp cumin
powder, 1 tsp coriander seeds, 1 tbs curry powder, 1 tbs
lemon juice, $\frac{1}{4}$ litre ($\frac{1}{2}$ pt) stock, 2 tbs tomato *purée*, 2 tbs oil,
garnish – lemon slices.

Rub chicken joints with seasoning and spices and let them
stand during the other preparations. Prepare and chop

apple, onion and pepper and *sauté* in oil. Drain and transfer to slow crock. Wash and drain raisins and mix them into the vegetables. Mix chutney, treacle, tomato *purée*, lemon juice and stock and pour into slow crock. *Sauté* chicken joints and place in crock with any other ingredients. Replace lid and cook on LOW for 6–8 hours until chicken is tender.

To serve, adjust seasoning to taste. Garnish with lemon slices.

Chicken Scrumpy   **10 hours LOW**

1½ kg (3 lb) boiling fowl, 3 medium cooking apples, 4 rashers streaky bacon, 3 small onions, 125 ml (¼ pt) cider or scrumpy, salt and pepper, 2 egg yolks, 2 tbs butter, 1 tbs brandy.

Prepare the chicken and place the apples, peeled and sliced, inside it. Place it in the slow crock. Fry the bacon gently until the fat melts and lay the rashers over the chicken. Peel and chop the onions and *sauté* in the butter and bacon fat, then drain and transfer to slow crock. Sprinkle the ingredients with salt and pepper, and pour the cider over the chicken. Replace lid and cook on LOW until bird is tender.

When cooked, remove bird and keep warm. Beat the egg yolks and add to the sauce with the brandy. Adjust seasoning and pour sauce over the chicken.

Chinese Style Chicken and Pork   **8 hours LOW**

4 chicken breasts, 375 g (¾ lb) lean pork, 60 g (2 oz) mushrooms, 1 medium onion, 90 g (3 oz) bamboo shoots, 1 small tin of bean sprouts, 2 tomatoes, 3 tbs soy sauce, 1 tbs sherry, 1 tbs each of cornflour and butter, 3 tbs water, salt and pepper.

Bone the chicken and cut into slices. Cut any excess fat

from pork and cut into cubes. Slice the onions, mushrooms, bean sprouts, bamboo shoots and tomatoes and place in base of slow crock. Place meat and chicken on top. Add soy sauce, and water. Replace lid and cook on LOW for 6–8 hours until dish is tender.

To serve, knead together the cornflour and butter and drop bit by bit into the slow crock. Stir well and allow to cook for 5 minutes or so. Stir in sherry and adjust seasoning. Serve.

Sweet and Sour Chicken   8 hours LOW

4 chicken joints, 1 large cooking apple, 125 g (4 oz) pineapple chunks, 1–2 garlic cloves, salt and pepper, 30 g (1 oz) each of cornflour and fat, 125 ml ($\frac{1}{4}$ pt) chicken stock, 1 tbs soy sauce, 3 tbs vinegar, 3 tbs sugar or honey, 4 tbs reserved pineapple juice, 3 tbs chopped parsley, 1 tbs ground ginger. *Optional*: a small bunch of grapes, 3 tbs blanched almonds.

Peel and slice apples and place in the base of the slow crock with the pineapple chunks. Rub chicken joints with garlic, ginger, salt and pepper and place in slow crock. Mix together the stock, soy sauce, vinegar and pineapple juice and pour over the chicken. Replace lid and cook on LOW for 6–8 hours until chicken is tender.

Half an hour before serving knead the cornflour with the fat and add in little bits to the slow crock. Also stir in the sugar or honey. To serve, adjust seasoning of sauce and garnish the dish with chopped parsley, also blanched almonds and grapes if wished.

Coq au Vin   10 hours LOW

$1\frac{1}{2}$ kg (3 lb) chicken, salt and pepper, 2 garlic cloves, juice of 1 lemon, 125 g (4 oz) butter, 215 g (4 oz) mushrooms, 10 shallots or button onions, 4 tbs brandy, 1 bottle of red wine

¾ litre (1¼ pt), 2 tbs flour, chicken giblets, watercress, bread *croûtons*.

Season the chicken with salt and pepper, rub in the garlic and sprinkle with lemon juice. Let it stand during the remaining preparations. Peel and chop onions or shallots and *sauté* them in half the butter, drain and transfer to slow crock. Do the same with the mushrooms. Then brown the chicken all over and place in the slow crock. Heat the brandy, set it alight and pour it over the chicken. Then add the wine and giblets. Replace lid and cook on LOW 8–10 hours until the chicken is tender.

Then, remove chicken and giblets, carve and keep warm. Spoon out the onions and mushrooms and place around the chicken. Skim fat. Thicken the sauce with a *beurre manié*. Adjust seasoning and pour over the chicken. Garnish with watercress and *croûtons* of fried bread.

Red and Orange Chicken   8[1] or 10[2] hours LOW

1–1½ kg (2–3 lb) roasting chicken[2] or chicken joints[1], 1 medium onion, 1 sweet red pepper, 1 large juicy orange, 60 g (2 oz) stuffed green olives, 1 tbs chopped parsley, salt and pepper, *bouquet garni*, 125 ml (¼ pt) white wine, 90 ml (3 fl oz) chicken stock, giblets, 2 tbs each of flour, butter and oil.

Peel and slice onion then *sauté* in the butter and flour until golden. Stir in the flour and cook but do not brown. Then slowly add the stock and wine. Heat until almost boiling, stirring continuously, then pour over the chicken in the slow crock. Add *bouquet garni* and seasoning. Replace lid and cook on LOW until chicken is tender.

Half an hour before serving slice and de-seed the pepper, and cook. Drain and set aside. Remove rind and pith from orange and slice into rounds. Chop the olives and parsley. To serve, remove the chicken from the slow crock and keep warm. Stir the pepper, orange and olives into the cooking sauce and adjust seasoning. Allow the mixture to heat thoroughly then pour it over the chicken. Garnish with parsley.

Chicken Bonne Femme   10 hours LOW

1½ kg (3 lb) boiling fowl, 125 g (4 oz) chicken liver, 200 g (6 oz) sausage meat, 1 tsp mixed herbs, pinch each of allspice and ground mace, salt and pepper, *bouquet garni* – sprig of thyme and sage, 2 celery leaves, 2 bay leaves, 3 small carrots, 1 small turnip, 4 small potatoes, ½ litre (1 pt) stock, 1 egg, 3 tbs flour and fat.

Clean chicken and season the inside of the carcass with salt. Then, peel and dice vegetables and parboil for 5 minutes in boiling water. Drain and transfer to slow crock. Chop chicken liver and mix with sausage meat, then add herbs, spices, seasoning and bind with an egg. Place this mixture inside the chicken, tie and secure firmly. Place in slow crock. Add *bouquet garni* and stock. Replace lid and cook on LOW for 8–10 hours until the chicken is tender.

To serve, remove chicken and keep warm, spoon out the vegetables and place around the chicken. Remove *bouquet garni*. Skim fat. Thicken with a *beurre manié*. Adjust seasoning, serve as a gravy or soup.

Rabbit or Chicken Stew   8 hours LOW

1 small chicken or rabbit jointed – approx. 1½ kg (3 lb), giblets, 2 rindless bacon rashers, 4 ripe tomatoes, 1 sweet red pepper, 3 medium onions, 1–2 tsp chilli or cayenne pepper, salt and pepper, 1 tsp thyme, 1 tbs Worcestershire sauce, 3 tbs flour and butter, ½ litre (1 pt) cider or stock.

Sprinkle the joints of meat with salt, pepper and chilli powder and set aside to stand for about an hour.

Heat bacon in a frying pan until fat melts, drain and set aside. Peel the onion, de-seed the pepper. Chop the vegetables and *sauté* pepper and onions in the fat then transfer to slow crock. Dredge the meat with flour and brown it in butter. Place in slow crock and lay the bacon on top. Add remaining ingredients and replace lid. Cook on LOW for 6–8 hours until the meat is tender. To serve, adjust seasoning.

Chicken Pudding (see Puddings, page 173)

Roast Stuffed Duck   **6–8 hours HIGH**

1½–2½ kg (3–5 lb) duck, 4–6 rashers of bacon, 1–2 garlic cloves, 2 tsp ground ginger, oil, small glass of sherry, 1–2 tbs redcurrant jelly.
Stuffing: 125 g (4 oz) seedless raisins, 125 g (4 oz) chopped onion, 125 g (4 oz) chopped walnuts, 200 g (6 oz) soft breadcrumbs, 60 g (2 oz) chopped celery, 2 eggs, salt and pepper to taste.

Grease the sides of the slow crock lightly with oil.
Combine the stuffing ingredients and bind with beaten eggs. Stuff duck loosely and secure with thread. Any remaining stuffing can be used by rolling it into small nut-size balls cooked alongside the roast. Rub the outside of the duck with garlic and dust with ginger. Place in slow crock and lay bacon rashers over. Replace lid and cook on HIGH 6–8 hours until tender.
When cooked, remove duck and keep warm. Skim fat from the surface of the cooking liquid. Stir sherry and redcurrant jelly into the gravy and adjust seasoning. Serve with a salad (orange, green pea and cress).

Chinese Style Roast Duck   **6–8 hours HIGH**

1½–2½ kg (3–5 lb) duck, salt and pepper, 2 tbs brandy or sherry, 1 tbs soy sauce, 2 tbs honey, sprig each of fresh mint and basil, a few chives, sliced ginger root, 3 tsp Worcester-shire sauce, oil.
Stuffing: 1–2 cooking apples, 1 tsp cinnamon, ¼ kg (½ lb) minced pork or veal, 60 g (2 oz) ham, 1 egg, 60 g (2 oz) breadcrumbs.

Rub the duck with salt and pepper inside and out and leave for an hour. To make the stuffing – mince or chop the ingredients finely and bind with beaten egg and bread-crumbs. Stuff the duck. Rub the inside of the slow crock lightly with oil and place duck on base. Add chopped chives, sprigs of mint and basil and ginger, pour on a little soy sauce. Replace lid and cook on HIGH for 6–8 hours until duck is tender.

To serve, remove duck and keep warm. Skim fat from surface of cooking liquid. Add sherry (or brandy), honey and Worcestershire sauce to gravy and stir until melted. Adjust seasoning. Serve.
Variation: Peel 4 large tomatoes and add to cooking liquid, sprinkled with paprika. An hour before the end add stuffed olives to the slow crock (about a dozen). To serve, mash the tomatoes into the gravy after skimming.

Casserole of Bacon and Rabbit   **6–8 hours LOW**

1 rabbit cut in joints, 125 g (4 oz) salt pork or bacon, 1–2 garlic cloves, salt and pepper, 1 bay leaf, 1 tbs tomato *purée*, 8–10 shallots or pickling onions, vinegar, water, 2 tbs each of oil and flour, ¼ litre (½ pt) stock.

Soak the rabbit overnight in salted water with a dash of vinegar then drain well and dry. Brown the rabbit and bacon joints in oil and add chopped onions sprinkled with flour.

Stir till flour is cooked then transfer to slow crock. Add seasoning, stock and herbs. Replace lid and cook on LOW for 6–8 hours. To serve, adjust seasoning.

Rabbit Prunella   **6–8 hours LOW**

1 rabbit cut into joints, 2 medium carrots, 2 medium onions, 125 ml ($\frac{1}{4}$ pt) each of beef stock and red wine, $\frac{1}{4}$ kg ($\frac{1}{2}$ lb) dried prunes, 90 g (3 oz) raisins, salt and pepper, *bouquet garni*, 2 tbs each of oil and flour, garnish – chopped parsley, fried bread *croûtons*.

Peel, slice and blanch vegetables and place in slow crock with washed fruit. Wipe joints and toss in seasoned flour, brown in oil, drain and transfer to slow crock. Add remaining ingredients. Replace lid and cook on LOW for 6–8 hours until rabbit is tender. To serve, adjust seasoning and garnish the dish with parsley and *croûtons* of bread.
Variations: Use mixed dried fruit instead of just prunes (including apples, apricots, figs, etc).

Cook the dish in cider and chicken stock instead of beef-stock and red wine.

Omit fruit entirely, rub the rabbit with 3 tbs French mustard, dredge in flour and brown in oil, and cook in chicken stock, with a tablespoon of vinegar and fresh chopped tarragon.

Cook dish in white wine and tomato juice, add 128 g (4 oz) mushrooms half an hour before serving.

Beer Hare   **6–8 hours LOW**

1 hare cut in joints, $\frac{1}{4}$ litre ($\frac{1}{2}$ pt) brown ale, 1 garlic clove crushed in salt, 1 bay leaf, 3 medium onions, $\frac{1}{4}$ tsp grated nutmeg, 1 tsp paprika, 1 tsp red wine vinegar, 1 grated carrot, 125 ml ($\frac{1}{4}$ pt) brown stock, 1 tbs each of butter and flour.

Wipe the hare joints and put them in a large bowl and cover them with beer, garlic, bay leaf, sliced onions and nutmeg. Mix together, cover and leave to marinate in refrigerator for 24 hours.

Then, drain joints and wipe dry. Roll them in seasoned flour (salt, pepper, paprika) and brown in butter. Transfer to slow crock, add stock, marinade and vinegar, grated carrot and nutmeg. Replace lid and cook on LOW for 6–8 hours. To serve, adjust seasoning and accompany with plain boiled potatoes.

Jugged Hare   **6–8 hours LOW**

1 hare cut in joints, marinade – 1 bottle red wine, 1 sprig each of thyme and rosemary, 2 onions, 1 carrot, 3 cloves, 1 bay leaf, 12 peppercorns, ½ tsp salt, pepper, pinch of nutmeg, ginger, cinnamon, 125 g (4 oz) mushrooms, *bouquet garni*, ¼ kg (½ lb) salt pork or bacon, 1 tbs redcurrant jelly, 2 tbs butter and flour.
Optional: small glass of brandy.

Place hare in a large bowl and cover with wine, herbs, sliced onion and carrot, then leave to marinade in refrigerator for 24 hours.

Then, drain joints and wipe dry. Strain marinade. Remove rind from bacon and cut into cubes. Brown it and transfer to slow crock. Toss hare in flour and brown that too, then transfer to slow crock. Add sliced mushrooms, spices and *bouquet garni* then pour strained marinade over. Replace lid and cook on LOW 6–8 hours until hare is tender. To serve, remove *bouquet garni*, stir in redcurrant jelly and adjust seasoning.

Pigeon Casserole   **8 hours LOW**

4 small pigeons, 125 g (4 oz) bacon, 2 small onions, 125 g
(4 oz) mushrooms, salt and pepper, 4 juniper berries, ¼ litre
(½ pt) stock, pinch of ginger and ground mace, 2 tbs oil and
flour, 2 tbs red wine.
Garnish: chopped parsley.

Clean pigeons and brown in oil. Transfer to slow crock.
Dice bacon and peel and chop onions, *sauté* in oil then add
these, the stock, seasoning and spices to slow crock. Replace
lid and cook on LOW 8 hours until pigeons are tender.

Half an hour before serving, *sauté* the sliced mushrooms
in oil, sprinkle on the flour and stir until cooked, then add to
slow crock. To serve, add the red wine, adjust seasoning and
garnish with chopped parsley.
Variations: Cook the pigeons in white wine and add 2 tbs
brandy at the end of the cooking period.

Sauté a celery stalk and add, with the onions, to the slow
crock.

Partridge with Celery   **8–10 hours LOW**

2 partridges, 2–3 celery stalks, 125 g (4 oz) green pitted
olives, 125 ml (¼ pt) tomato juice, 3 tbs oil, juice of 1 lemon,
salt and pepper to taste, pinch each of ginger and cumin.

Clean partridges, rub with lemon and cut into portions.
Heat oil in a frying pan and brown meat all over. Wash and
chop celery and *sauté* lightly in oil. Transfer celery and
partridge to slow crock, add seasoning, spices and tomato
juice. Replace lid and cook on LOW for 8–10 hours until bird
is tender. An hour before serving, add the olives to the
cooking liquid. To serve, adjust seasoning.

Pheasant with Apples   **8 hours LOW**

1 pheasant plucked and drawn, 6 medium sized dessert apples, salt and pepper, cinnamon, 1 bay leaf, $\frac{1}{4}$ litre ($\frac{1}{2}$ pt) chicken stock, 1 tbs whisky, 2–3 tbs cream, 2 tbs butter.

Peel, core and slice apples, then brown them lightly in butter and place in slow crock. Sprinkle with cinnamon. Season bird with salt and pepper and brown until golden in butter and place in slow crock. Add chicken stock, bay leaf, then replace lid and cook on LOW 8 hours until pheasant is tender.

To serve, remove pheasant and keep warm. Remove bay leaf. Add whisky and cream to stock and adjust seasoning. Serve.

Variations: Instead of whisky, add a small glass of sherry.

Pigeon Pudding (see Puddings, page 174)

Partridge Pudding (see Puddings, page 175)

Grouse Pudding (see Puddings, page 175)

Rabbit Pudding (see Puddings, page 176)

OFFAL RECIPES

Generally the term 'offal' refers to liver, kidney, brains, head, tongue, sweetbreads, heart, tripe and trotters. They must not always be eaten while absolutely fresh. This term also includes other parts cut off as waste from the carcass – such as the tail.

Stuffed Hearts   **8 hours LOW**

1–1½ kg (2–3 lb) hearts, eg 4 pigs' hearts, 6 lambs', or 1 ox heart, 6 rashers bacon, scant 125 ml (¼ pt) wine or beer.
Stuffing: ¼ kg (½ lb) sausage meat, 1 celery stalk, 30 g (1 oz) nuts, ½ tsp sage, 1 small onion, 90 g (3 oz) breadcrumbs, 1 egg, salt and pepper to taste.

Wash and clean hearts. Remove gristle, valves and membrane from cavity. Soak in cold water with a tablespoon of vinegar for an hour at least. Then rinse, drain and pat dry.

Meanwhile, mix together ingredients for stuffing. Chop the vegetables very small and then combine with the sausage meat, breadcrumbs, chopped nuts and herbs. Season to taste and bind with an egg.

Take each heart and cut the two cavities into one by slitting the centre wall. Then fill each carefully with stuffing. Wrap a rasher of bacon around the heart and secure with a cocktail stick. Place in slow crock and pour liquid around. Replace lid and cook on LOW for 8 hours until hearts are tender.
Variation: Add 1–2 tbs redcurrant jelly to the gravy.
Alternative stuffings for hearts recipe:
1: *Prune and apple* 10 prunes, 2 medium apples, 125 g (4 oz) breadcrumbs, 1 tsp grated lemon rind, juice of ½ lemon, 1 beaten egg, salt and pepper, 60 g (2 oz) chopped nuts, 60 g (2 oz) melted butter.

Grate apples and chop prunes, or mince both. Mix dry ingredients, add seasoning to taste, lemon juice and rind. Bind with melted butter and beaten egg. Follow recipe as above.

2: *Sage and onion* ¼ kg (½ lb) onions, 8–10 sage leaves, 125 g (4 oz) fresh breadcrumbs, salt and pepper, 1 egg, grated rind of ½ lemon, squeeze of lemon juice, 60 g (2 oz) butter, 3–4 pickled walnuts, 1 large apple, peeled, cored and diced.

Peel and chop onions and boil for 5 minutes in enough water to cover them. Drain. Mix together breadcrumbs, onion, chopped sage leaves, chopped apple, and season the mixture to taste. Bind with beaten egg and melted butter and stir in lemon juice and rind. Add walnuts cut in four. If mixture is too dry, add cider or stock to moisten.

Braised Liver   6–8 hours LOW

½ kg (1 lb) liver, 125 ml (¼ pt) white wine, 4 medium onions, 2 tsp paprika, salt and pepper, 1 bay leaf, 2 tbs butter and flour. *Garnish* – 2 tbs chopped parsley.
Optional: 1 carton of cream.

Peel and slice onions then *sauté* in butter and transfer to slow crock. Toss slices or cubes of liver in seasoned flour and brown gently in butter then place in slow crock. Add remaining ingredients. Replace lid and cook on LOW for 6–8 hours until ingredients are thoroughly cooked. To serve, stir in cream and garnish with chopped parsley, adjust seasoning.

Liver and Aubergine   6 hours LOW

½ kg (1 lb) liver, 3 aubergines, 2 onions, 3 tbs oil, 1–2 tbs vinegar, salt and pepper, 125 ml (¼ pt) tomato juice, squeeze of lemon juice, dash of Worcestershire sauce, 1–2 tbs flour.
Optional: 1 garlic clove.

Slice aubergine, sprinkle with salt for about an hour so that the bitter juices escape. Then wash in cold water and drain. Peel and slice onions. Heat some of the oil in a frying pan and first *sauté* onions then aubergine until brown, together with crushed garlic if used. Drain and transfer to slow crock. Toss sliced or cubed liver in seasoned flour then *sauté* quickly in oil and transfer to slow crock. Make *roux* from remaining oil and flour and gradually add tomato juice, then pour into slow crock with remaining ingredients. Replace lid and cook on LOW for about 6 hours until the aubergine is tender. To serve, adjust seasoning.

Liver Roll   **4–6 hours HIGH**

200 g (6 oz) each of calf's liver and bacon, salt and pepper, 1 tsp chopped parsley, $\frac{1}{4}$ kg ($\frac{1}{2}$ lb) self-raising flour, 120 g (4 oz) shredded suet, water, salt and pepper.
Metal foil, boiling water, trivet.

Make a soft and slightly moist suet pastry, seasoning to taste. Then roll out on a floured board into an oblong with a width that will fit your slow crock.

Chop finely or mince the liver and bacon, add herbs and seasoning to taste. Spread the mixture over the pastry, but not too near the edges. Moisten the edges of the pastry with water then roll up.

Wrap the roll in greaseproof paper or metal foil and place on a trivet in the slow crock. Pour about 125 ml ($\frac{1}{4}$ pt) boiling water in. Replace lid and cook on HIGH for at least 4 hours until the suet pastry is cooked.

Spanish Style Liver   **6 hours LOW**

$\frac{1}{2}$ kg (1 lb) liver, 4 rashers bacon, 1 onion, 2 carrots, 1 tbs tomato paste, 2–3 tbs dry sherry, $\frac{1}{4}$ litre ($\frac{1}{2}$ pt) beef stock, salt and pepper, 1 tbs flour and oil.

Heat bacon in a pan until the fat melts, then place in slow crock. Cut liver into strips, slices or cubes and toss in seasoned flour. *Sauté* liver in the bacon fat, then drain and set aside. Peel and slice vegetables and *sauté* quickly in oil and place in slow crock with liver on top. Mix tomato paste with beef stock and pour onto dish. Replace lid and cook on

LOW for about 6 hours until the vegetables are tender. To serve, pour in the sherry, and adjust seasoning.

Venetian Casserole   **6 hours LOW**

½ kg (1 lb) lamb's liver, 125 g (4 oz) each of mushrooms and tomatoes, 4 bacon rashers, 3 onions, 120 g (4 oz) black pitted olives, 1 tsp dry mustard, juice of ½ lemon, ¼ litre (½ pt) chicken stock, 30 g (1 oz) each of flour and oil, salt and pepper.

Remove rind and chop bacon then heat in a frying pan until the fat melts. Transfer to slow crock. Slice the liver and toss in seasoned flour then *sauté* quickly in bacon fat and transfer to slow crock. Peel and chop remaining vegetables, *sauté* and place in slow crock. Make a *roux* from the remaining flour and oil and stir in a little of the stock. Pour this into slow crock. Replace lid and cook on LOW for about 6 hours until ingredients are thoroughly cooked. To serve, add lemon juice and adjust seasoning.

Mock Goose   **6–8 hours LOW**

½ kg (1 lb) pig's liver, ½ kg (1 lb) potatoes, 1 large onion, 1 tbs flour and oil, salt and pepper, 1 tsp sage, ¼ litre (½ pt) vegetable stock.

Peel and slice potatoes and onions and parboil for 5 minutes then drain and set aside. Reserve potato stock.
Slice or cube liver and toss in seasoned flour then *sauté* gently in oil, drain and set aside. Arrange the vegetables and liver in alternate layers in slow crock, beginning and ending with potatoes. Season each layer. Pour vegetable stock over (including the potato water). Replace lid and cook on LOW for 6–8 hours until the potatoes are tender. To serve, adjust seasoning.

Braised French Oxtail   8–10 hours LOW

1 kg (2 lb) oxtail joints, 125 g (4 oz) salt pork or bacon, 1 tbs
tomato paste, 1 carrot and onion, scant 125 ml (¼ pt) each
of dry red wine and beef stock, salt and pepper, pinch of
mace and allspice, ½ tbs each of flour and oil, 2 garlic cloves,
bouquet garni (bay leaf, parsley, thyme), garnish – 1 tbs
chopped parsley.

Peel and chop vegetables and *sauté* quickly in hot oil and
place on bottom of slow crock. Dredge oxtail joints in flour
and brown in oil. Transfer to slow crock. Add tomato paste
mixed with stock and wine, plus remaining ingredients.
Replace lid and cook on LOW for 8–10 hours until meat is
falling away from the joints. To serve, remove *bouquet garni*,
skim excess fat from liquid, adjust seasoning.

The above two recipes can be served with onion dumplings
added an hour before the end of cooking time.
Onion dumplings for oxtail stews
200 g (6 oz) self-raising flour, 90 g (3 oz) fat, 1 tbs finely
minced onion, egg to bind, salt and pepper, pinch of mixed
herbs.
    Mix all the ingredients together and bind with an egg.
Shape into small balls and add to slow crock an hour before
the end of cooking time.

West Indian Style Oxtail Stew   8–10 hours LOW

1 kg (2 lb) oxtail joints, 125 g (4 oz) each of raisins and pitted
black olives, 1 green pepper, 2 celery stalks, salt and pepper,
1 tbs each of chilli powder, oil and flour, ½ tbs dry mustard,
bouquet garni (bay leaf, thyme, parsley, strip of orange peel),

1 tbs lemon juice, 125 ml (¼ pt) each of natural or fresh orange juice and beef stock, *garnish* – watercress.

De-seed pepper, wash and chop vegetables and place in bottom of slow crock with raisins and olives. Dredge oxtail joints with the flour. Heat oil in a frying pan and brown the oxtail. Sprinkle on the spices and cook for a minute. Transfer to slow crock. Heat the juice and stock in the frying pan then pour into slow crock. Add *bouquet garni*, and lemon juice. Replace lid. Cook on LOW for 8–10 hours until oxtail is cooked and meat is falling away from the bones. To serve, remove *bouquet garni*. Skim fat off the surface of the stew with absorbent paper towels. Adjust seasoning. Garnish with watercress.

Kidney Casserole   **6 hours LOW**

¾ kg (1½ lb) ox kidney, 2 onions, 1 tbs chopped parsley, 1 tsp sweet basil, ¼ litre (½ pt) beef stock, salt and pepper, 30 g (1 oz) each of fat and flour.

Skin, trim and core kidney. Cut into small pieces and toss in seasoned flour. Melt fat and brown kidneys. Drain and set aside. *Sauté* peeled and chopped onions quickly and place in base of slow crock with kidney on top. Make a *roux* with the remaining fat and flour and gradually add stock, and heat. Pour into slow crock. Add seasoning and herbs. Replace lid and cook on LOW for about 6 hours until kidneys are tender. To serve, adjust seasoning and garnish with chopped parsley.

Variation: Instead of making a *roux*, just mix the stock with 3 tbs tomato paste and pour onto dish.

Kidneys in Wine   **6 hours LOW**

¾ kg (1½ lb) lamb's or calf's kidney, 200 g (6 oz) mushrooms,
1 carrot, 1 celery stalk, 125 ml (¼ pt) each of white wine and
beef stock, 1 tbs butter and flour.
Optional: 1 carton of single cream, 2 tbs brandy, 1–2 garlic
cloves, *garnish* – fried bread *croûtons*, salt and pepper.

Skin kidneys and cut in half. Toss in seasoned flour. Melt
butter in a frying pan and *sauté* the kidneys then drain and
set aside. Peel and chop vegetables and *sauté* lightly then
place in base of slow crock with kidneys on top. Make a
roux with the remaining flour and butter and heat stock.
Pour wine and *roux* into slow crock, add crushed garlic if
wished. Replace lid and cook on LOW for about 6 hours until
kidneys are tender. To serve, strain off cooking juice and
reduce in a pan, remove from heat and stir in cream and
brandy. Adjust seasoning. Pour the sauce back over the
kidneys. Garnish with *croûtons* of fried bread.

Boiled Tongue   **12–14 hours/overnight LOW**

1½–2½ kg (3–5 lb) tongue, 6 peppercorns, *bouquet garni*, 2
onions, 2 carrots, 1 celery stalk, cold water.

A salt tongue should be rinsed in fresh water before
cooking. A fresh tongue should be soaked in salt water for
an hour before cooking. Ask butcher to remove the root and
gristle from the tongue.
Place tongue in slow crock, curled around the base. Add
peeled and chopped vegetables and *bouquet garni*. If tongue
is fresh add salt, otherwise add no salt. Cover tongue with
cold water. Replace lid and cook on LOW overnight or for
12–14 hours until it can be easily pierced with a toothpick.
When cooked, remove tongue and peel skin off. Then
place it in a round tin and press down with weights. To
serve, slice thinly at a slant. Strain off stock and use as the

basis of a sauce for the tongue (see below), or as the stock for any soup and stew that requires a good strong basis.

Tongue can be served hot or cold.

Devilled Tongue   2–3 hours LOW

1 cooked skinned tongue (see recipe, page 152), 1 tbs flour, 1 tbs vinegar, 2 tbs tomato ketchup, dash of Worcestershire sauce, ½ tsp dry mustard, ¼ tsp ground ginger, 125 ml (¼ pt) each of tongue stock and water, *garnish*: – watercress.

Rinse out the slow crock and place sliced tongue in the base. Make a flour paste with a little water, then mix with remaining ingredients, and add to slow crock. Replace lid and heat on LOW for 2–3 hours. To serve, garnish with watercress.

Chinese Style Tongue   2–3 hours LOW

1 cooked tongue (see recipe, page 152), 2 tbs cornflour, 90 ml (3 fl oz) soy sauce, 2 tbs sherry, 1 garlic clove, 2 tsp sugar, ¼ tsp tarragon, ¼ tsp ground ginger, 125 ml (¼ pt) each of reserved tongue stock and water.

Slice the tongue thinly. Rinse out slow crock and place tongue in the base. Mix remaining ingredients into a paste, adding stock gradually to avoid lumpy flour paste. Pour into slow crock. Replace lid and heat on LOW for 2–3 hours.

PÂTÉS

The correct name for a preparation of meat, fish or game baked in a piedish, and layered with strips or rashers of bacon, is a terrine (although it is commonly known as a pâté). A pâté is strictly a meat dish encased in pastry, like a pork pie. Terrines are usually served cold, whereas a real pâté can be served hot or cold.

One basic pâté recipe can be varied by the subtle interchange of different alcohols, or by different combinations of spices and herbs. You can also pour off the fat after cooking and substitute a jelly made from chicken or game bones, or flavoured with sherry or lemon juice.

The texture of the pâté can be altered by mincing the meats finely, or chopping them roughly to give a smooth or a chunky pâté respectively. By layering the different ingredients alternately you can get a marbled or mottled effect.

The flavour of the pâté will be altered by keeping it for a couple of days or weeks – not in a deep freeze but just in a cool place. A pâté should always be prepared at least 12 hours in advance of eating.

Basic Ingredients for Pâté

LIVER	Use up to ¾ kg (1½ lb) depending on the size of your container. Goose is the traditional and the best for *pâté* but the most difficult to get. Chicken is second best and produces a smooth and delicate *pâté*. Ox, pig's and lamb's liver are all very good but have a stronger and coarser taste.
BACON	Use up to ¼ kg (½ lb), that is a third in weight of the main liver ingredient.
VEGETABLES	Onion and garlic are used as essential flavouring to the liver *pâté*. Mushroom and carrot slices are used to garnish the top.
HERBS	Bay leaf is placed on top of the *pâté* and removed before serving. Thyme, parsley, rosemary and mace are used in varying proportions depending on the *pâté*.
SPICES	A clove or two can be poked into the top of the *pâté* and removed before serving, and allspice and nutmeg added in pinches to the ingredients.

SEASONING	Salt and black pepper should be used with caution – about $\frac{1}{2}$ tsp of black pepper per $\frac{3}{4}$ kg ($1\frac{1}{2}$ lb) of *pâté*. If the bacon is smoked, the salt will not be needed in large quantities either.
ALCOHOL	1–2 tsp of brandy or sherry can be sprinkled over the *pâté* while it is maturing.
GARNISH	To serve *pâté* with a brightly coloured salad adds to its appeal. Radishes, tomatoes and cucumbers cut in chunks look good. Chopped parsley and cress look as well as taste interesting. The *pâté* itself can be served on a bed of lettuce. Lemon slices add yet another streak of colour.
EGG	1 egg can be added for that extra smoothness and as a binding agent.
OTHER MEATS	Instead of the traditional liver ingredient, other meats such as rabbit, veal, beef can be used although strictly speaking this could mean that you were making a galantine or meat loaf.
VEGETARIAN	*Pâtés* can be made using beans. See chapter on vegetables, page 159.

Basic Method for Pâté in the Slow Crock

1. During preparations switch on the slow crock to HIGH.
2. Choose a container that easily fits into the slow crock and grease it. Then line it with bacon rashers. Use remaining rashers in the body of the pâté.
3. All the ingredients must be finely sieved or chopped. To make the liver firm enough for this, plunge it into very hot water until it changes colour. Mix all the ingredients together into a smooth liquid-paste and add the seasoning and ground spices. Mix in lightly beaten egg.
4. Place bay leaf and cloves in pâté dish, and add garnish of carrot and mushroom slices. Pour the mixture into the pâté dish. Cover container with metal foil and place in

slow crock. Pour boiling water around until it reaches half-way up the side.

5. Replace lid and cook on HIGH for 3–4 hours. Remove container from slow crock and press the pâté down with weights. If possible, leave for a day to mature in a cool place or a refrigerator. To serve, turn it out onto a flat board.

PÂTÉ RECIPES

Chicken Liver Pâté   **3–4 hours HIGH**

¾ kg (1½ lb) chicken livers, ¼ kg (½ lb) streaky bacon, 2 medium onions, ½ tsp black pepper, 1 tsp salt, 2–3 cloves garlic, pinch each of mace and thyme, 4 whole cloves, 1 bay leaf, 1 egg. *Garnish* – sliced mushrooms and carrot. Boiling water, metal foil, container, margarine or lard.
Optional: 1–2 tsp brandy or sherry.

Switch slow crock to HIGH during preparations.
Follow instructions for basic method above (page 155) and cook on HIGH for 3–4 hours. Sprinkle brandy or sherry over pâté while it is cooling and maturing.

Ox Liver Pâté   **3–4 hours HIGH**

¾ kg (1½ lb) ox liver, 125 g (4 oz) streaky bacon, 1 garlic clove, 5 anchovy fillets or 1 tsp anchovy essence, pinch each of salt and pepper, ½ tsp each of rosemary and parsley, 1 large bay leaf, 1 egg, *garnish* – slices of carrot and mushroom.

Switch slow crock to HIGH during preparations.
Follow basic method for pâté (see page 155) and cook on HIGH for 3–4 hours.

Meat Pâté   **3–4 hours HIGH**

¼ kg (½ lb) minced beef, veal or lamb, 200 g (6 oz) sausage meat, 2 slices of bread, 2 small onions or shallots, 3 tbs chopped parsley, 1 tbs chervil, 2 egg yolks, salt and pepper, butter, *garnish* – slices of gherkin, boiling water, metal foil, container.

Switch slow crock to HIGH during preparation.

Soak bread in a little water and squeeze dry. Mince the meat finely with the sausage meat. Peel and chop onions and herbs. Mix all these together, adding salt and pepper to taste, and the egg yolks.

Grease a tin that fits your slow crock, and pat the mixture firmly into it. Cover with foil and place in slow crock. Pour boiling water around until it reaches half-way up the sides. Replace lid and cook on HIGH for 3–4 hours. To serve, remove container from slow crock and allow to cool and mature. Garnish with slices of gherkin.

Veal and Beef Pâté   **3–4 hours HIGH**

¼ kg (½ lb) each of lean minced beef and veal, salt and pepper, ½ tsp ground mace, pinch of allspice and chilli powder, 30 g (1 oz) butter or margarine, boiling water, metal foil, container.

Switch slow crock to HIGH during preparations.

Grease a tin that will fit into your slow crock. Mix all the ingredients together in a bowl and transfer to the tin. Smooth mixture down. Cover with metal foil and place in slow crock. Pour boiling water around and replace lid. Cook on HIGH for 3–4 hours. To serve, allow to cool then pound all the ingredients till smooth. Adjust seasoning with more pepper. Work in some extra butter to give a smoother texture. Press mixture into a jar or terrine and cover with clarified butter. Serve with hot toast.

Faggots   **3–4 hours HIGH**

200 g (6 oz) each of pig's liver, calf's liver and fresh pork, 125 g (4 oz) breadcrumbs, 1 onion, salt and pepper, 1 egg yolk, ½ tsp thyme and parsley, pinch of allspice.

Switch slow crock to HIGH during preparations.

Follow basic method for pâté (see above, page 155) and cook on HIGH for 3–4 hours.

7 VEGETABLES AND VEGETARIAN

Although the slow crock is not at its best as a vegetable cooker there are inevitably dishes that need the addition of one or two for flavour and here there are two simple rules to follow as regards preparation.
1. Root and starchy vegetables should be parboiled or blanched before being added to the slow crock to ensure that they soften properly over the long cooking period.
2. Green vegetables, onions and garlic should be *sautéed* in oil or butter, and then added to the slow crock.

Elsewhere in the book where vegetables are part of the ingredients of a composite dish (eg soup, meat stew) I have dealt with their preparation as part of the method of the whole recipe, and you will probably find that you will naturally incorporate the pre-cooking of vegetables into the normal routine of assembling a slow crock dish.

Beans and rice both cook in the slow crock on the HIGH setting. Dried beans, as usual, need to be soaked overnight in cold water and when cooking them you should not add salt to the water until the end as this hinders the softening process. Bicarbonate of soda can be added – a pinch or two – to aid softening but this reduces the nutritional value.* Beans take nearly a day to cook in the slow crock, that is, if you start the whole cooking process from cold in the slow crock, ie add beans, cold water to cover, remaining ingredients and leave to cook on HIGH. If you want to reduce that overall timing, you simply bring all the ingredients to boiling point in a separate container and add to a pre-heated slow crock; timing is then reduced by a half.

Rice, if you use the wrong kind, will 'explode' in the slow crock – that is, stick together in an unappealing mush. 'Easy-cook' rice works the best, and so does brown rice. The timing is very short (1–2 hours) and you will perhaps find it

* No longer recommended.

more logical to use rice as the component of another dish rather than cook it alone.

This chapter also includes a range of food not strictly vegetable and not totally vegetarian, but with enough of each to warrant being included under the same heading – so there are egg curries and some suggestions about stuffed vegetables, which cook just fine in the slow crock.

Leek (and Mushroom) Pudding (see Puddings, Chapter 176)

Baked Onions   **2–3 hours HIGH**

6–8 medium onions, 2 tbs oil, water, salt and pepper, sprig of thyme or 1 bay leaf.

Peel and halve the onions and fry in oil until golden brown. Place in slow crock and add water to cover the base. Add herbs. Replace lid and cook on HIGH 2–3 hours until onions are tender and succulent. To serve, adjust seasoning with salt and pepper.

Baked Beetroot   **8 hours HIGH**

4–6 beetroot, water to cover base.

Scrub beetroot and place on base of slow crock. Add water to cover base. Cook on HIGH 8 hours. Peel and serve hot or cold.

Baked Potatoes   **10–12 hours LOW**

10–12 medium potatoes, butter or oil.

Scrub potatoes. Grease the inside of the slow crock with

butter or oil. Place rinsed (but not dried) potatoes in slow crock. Replace lid and cook on LOW 10–12 hours until soft. To serve, cut in half and place a knob of butter or sour cream on each half.

STUFFED VEGETABLES

In order to keep their shape and firmness while cooking it is a good idea to place stuffed vegetables on a trivet or crumpled metal foil in the slow crock. Always choose a shape that will fit your slow crock (eg peppers come tall and fat or long and thin).

Stuffed Peppers   3 hours LOW

4 green or red peppers, boiling water.

Stuffing 1: 1 onion, 3 sweet apples, butter, salt and pepper, tomato *purée*, 1 small can of frankfurters.

Stuffing 2: 60 g (2 oz) chopped bacon, 125 g (4 oz) chopped mushrooms, 60 g (2 oz) cooked rice, seasoning, 1 tsp butter.

Stuffing 3: 125 g (4 oz) cooked rice, juice of ½ lemon, 2–3 tbs chopped parsley, pinch of thyme and marjoram, salt and pepper, pinch of turmeric or saffron for colour, 1 tsp oil.

Method for stuffed peppers

Pre-heat slow crock on HIGH during preparations.

Cut tops from peppers, remove seeds and core. Plunge into boiling salted water for 3 minutes. Drain and set aside.

Chop and *sauté* all the stuffing ingredients and fill the peppers with the mixture.

Place the stuffed peppers on a trivet or crumpled metal foil in crock and pour boiling water in to the depth of 1 cm (½″). Replace lid and cook on LOW for 3 hours.

T–F

Stuffed Tomatoes   **3 hours LOW**

8 large tomatoes, seasoning, 60 g (2 oz) chopped walnuts, 1
tbs chopped onions or spring onions, chives and parsley,
125 g (4 oz) minced meat, 4 tbs breadcrumbs, boiling water.

Pre-heat slow crock on HIGH during preparations.

Cut the tops off the tomatoes and scoop out the pulp
which should be reserved. Season the cases lightly with salt
and pepper. Mix the ingredients for the stuffing together,
including the tomato pulp, and fill the cases. Place the lids
of the tomato tops back on. Place tomatoes on a trivet or
crumpled metal foil in the slow crock. Pour boiling water
onto the base to the depth of 1 cm ($\frac{1}{2}''$). Replace lid and cook
on LOW for 3 hours until tender.

N.B. Instead of minced meat, *sautéed* chopped bacon can be
used.

Stuffed Marrow   **4–5 hours LOW**

1 medium marrow, boiling water.
For stuffing: 1 red pepper, 1 medium onion, 125 g (4 oz)
cooked chopped ham, 1 tbs butter, 1 tbs flour, seasoning,
chopped parsley, grated cheese, 125 g (4 oz) mushrooms.

Pre-heat slow crock on HIGH during preparations. Peel
the marrow and cut it into 4 or 8 slices, depending on the
size and shape of your slow crock. Remove the seeds and
then plunge it into boiling salted water for 5–6 minutes.
Drain and set aside.

To make stuffing, de-seed the pepper, peel and chop the
vegetables and *sauté* in butter, then sprinkle with flour, and
cook. Mix this with the chopped ham. Add seasoning and
herbs. Fill the marrow with this mixture then place the
slices on a trivet or crumpled metal foil in the slow crock.
Pour boiling water in to depth of 1 cm ($\frac{1}{2}''$). Replace lid and

cook on LOW for 4–5 hours until tender. To serve, sprinkle with grated cheese and allow it to melt.

N.B. This stuffing can also be used for aubergines and peppers, which would also need plunging in boiling salted water before stuffing.

Stuffed Aubergine   3–4 hours LOW

4 aubergines, boiling water, *stuffing* – 1 green pepper, 1 onion, 1–2 garlic cloves, 60 g (2 oz) fresh breadcrumbs, $\frac{1}{4}$ kg ($\frac{1}{2}$ lb) minced meat or chopped bacon, 3 tbs tomato paste, 60 g (2 oz) grated cheese, salt and pepper, 4 tbs olive oil, 1 tsp mixed herbs, chopped parsley.

Pre-heat slow crock on HIGH during preparations.

Depending on shape of slow crock either cut aubergines in half lengthways or cut the tops off and scoop out the centre. Plunge into boiling salted water for 3 minutes. Drain and set aside. To make the stuffing *sauté* chopped onion and pepper, garlic and meat or bacon then mix it with the remaining ingredients and season. Stuff the aubergines. Place on a trivet or crumpled metal foil in the slow crock and pour in boiling water to the depth of 1 cm ($\frac{1}{2}$"). Replace lid and cook on LOW for 3–4 hours until tender. To serve, garnish with cheese and sprinkle with chopped parsley.

BEANS, PULSE AND GRAIN

Beans are among the more suitable vegetables for the slow crock and without any unusual preparation they can make fine dishes. All pulses and grains should be cooked on the HIGH setting. In the old days a pinch of bicarbonate of soda or a lump of clean coal was recommended to aid the softening process or, for the more specialized wholefood cooks, a strip of seaweed, preferably fresh. Pulses still have to be soaked overnight, then rinsed and drained before

cooking for a 6–8 hour period in the slow crock. Rice
doesn't take as long although I can only imagine it as part
of a combined slow crock dish, not worth cooking on its own
unless there is no other appliance for doing so.

Basic Method for Slow Crock Beans   6–8 hours HIGH

Soak beans overnight in cold water then rinse, drain and
transfer to slow crock.

Any vegetables should be peeled or de-seeded as appropriate, then *sautéed* lightly in oil. Flour and spices should
then be sprinkled over and cooked slightly with the vegetables before all is transferred to the slow crock.

Add cold, unsalted water* to barely cover the beans.
Excess moisture can be reduced at the end by cooling with
the lid off to evaporate.

Beans are traditionally cooked with a bacon bone, salt
pork or bacon for flavour. At the end of the cooking period
the bean dish can be sweetened with honey, sugar, molasses,
black treacle or syrup.

The dish can be spiced with chilli powder, fresh chillies or
Tabasco sauce, added at the beginning of the cooking period.
Herbs are also added at the beginning.

If possible, stir the beans once or twice during the final
hours of cooking as this helps them to cook evenly. Adjust
seasoning at the end.

Boston Baked Beans   6–8 hours HIGH

½ kg (1 lb) haricot beans, 125 g (4 oz) salt pork or bacon,
1 medium onion, salt and pepper, small tin of tomato paste,
dash of Worcestershire sauce, ½ tsp marjoram, 125 ml (¼ pt)
or so of water, 1 bay leaf, 2 tsp dry mustard, 2–4 tbs black
treacle, molasses or syrup, pinch of bicarbonate of soda.

* Alternative method for beans: add *boiling* water to a *pre-heated* slow
crock and reduce timing by half.

Soak beans overnight in cold water, then rinse and drain and place in base of slow crock. Trim fat from pork or bacon and cut into cubes. Slice onion thinly. Add these to the crock. Finally, add water to moisten the beans, barely covering them. Do not add salt at this point as it tends to harden them. Add pinch of bicarb, herbs and spices. Replace lid and cook on HIGH for 6–8 hours, stirring once during the last few hours if possible to ensure even cooking. Cook beans until they are tender. Half an hour before serving, stir in the tomato paste, sweetening and adjust seasoning, adding a little more mustard for a spicier taste, etc. Add salt at this point if wished. To serve, stir beans well, remove bay leaf. If there is too much water allow it to steam off without the lid. If there is too little water, add a little at a time until the right consistency is achieved.

Bean Loaf   **3–4 hours HIGH**

½ kg (1 lb) mixed beans (black eye, kidney, chick, split pea, etc), 3 tbs sesame seeds, 3 tbs oil, 3 tbs water or milk, 1 tbs honey, 2 tbs Parmesan cheese, 2 medium onions, 1 tsp celery seeds, ¼ tsp each of parsley, sage and thyme, 3 garlic cloves, salt and pepper, container that fits your slow crock, metal foil, hot water.

Soak beans overnight in cold water then rinse and drain. Pre-heat slow crock on HIGH during preparations. Boil the beans in water next day until soft, then sieve them with the onions into a large bowl. Add herbs, seasoning, cheese and minced garlic and mix thoroughly. Bind the mixture with oil and honey, if too dry add a little water or milk.

Grease your container with oil and place the mixture firmly in, smooth it down and cover with metal foil. Place tin in slow crock and pour boiling water around until it reaches half-way up the side. Replace lid and cook on HIGH for 3–4 hours until firm to touch. Then remove and allow to cool, pressing down with weights during this process. To serve, turn out onto a salad-lined platter.

Chilli Beans   **6–8 hours HIGH**

½ kg (1 lb) red kidney beans, 1 red pepper, 1 onion, 1 green chilli, 1 tsp ground cumin, 1 tsp coriander seeds, 1 tsp or so of Tabasco sauce, dash of vinegar or Worcestershire sauce, 1 tbs brown sugar, ½ tsp celery seed or 1 stalk celery, 2 tbs each of oil and flour, water.
Optional: piece of ginger root, grated.

Soak beans overnight in cold water, then rinse and drain and place in slow crock. *Sauté* the chopped vegetables in oil and sprinkle on flour and ground spices. Transfer to slow crock and add water to barely cover beans. Add Tabasco, etc. Replace lid and cook on HIGH for 6–8 hours until the beans are tender. To serve, stir in sugar if wished and adjust seasoning. Be careful not to make this dish too hot if you're not used to it – reduce the hot spices if wished, especially Tabasco.

Beans and Rice   **6–8 hours HIGH**

¼ kg (½ lb) red kidney beans, ¼ kg (½ lb) brown rice, 2 onions, 3 garlic cloves, 1 tsp chervil, salt and pepper, water, 3–4 tbs tomato paste, 1 cracked ham bone, 1 tbs oil.
Optional: pinch of bicarbonate of soda.
Soak beans overnight in cold water, rinse, drain and transfer to slow crock. Wash the rice and stir it in with the beans. *Sauté* the chopped onion and garlic and add to slow crock with tomato paste and ham bone, pour on water to barely cover the mixture, add a pinch of bicarbonate if you wish. Replace lid and cook on HIGH for 6–8 hours until beans are tender. Stir the dish once or twice during the final hours to ensure even cooking. To serve, remove ham bone and add seasoning to taste.

Spiced Lentils 4–6 hours HIGH

¼ kg (½ lb) red lentils, 2 tbs butter or margarine, 1 onion, ½ tsp turmeric, 1 tsp salt, ½ tsp paprika or chilli powder, 1 tsp mustard seeds or dry mustard, ½ tsp ground cumin, 1 tsp garam masala, or alternatively 1 tbs curry powder instead of all these different spices, water, 1 bay leaf.
Optional: ¼ kg (½ lb) spinach.

Rinse the lentils and place in base of slow crock. Heat the butter and fry chopped onion with all the ground or pounded spices then transfer to slow crock. Add water to barely cover the ingredients. Replace lid and cook on HIGH for 4–6 hours until the lentils are cooked. To serve, remove bay leaf and adjust seasoning.

If using spinach, wash, drain and chop it then stew it for 5–10 minutes in butter and stir it in thoroughly with the lentils.

Variation: Add 2 fresh green chillies and use juice of 1 lemon.

Beans in Wine 6–8 hours HIGH

½ kg (1 lb) beans (red kidney, black eye, haricot), 1 onion, 2 garlic cloves, *bouquet garni*, 125 g (4 oz) salt pork or bacon, 2 tbs oil and flour, 125 ml (¼ pt) red wine, water, salt and pepper.
Optional: bicarbonate of soda.

Soak beans overnight in cold water then rinse, drain and transfer to slow crock. *Sauté* chopped onion and salt pork in oil and sprinkle on flour and minced garlic – stir for a minute or so and transfer to slow crock. Pour on water to barely cover beans, and add *bouquet garni*. Replace lid and cook on HIGH for 6–8 hours until beans are tender. Then, lift the lid, add seasoning, allow excess moisture to evaporate then add wine. Remove *bouquet garni*. Serve.

Succotash   **6–8 hours HIGH**

½ kg (1 lb) haricot beans, 125 g (4 oz) salt pork or bacon, oil, salt and pepper, water, 1 carton of single cream, 15 g (½ oz) butter, ¼ kg (½ lb) packet of sweet corn or corn on the cob. *Optional*: pinch of bicarbonate of soda.

Soak beans overnight in cold water, rinse, drain and transfer to slow crock. Trim fat from pork or bacon, chop and *sauté* in a little oil and mix into the beans. Add water to barely cover and a pinch of bicarbonate if you wish. Replace lid and cook on HIGH until beans are tender. Half an hour before serving add the sweet corn or corn scraped off the cob. Adjust seasoning and then stir in the cream mixed with butter.

Tarragon Egg Casserole   **3–4 hours LOW**

8–10 hard-boiled eggs, ½ tsp dried tarragon, 1 tbs minced onion, 125 g (4 oz) mushrooms, 125 ml (¼ pt) white wine, salt and pepper, 2 tbs each of flour and butter, 125 ml (¼ pt) milk.

Place shelled and sliced eggs in base of slow crock. Knead butter and flour together and then add salt, pepper and herbs, gradually blend in milk and wine, stirring until smooth. Pour this mixture into slow crock. *Sauté* the sliced mushrooms and minced onion lightly in butter and stir into crock. Replace lid and cook on LOW 3–4 hours until mixture has thoroughly blended. To serve, adjust seasoning. Garnish with chopped chives.

Egg Curry   **3–4 hours LOW**

8–10 hard-boiled eggs, 3–4 garlic cloves, ½ tsp each of chilli powder and ground ginger, 1 tsp each of salt and ground cumin, 2 medium onions, 1 tsp garam masala, 1 tbs brown sugar, generous pinch of cinnamon, 90 ml (3 fl oz) each of vinegar and water, 2 tbs each of cornflour and butter.

Shell eggs and cut them in half then place them on the base of slow crock. Peel and chop onion and garlic and *sauté* in butter, then sprinkle on cornflour, spices and salt with a little liquid to make a dry paste. Stir in sugar and remainder of liquid. Transfer this mixture to slow crock after 2–3 minutes. Replace lid and cook on LOW for 3–4 hours until ingredients are thoroughly blended. To serve, adjust seasoning. Serve with plain boiled rice. If the curry is too dry add a little more water.

Vegetarian Moussaka   4 hours LOW

2–3 medium or large aubergines, 2–3 courgettes, 1 medium onion, 1 tomato, 2 tbs tomato paste, $\frac{1}{2}$ tsp allspice or 1 tsp cinnamon, salt and pepper to taste, 2 tbs minced parsley, $\frac{1}{4}$ litre ($\frac{1}{2}$ pt) Béchamel sauce (see page 95), 3 tbs red wine, 90 g (3 oz) grated Cheddar cheese, 4 tbs oil.

Peel and slice aubergines thinly, or slice them unpeeled. Salt them and allow to drain for an hour or so to allow bitter juices out. Rinse and dry. Then *sauté* the aubergines in oil and set aside.

Peel and slice onion and courgettes and *sauté* until golden. Drain and set aside.

Beginning and ending with the aubergine, make alternate layers in the crock with the vegetables. Mix together the spices, seasoning, herbs, tomato paste, wine and sauce and pour it over the dish. Replace lid and cook on LOW for 4 hours until the layers have blended. Half an hour before serving, sprinkle grated cheese over the dish and allow it to melt.

Variations: A layer of mashed potato can also be added at the time of the grated cheese to make a more filling dish.

A richer moussaka can be made by covering each layer with grated Parmesan or slices of Gruyère.

Ratatouille　　　　　　　　　　**4–6 hours LOW**

2 medium onions, 2 large aubergines, 2 sweet red peppers,
2 courgettes, 2 large tomatoes, 2 garlic cloves, salt and
pepper, 1 tsp coriander seeds, sprigs of fresh basil, parsley
and chives, 90 ml (3 fl oz) oil, *garnish* – black olives, chopped
anchovy.

De-seed peppers, peel and slice all vegetables and *sauté*
well in oil, sprinkling with herbs and seasoning. Transfer to
slow crock when they are golden, replace lid and cook until
tender on LOW 4–6 hours. Garnish with anchovy and black
olives.

Pickled Onions　　　　　　　　　**8–10 hours LOW**

1 kg (2 lb) pickling onions, 125 g (4 oz) sugar and salt, 1 tbs
mixed spice, 6 cloves and peppercorns, 1 litre (2 pt) malt
vinegar.

Peel onions and place in a bowl. Sprinkle with salt and let
stand overnight. Then rinse well, dry and place in slow
crock. Add sugar, spices and vinegar. Replace lid and cook
on LOW 8–10 hours. Then, pack the onions into jars and
cover with the strained vinegar. Allow to cool and cover
closely.

Aubergines with Tomatoes　　　　**4–6 hours LOW**

2 large aubergines, ½ kg (1 lb) tomatoes, 2 medium onions,
90 g (3 oz) breadcrumbs, 2 tbs chopped parsley, 2 garlic
cloves, pinch of marjoram and basil, 4 tbs oil, 3 tbs white
wine, salt and pepper.

Chop the onions and aubergines roughly and plunge into
boiling salted water for 3 minutes, drain and transfer to

slow crock. Chop the tomatoes roughly and *sauté* in oil. Transfer to slow crock. Sprinkle with seasoning, herbs and crushed garlic. Replace lid and cook on LOW for 4–6 hours. To serve, stir in white wine, adjust seasoning and sprinkle with browned breadcrumbs and chopped parsley.

8 SAVOURY AND SUET PUDDINGS

SUET PUDDINGS

These can be sweet or savoury depending on the filling you choose (for sweet steamed puddings see chapter 9). Line your pudding bowl with a suet pastry and add a steak-and-kidney or an apple-and-raisin filling, put a pastry crust on, then cover the container with metal foil and steam it for 6 hours on HIGH. The result is delicious.

You will find a basic suet pastry recipe below which will apply to all the suet pudding recipes.

First, choose a bowl that fits your slow crock and allows the lid to sit properly on the rim with enough room for you to pour boiling water around the side. Always pre-heat the slow crock on HIGH during preparations. Remember that after cooking you have to be able to remove the container without too much trouble, so either choose one that is easily lifted out or make a handle with string or twisted cloth or foil.

Basic Suet Pastry for Puddings
The proportion of pastry to filling is usually ½ pastry to filling, ie ¼ kg (½ lb) pastry to ½ kg (1 lb) filling.

The recipe that follows makes 400 g (¾ lb) suet pastry, suitable for a 1 litre (2 pt) bowl. Depending on the capacity of your slow crock and the size of a container that will fit, you will have to adjust the amounts accordingly.

200 g (6 oz) self-raising flour, 100 g (3 oz) shredded suet, cold water to mix (about 100 ml, 4 fl oz), pinch of salt, either a pinch of mixed herbs for a savoury pudding, or a pinch of mixed spice for a sweet pudding.

Mix self-raising flour with suet and add a pinch of salt and water to moisten. Mix ingredients into a spongy, but not too moist, light dough. Divide dough into 2, with one piece twice the size of the other, and roll out on a floured board into round shapes. Then line a greased bowl with the large round of pastry, reserving the smaller one for the crust. Place pudding filling in the middle (see individual recipes) and place pastry on top. Cover the bowl with metal foil. Then proceed as recipe instructs for method and timing.

SAVOURY, SUET PUDDING RECIPES

Steak and Kidney Pudding   **6 hours HIGH**

400 g (¾ lb) stewing steak, 200 g (6 oz) kidney, 1 onion, 125 g (4 oz) mushrooms, pinch of mixed herbs, 1 bay leaf, generous pinch of dry mustard, dash of Worcestershire sauce, salt and pepper.
Optional: 1 garlic clove, 2 tsp paprika, 3 tbs Guinness or beef stock, 400 g (¾ lb) suet pastry (see recipe page 172).

Pre-heat slow crock on HIGH during preparations. Make suet pastry and line a greased bowl with it.

Cube the meat and kidney and mix them together with the chopped onion, sliced mushrooms, seasoning and spices. Place the mixture in the lined bowl and moisten with stock or beer if wished. Place a suet lid on the pudding and press it well to the sides. Cover with metal foil. Place bowl in slow crock and pour boiling water around until it reaches half-way up the side. Replace lid and cook on HIGH for 6 hours or until the meat feels tender when you test it with a pointed knife, and there is no sticky pastry on the knife.

Chicken Pudding   **6 hours HIGH**

½ kg (1 lb) boneless chicken, 125 g (4 oz) cooked ham, 125 g (4 oz) mushrooms, 1 small onion, ¼ tsp tarragon, generous pinch of paprika, 1 bay leaf, ½ tbs chopped parsley, salt and pepper, 4 tbs white wine, suet pastry – 200 g (6 oz) self-raising flour, 90 g (3 oz) shredded suet, salt and pepper, pinch of mixed herbs, water, bowl, metal foil, boiling water.

Choose a bowl that will fit your slow crock and grease it. Switch slow crock to HIGH while preparing the ingredients. Make a suet pastry – mix flour with suet and add water to make a light and spongy dough but not sticky. Add seasoning and herbs. Roll out the dough on a floured board and then line the bowl with it (see page 172).

Peel and chop vegetables and combine with the chopped meat and seasoning. Mix well and fill the bowl. Add the wine and cover the bowl with a suet crust. Cover the whole top with a layer of metal foil and place bowl in slow crock. Pour boiling water into the slow crock until it reaches half-way up the side. Replace lid and cook on HIGH for 6 hours until the chicken is tender.

Other fillings: used in the following proportions: $\frac{1}{2}$ kg (1 lb) for main ingredients, 125 g (4 oz) for secondary ingredients plus one or two vegetables, seasoning to taste, with a tablespoon or two of flavoursome liquid (beer or wine) to moisten.
1. Pork, onion and apple with a pinch of sage.
2. Pork sausage and bacon, with tomatoes and leeks, pinch of basil and minced garlic.
3. Rabbit or partridge, with dried raisins, red wine, celery and carrot.

Pigeon Pudding   **6 hours HIGH**

2 pigeons, 200 g (6 oz) steak, 2 hard-boiled eggs, salt and pepper, 2 tbs strong stock, 1 tbs flour, 400 g ($\frac{3}{4}$ lb) suet pastry.

Make suet pastry (see recipe above, page 172) and line a greased container that fits your slow crock. Pre-heat crock on HIGH.

Split the pigeons in half and remove skin. Cube the steak and roll these meats in seasoned flour. Shell and quarter the hard-boiled eggs. Place the ingredients in the pastry-lined bowl, add stock, and put a suet crust on top. Cover the bowl with metal foil and place in slow crock. Surround with boiling water. Replace lid and cook on HIGH for 6 hours until meats are tender.

Grouse Pudding   **6 hours HIGH**

1 young grouse, $\frac{1}{4}$ kg ($\frac{1}{2}$ lb) steak, 1 onion, 60 g (2 oz) mushrooms, 2 tbs each of red wine and strong stock, salt and pepper, 1 tbs flour, 400 g ($\frac{3}{4}$ lb) suet pastry.

Make suet pastry (see recipe above, page 172) and line a greased container that fits your slow crock. Pre-heat slow crock on HIGH.

Cut the steak and the flesh from the bird into cubes anp toss in seasoned flour. Chop onion and mushrooms and fill the pastry-lined bowl with the ingredients. Place a suet crust on top, and cover with foil. Place in slow crock and pour boiling water around until it reaches half-way up side. Replace lid and cook on HIGH until meat is tender. Older grouse will take longer.

Partridge Pudding   **6–8 hours HIGH**

1 partridge, salt and pepper, 1 tbs flour, 125 g (4 oz) mushrooms, 2 shallots, 2 cloves, 2 bacon rashers, 90 ml (3 fl oz) stock and beer.
Optional: $\frac{1}{2}$ dozen oysters, 400 g ($\frac{3}{4}$ lb) suet pastry.

Make suet pastry (see recipe on page 172) and line a greased container that fits your slow crock. Pre-heat crock on HIGH.

Cut the bird into joints and toss in seasoned flour. Place in pastry-lined bowl with sliced mushrooms, bacon rashers, chopped shallots, cloves and oysters, if used. Add stock. Place suet crust on top and cover with metal foil. Place in slow crock and replace lid. Cook on HIGH for 6–8 hours until meat is tender.

Rabbit Pudding   **6–8 hours HIGH**

1 rabbit cut into joints, 2–3 bacon rashers or cooked ham slices, 4 sage leaves, 1 tbs chopped onion, salt and pepper, 125 g (4 oz) mushrooms, 90 ml (3 fl oz) stock and red wine, 2 tbs flour, 400 g ($\frac{3}{4}$ lb) suet pastry.

Make suet pastry (see recipe on page 172) and line a greased container that fits your slow crock. Pre-heat slow crock on HIGH.

Toss the rabbit joints in seasoned flour. Chop the sage leaves and mushrooms. Put in a layer of rabbit, chopped sage and onion, then a layer of mushrooms and continue until pastry-lined bowl is full. Add stock and wine and bacon. Place a suet crust on top and cover with metal foil. Place in slow crock and replace lid. Cook on HIGH for 6 hours until meat is tender.

Leek Pudding   **6 hours HIGH**

4–6 leeks, salt and pepper, 400 g ($\frac{3}{4}$ lb) suet pastry (see recipe on page 172), dots of butter.
Optional: 125 g (4 oz) washed and sliced mushrooms.

Make suet pastry (see recipe and method on page 172) and line a greased bowl that fits your slow crock with it, reserving a little for the crust. Pre-heat slow crock on HIGH.

Wash the leeks thoroughly then slice them very thinly and fill the lined bowl, seasoning as you go along, and adding the mushrooms in layers. Dot with butter. Place crust on top and cover container with metal foil. Place in slow crock and pour boiling water around until it reaches half-way up the side. Replace lid and cook on LOW 6–8 hours, until a knife inserted penetrates the ingredients easily.

9 DESSERTS

SWEET PUDDINGS, CAKES AND BREAD

Steamed puddings have a roly poly texture and look about
them and they taste roly poly when you eat them. The slow
crock cooks very roly poly puddings and they're easy to
make. They are steamed in a bowl covered with metal foil
and surrounded with hot water on a HIGH setting for 4–6
hours. A Christmas pudding takes longer (8 hours HIGH).
All puddings like these can be re-heated, which takes about
2–3 hours. So even if you haven't actually cooked your
pudding in a slow crock you can re-heat it by this method.

Some sweet puddings have more or less the same ingredients as sweet cakes, and the only difference between
them is that one is steamed and the other is baked. The slow
crock does not 'bake' as such because you always have to
add some moisture to it to avoid the risk of cracking. So,
you will find that although I have included recipes for what
I call 'cakes' they will in fact taste rather like puddings owing
to the steam method. This applies to bread as well.

Basic Method for a Sweet Steam-Baked Pudding
¼ kg (½ lb) self-raising flour, 125 g (4 oz) each of sugar and
margarine (or butter), 1 egg, 125 ml (¼ pt) milk, pinch of salt
and nutmeg, a few drops of vanilla essence.

Choose a container that will easily fit into your slow
crock and grease it lightly. Pre-heat crock on HIGH during
preparations.

Sift the flour into a bowl and rub in with the margarine.
Add sugar and spices with a pinch of salt. Stir in egg beaten
with milk. Beat well. Add other ingredients (see below) and
pour mixture into the greased pudding bowl. Cover with
metal foil and place in slow crock. Pour boiling water

around until it reaches half-way up the side. Replace lid and cook on HIGH for 3–4 hours until a skewer or knife inserted in it comes out clean. To serve, turn pudding out onto a warm flat plate.

Chocolate Pudding: Add 3 tbs sifted cocoa powder to mixture. To serve, garnish with glacé cherries.

Raisin and Chocolate Chip Pudding: Add 90 g (3 oz) each of raisins and chocolate chips.

Coffee Raisin Pudding: 3 tbs strong coffee, 90 g (3 oz) raisins, mixed fruit or chopped dates.

Gingerbread and Plum Pudding: Add 1 tsp ground ginger and mixed spice. Line the bottom of the pudding bowl with plums. Halve the sugar and make it up to 125 g (4 oz) with black treacle and syrup.

Apricot Nut Pudding: Line the base of the pudding bowl with fresh apricots (or peaches, damsons, etc) mixed with chopped nuts.

Ginger Pear Pudding: Add 1 tsp ground ginger to mixture and line the bottom of the pudding bowl with 2 pears peeled and sliced, mixed with a little jam or marmalade, 30 g (1 oz) each preserved ginger, maraschino cherries.

Golden Pudding: Make basic pudding as above and when you turn it out to serve, top it with 2–3 tbs hot golden syrup.

Lemon Apple Pudding: Add juice and grated rind of 1 lemon to pudding mixture and 1 large eating apple peeled and grated.

Christmas Pudding   **8–10 hours HIGH**

This recipe is enough for 2 good sized puddings, ¾ litre (1½ pt each) or 3 ½ litre (1 pt) basins.

¾ kg (½ lb) currants, 125 g (4 oz) raisins, ¼ kg (½ lb) sultanas, 125 g (4 oz) dates, 90 g (3 oz) mixed peel, ¼ kg (½ lb) suet, 3 eggs, ¼ kg (½ lb) flour, 120 g (4 oz) breadcrumbs, ¼ kg (½ lb) sugar, ½ tsp grated nutmeg, ½ tsp mixed spice, grated rind of 1 lemon, 30 g (1 oz) finely chopped almonds, brandy, stout or milk, boiling water.

Pre-heat slow crock on HIGH during preparations. Wash and prepare the fruit. Stone raisins, chop dates and suet, beat eggs well. Put dry ingredients into a bowl and mix thoroughly. Stir in eggs. Add enough brandy, milk or stout to moisten the mixture. Put into well-greased pudding basins. Cover with greaseproof paper and metal foil. Place container in slow crock and pour boiling water around until it reaches half-way up the side. Replace lid and cook on HIGH 8–10 hours.

When cooked, remove the container from the slow crock, take off the paper and foil and let it cool. When cool re-cover it with clean, dry metal foil. Let the pudding mature in a dry cupboard; the longer the better. For quick maturing, prick the top of the pudding with a knitting needle or spike and carefully pour on 1 tbs brandy or rum.

Apple Turnover   **4–6 hours HIGH**

400 g (¾ lb) suet pastry (see recipe on page 171), ½ kg (1 lb) apples, sugar to taste, 1 tsp cinnamon, ½ tsp grated lemon or orange peel.
Optional: 125 g (4 oz) raisins. Cook as for basic suet pudding (see above). Any fresh mixed fruits can be used. Serve with hot custard or cold cream.

Rice Pudding   **3–4 hours LOW**

90 g (3 oz) round pudding rice, 30 g (1 oz) sugar, ½ litre (1 pt) milk, knob of butter.
Optional: cinnamon, juice and grated rind of 1 lemon, mixed dried fruit.

Wash the rice and place in slow crock with sugar, milk and butter. Replace lid and cook on LOW for 3–4 hours. Stir before serving. The cinnamon can be sprinkled on at the end for a garnish. The other optional ingredients should be

added at the beginning of the cooking period. N.B. This recipe is best when using rich creamy gold top milk.
Variations: This basic method can be used for tapioca, sago, semolina.

Porridge , **overnight/LOW**

125 g (4 oz) porridge oats or oatmeal, ½ litre (1 pt) water or milk, pinch of salt, sugar to taste.

Lightly grease the inside of the slow crock and place oats, liquid and salt in. Stir well. Replace lid and cook on LOW overnight. To serve, add sugar to taste.

Bread and Butter Pudding   **3 hours LOW**

12 slices of bread, 125 g (4 oz) seedless raisins, 2 tbs each of grated lemon and orange peel, 4 tbs sugar, 1 egg, generous 125 ml (¼ pt) milk, ½ tsp ground cinnamon, nutmeg or mixed spice.
Optional ingredients: 2 bananas, 60 g (2 oz) butter.

Butter the bread and place it in a shallow dish. Beat together the egg and milk and pour it over the bread allowing it to soak up the liquid.

Grease the inside of the slow crock lightly then place the bread slices in alternate layers with the raisins, spices, sugar, fruit, peel and sliced bananas. When finished pour over a little extra milk if wished. Replace lid and cook on LOW for 3 hours until the ingredients are soft and slightly blended, but the liquid is set.

Egg Custard   **4–6 hours LOW**

3–4 eggs or egg yolks, 30 g (1 oz) sugar, ½ litre (1 pt) milk, grated nutmeg, a few drops of vanilla essence.

Pre-heat slow crock on HIGH during preparations. Grease a container that will fit your slow crock. Beat together lightly the eggs and sugar and add the milk slightly warmed. Stir in essence. Sprinkle with nutmeg. Cover the dish with metal foil. Place container in slow crock and pour boiling water around until it reaches half-way up the side. Replace lid and cook on LOW for 4–6 hours until a knife inserted in the custard comes out clean. Allow to cool and serve with canned or stewed fruit.

Caramel Custard   4–6 hours LOW

30 g (1 oz) butter, 90 g (3 oz) brown sugar.

Make an egg custard mixture as above and add a caramel as follows: Melt butter in a saucepan and add brown sugar and 3 tbs water. Stir over a low heat until sugar is dissolved, then boil until there is a golden brown caramel. Add another 3 tbs of water and boil until the caramel is dissolved in this. Stir the caramel into the egg custard mixture, or pour the caramel into the greased container first to coat the bottom and sides, and add the egg custard last. Bake as for egg custard. Allow to cool before serving.

Fluffin   3–4 hours LOW

60 g (2 oz) pearl barley, 60 g (2 oz) sugar, $\frac{3}{4}$ tsp grated nutmeg, $\frac{1}{2}$ litre (1 pt) milk, a few drops of brandy.

Wash the barley and place in slow crock with milk. Cook on LOW 3–4 hours. To serve add the nutmeg, sugar and brandy. Stir.

Malt Bread   4–6 hours HIGH

This is a batter bread that doesn't need proving (ie leaving to rise). Fruit makes it more interesting.

½ kg (1 lb) wholewheat flour, ½ tsp salt, 3 tbs warm water, 1 tsp dried yeast, 1 tsp brown sugar or honey, ¼ litre (½ pt) warm water, 2 tbs malt.
Optional: 90 g (3 oz) raisins.

Pre-heat slow crock on HIGH during preparations. Grease a container that fits your slow crock.

Mix together flour and salt. Place 3 tbs warm water in a bowl, sprinkle on yeast and whisk until dissolved. Add the sugar or honey. Leave the mixture to froth for 15 minutes then pour it into the centre of the flour and add the remaining ¼ litre (½ pt) of warm water. Knead well until the dough is elastic and leaves the side of the bowl clean then place it in the greased container. Cover with metal foil. Place in slow crock and pour boiling water around until it reaches half-way up the side. Replace lid and cook on HIGH 4–6 hours until cocktail stick inserted comes out clean.
Variations: Instead of wholewheat flour alone, a mixture of flours can be used, eg 125 g (4 oz) each of medium rye flour, cornmeal, wholewheat and self-raising.

Instead of warm water use ¼ litre (½ pt) buttermilk. Bread will have a steamed consistency but in order to reduce this steamed effect you can put layers of absorbent paper towels and greaseproof paper over the container before covering with metal foil. Secure these layers with a piece of string before cooking.

10 SWEET AND SAVOURY SAUCES AND FONDUES

SWEET AND SAVOURY SAUCES

There are two ways to prepare sauces in the slow crock. The first method involves using the slow crock as a double boiler (*bain-marie*), that is, adding boiling water to a pre-heated slow crock and placing a small container on the base with the ingredients inside. This method is useful for sauces that curdle easily, eg those containing eggs. The boiling water surrounding the container provides sustained and indirect heat and allows the sauce to cook without curdling. The second method involves cooking the sauce directly in the slow crock.

SAVOURY SAUCES

Tomato Sauce   **3–4 hours LOW**

1–1½ kg (2–3 lb) ripe tomatoes, 1–2 tsp each of sugar and salt, pinch of ground ginger or cinnamon, 1–2 garlic cloves, basil and marjoram, 1–2 tbs sherry or port.

Place the tomatoes whole and unskinned in slow crock with enough water to cover the base and cook on LOW until soft. Then *purée* and return to slow crock. Add remaining ingredients and stir well.

Butter Sauce

2 tsp flour, 60–90 g (2–3 oz) butter, 125 ml (¼ pt) water.

Pre-heat slow crock on HIGH and after 20 minutes pour in

boiling water to reach half-way up the side of a small container placed on the base.

Mix flour and water to a thin paste in the container, add a good pinch of salt and stir mixture over the water. When smooth add butter in small pieces. Stir with wooden spoon until creamy and thick.

This basic sauce with the additional few drops of lemon is good with fish. Make it in the quantity required as it will not re-heat well.

Cucumber Sauce

Make as above, add 30 g (1 oz) chopped and de-seeded cucumber *sautéed* in butter, with lemon juice and a sprinkling of parsley and chives.

Shrimp Sauce

Make a butter sauce (see above) and add 125 ml (¼ pt) freshly boiled shrimp with a pinch of ground mace and cayenne.

Mustard Sauce

Add 1 tsp strong yellow mustard to a 125 ml (¼ pt) butter sauce (see above).

Basic White Sauce (Roux Method)

30 g (1 oz) margarine or butter, 30 g (1 oz) flour, ¼ litre (½ pt) milk *or* 125 ml (¼ pt) each of milk and stock, salt and pepper to taste.

Melt fat and stir in flour to form a thick *roux*. Cook over a low heat for 1–2 minutes until crumbly, resembling breadcrumbs. Remove from heat and gradually stir in half the liquid, beating well until smooth. Add remaining liquid, stirring well. When smooth return to heat and bring slowly to boil, stirring continuously. Adjust consistency by adding liquid or reducing by boiling. Adjust seasoning to taste.

Basic Brown Sauce

1½ tbs fat or dripping, 1 small carrot and onion, 1½ tbs flour, ¼ litre (½ pt) stock, ½ tsp yeast (Marmite) or meat extract (Bovril), piece of brown onion skin, salt and pepper.

Melt fat and fry sliced onion and carrot until brown. Stir in flour and cook on a low heat until tan coloured. Add half of the liquid gradually, beating well until smooth. Add remaining liquid, stirring continuously until it boils. Add remaining ingredients and simmer gently for 20–30 minutes. Adjust seasoning. Remove onion skin.

Gravy

For an unthickened gravy, simply skim the fat from the meat juices, taste and correct seasoning, then re-heat and serve. Vegetable or meat stock may be added, or water.

For a thickened gravy, skim, taste and re-heat as above, adding liquid if required, then thicken with a *beurre manié* using flour or cornflour.

Sweet and Sour Sauce for Tongue   ½–1 hour HIGH

125 ml (¼ pt) each of tongue stock and water, 200 g (6 oz) brown sugar, 90 g (3 oz) raisins, 4 tbs minced onion, ½ tsp each of cinnamon and ground cloves, 1 tsp ginger, juice of ½ lemon, 2 tbs each of flour and butter.

Combine all ingredients except flour and butter and place

in a clean slow crock. Replace lid and heat on HIGH for ½–1 hour (depending on whether stock and slow crock are still hot from previous use). Thicken with *beurre manié*.

SWEET SAUCES

Clotted Cream

1–1½ litres (2–3 pt) Gold top or Channel Island milk.

Let the milk stand for 24 hours in winter, 12 hours in summer. Then place it in the slow crock and cook on LOW *with the lid off* for 8–10 hours. Then switch the slow crock off and let it stand overnight in a cool place (*not* in fridge). In the morning the cream will be very thick. Scoop it off the top and use.

Ice Cream

¼ litre (½ pt) single cream or rich milk, 1 vanilla pod or vanilla essence, 3 egg yolks, sugar, ¼ litre (½ pt) double cream.

Pre-heat slow crock on HIGH for 20 minutes. Bring milk or single cream slowly to the boil in a saucepan and add vanilla pod or a few drops of vanilla essence. Beat the egg yolks and whisk the hot milk into them. Transfer mixture to a container that will fit your slow crock and pour boiling water into slow crock so that it reaches half-way up the side of the container. Stir the mixture until it coats the spoon. Sweeten to taste. Cool. Remove vanilla pod if used. Stir the mixture gradually into the whipped double cream. Sweeten to taste. Then freeze the mixture.

Vanilla Custard

400 ml (¾ pt) milk, ½ tsp vanilla essence, 4 tbs sugar, 4 egg yolks, ¼ tsp salt.

Pre-heat slow crock on HIGH for 20 minutes. In a saucepan heat milk until almost boiling and stir in vanilla essence. Combine sugar, egg yolks and salt and beat until fluffy and yellow. Pour a little of the hot milk into mixture, blend and stir it into the hot milk in the saucepan.

Place a container in the slow crock and pour boiling water around. Pour the custard into the bowl and stir continuously until mixture coats spoon. Serve.

For a less rich custard use the following recipe:
½ litre (1 pt) milk, 3 eggs, ½ tsp vanilla essence, ¼ tsp salt, 3–4 tbs sugar.

Chocolate Cream Sauce

2 tbs rum, 125 g (4 oz) plain chocolate, 125 g (4 oz) butter, 125 g (4 oz) icing sugar, 4 egg yolks.

Pre-heat slow crock on HIGH for 20 minutes. Choose a container that fits your slow crock and place it on the base. Pour boiling water around until it reaches half-way up the side. Break the chocolate into this container and stir until it is melted and smooth. Cream the butter and sugar until light then beat in the egg yolks one at a time, then add rum and finally stir this mixture into the melted chocolate.

Brandy Sauce

2 egg yolks, 4–6 tbs double cream, water and brandy, 1 tbs sugar.

Pre-heat slow crock on high for 20 minutes. Place a

container in the crock and pour boiling water around until
it reaches half-way up the side. Combine all the ingredients
in the container and whisk over the hot water until sauce
is thick and frothy.

Rich Brandy Sauce (for Christmas cake or pudding).

5 egg yolks, 125 g ($\frac{1}{4}$ lb) icing sugar, 2 tbs plain flour, $\frac{1}{4}$ litre
($\frac{1}{2}$ pt) milk, $\frac{1}{2}$ tsp vanilla essence, 125 ml ($\frac{1}{4}$ pt) double cream,
sugar to taste, brandy to taste.

Pre-heat slow crock on HIGH for 20 minutes. Whisk the
egg yolks with icing sugar then beat in the flour. Bring the
milk to the boil, add vanilla essence and stir it into the egg
and sugar. Transfer ingredients to a container that fits your
slow crock and pour boiling water around the container in
the slow crock until it reaches half-way up the side. Stir the
mixture continuously until smooth and thick. Remove and
add cream. Add sugar and brandy to taste.

Lemon Curd   2–3 hours HIGH

Juice and grated rind of 4–6 lemons, $\frac{1}{2}$ kg (1 lb) castor sugar,
125 g (4 oz) butter, 4 egg yolks.

Pre-heat slow crock on HIGH for 20 minutes. Melt butter
in a separate saucepan, add lemon juice, rind and sugar.
Stir until dissolved. Choose a container that will fit into your
slow crock and pour this mixture into it, allow it to cool
then add beaten eggs. Place container covered with metal
foil in slow crock and pour boiling water around until it
reaches half-way up the side. Replace lid and cook on HIGH
2–3 hours, or LOW 4–6 hours, until curd is the thickness of
butter. Bottle and cover with wax disc and cellophane
paper, or use soon after making.

FONDUES

The word fondue comes from the French word meaning to melt. The slow crock can be used as a melting pot. The simplest kind of fondue is made by adding wine or cider and grated cheese to the slow crock, plus seasoning, and cooking on HIGH or LOW until the cheese has melted and the wine is hot; then, to serve, stirring the mixture, adjusting the seasoning and scooping it out with chunks of bread or spears of carrot, cucumber, cauliflower, etc.

Cheddar Cheese Fondue   2 hours HIGH

½ kg (1 lb) grated Cheddar cheese, ¼ litre (½ pt) dry cider or white wine, ½ tsp Worcestershire sauce, salt and cayenne pepper, 2 tsp cornflour, 1 garlic clove.

Grease the slow crock lightly with butter and rub the inside with a cut garlic clove. Add the cheese and wine or cider and replace lid. Cook on HIGH for 2 hours stirring once or twice until cheese has melted. Add the cornflour mixed with a little liquid. Season and keep hot, stirring occasionally. Use within an hour or so. Serve by dipping chunks of French bread into it. Keep it warm on LOW for serving.

Swiss Fondue   2 hours HIGH

½ kg (1 lb) Swiss cheese, 200 g (6 oz) Gruyère, 2 tsp cornflour, 1 garlic clove, ½ litre (1 pt) white wine, 1 tbs lemon juice.

Grate the cheeses and combine them with the cornflour. Rub the inside of the slow crock with cut clove of garlic. Pour wine and lemon juice into crock and switch to HIGH. Add cheese and stir. Replace lid and cook on HIGH for 2 hours until cheese is melted and wine is hot. Adjust seasoning with salt and pepper. Use within an hour or so. Keep it warm on LOW for serving. Serve by dipping in with chunks of French bread. If fondue gets too thick add a tablespoon or two of warm wine, and stir.

Chocolate Fondue

125 g (4 oz) unsweetened chocolate, 125 g (4 oz) sugar, $\frac{1}{4}$ litre ($\frac{1}{2}$ pt) single cream, 90 g (3 oz) butter, pinch of salt, 3 tbs coffee liqueur or coffee essence, sponge fingers.

Switch slow crock to HIGH. Break chocolate into chunks and add to slow crock, replace lid and wait about $\frac{1}{2}$ hour until chocolate melts. Add sugar, butter and cream and stir continuously until blended. Add coffee flavouring. Switch slow crock to LOW. To serve, dip sponge fingers into the mixture.

11 HOT DRINKS

One use of a slow crock is that of heating up liquid slowly. After 2 hours wine or fruit juice will be hot enough to drink, yet even after 5 hours (unless it has been refilled) it's not spoiled by overheating. For whatever reasons you may want to keep a supply of hot wine or juice going for long periods of time (Bonfire Night? Hallowe'en?) you can certainly use the slow crock for this purpose – either to keep a liquid continuously hot or to continually refill the slow crock with more ingredients when it's empty.

Mulled wine and hot punches have been spiritual boosters for centuries although they are somewhat taboo with the connoisseurs responsible for maintaining the hallowed traditions that surround alcohol. Heat destroys it they say. And the addition of sugar, necessary to allay the bitterness, perverts the character and body of a good wine or spirit. You never use your best wine or spirit for a mull or punch anyway, it would be a waste. The whole idea is to mix together certain amounts of enhancing flavours that include a proportion of alcohol and heat them as slowly as possible with little evaporation. The slow crock with its tight fitting lid lets little escape and produces the right effect for this kind of drink.

Besides harmless fruit and vegetable bouillons which do more to revive the spirit than dull the senses, there are such long forgotten things as beef tea and lemon barley both of which have been preserved by healthfood enthusiasts. They require little preparation and are worthwhile preparing before a country walk in the winter or after any strenuous work/exercise in the cold.

If you have the time and inclination you will find that many mixtures improve if they are made and heated sometime beforehand, allowed to cool and then re-heated. This is all possible by just switching the slow crock on and off and on again with time gaps in between. The best plan would be to heat it in the evening, then allow it to cool and stand overnight. Then when required (presumably the next day) heat again.

The main liquid ingredients will be fruit juice, alcohol, stock. Usually some water will be needed. The solid ingredients will include sliced fruit and vegetables, and sometimes meat and grain. Flavours from spices, sweetening or herbs will vary according to the recipe. Flavouring that doesn't dissolve should be tied in a muslin sachet so that it can be easily extracted at the end of the heating period.

The advantage of this method of preparation is that you are heating without boiling and thus preserving in a very gentle way the best of a hot drink.

The timings given are the minimum required to produce a satisfactory temperature for a hot drink, but in fact timings can be extended as wished.

FRUIT DRINKS

Spiced Grape Juice   **2 hours HIGH/4 hours LOW**

1¼ litres (2½ pt) grape juice, 125 g (4 oz) sugar, 2 small cinnamon sticks, 12 whole cloves, generous pinch of salt. *Optional*: lemon juice to taste.

Mix all the ingredients in the slow crock, except lemon juice. Tie spices in a muslin sachet if wished. Replace lid and heat on HIGH or LOW for 2 or 4 hours, minimum. Strain and allow to cool. When ready to serve, rinse out slow crock and refill it with the juice, add lemon to taste, reheat again on LOW for 2 hours or HIGH for 1 hour.

Spiced Apple Juice   **2 hours HIGH/4 hours LOW**

1¼ litres (2½ pt) apple juice, 60 g (2 oz) sugar, 8 small cinnamon sticks, 12 whole cloves, 8 whole allspice.

Place all the ingredients in the slow crock. Tie the spices in a muslin sachet if wished. Replace lid and cook on HIGH or LOW for 2 or 4 hours, minimum. Then, remove spices, strain and allow to cool for several hours. To serve, rinse out slow crock, refill it with liquid and reheat again on LOW for 2 hours or HIGH for 1 hour.

Jaffa Mix   2–4 hours HIGH/LOW

½ litre (1 pt) each of natural unsweetened orange, grapefruit juice and water, 1 small cinnamon stick, 3 whole cloves, squeeze of lemon juice, 1 tbs rosewater (optional), honey or sugar to taste, a few fresh mint leaves.

Combine all ingredients in slow crock and heat on HIGH or LOW for 2 or 4 hours. To serve, remove spices and adjust sweetness with honey or sugar.

Lemon Barley Concentrate   4–6 hours HIGH/LOW

60 g (2 oz) pearl barley, 60 g (2 oz) seedless raisins, 60 g (2 oz) sliced figs, 15 g (½ oz) liquorice root, juice of 6–8 lemons or more, 1 litre (2 pt) water, brown sugar, glucose or honey, to taste.

Wash barley and place in slow crock. Add water, raisins and figs. Replace lid and cook on HIGH or LOW for 4 or 6 hours. Add liquorice root and lemon juice to taste in the final half hour. When cooking is completed, strain the liquid and adjust flavour with brown sugar, glucose or honey. This drink can be diluted or served in small undiluted amounts. Traditionally used as a nourishing drink for invalids and those with fevers or stomach upsets.

T–G

Constable's Apple Drink   **4 hours LOW**

1 litre (2 pt) ale, 4 cooking apples, 3 cloves, ½ tsp ground ginger, 30 g (1 oz) butter, 4–6 tbs sugar, 60 g (2 oz) raisins.

Peel, core and slice cooking apples, add these with the other ingredients to slow crock, with sugar to taste. Replace lid and cook on LOW for 4 hours until the apples are tender. To serve, adjust sweetening and remove cloves.

ALCOHOLIC DRINKS

Mulled Wine   **4 hours LOW**

1¼ litres (2½ pt) red wine, 2 lemons, 20 whole cloves, ¼ litre (½ pt) water, 3 cinnamon sticks, 12 whole allspice, 120 g (4 oz) sugar.

Slice lemon thinly and stud with cloves. Place all ingredients in slow crock, replace lid and heat on LOW for 4 hours minimum. Serve when hot.

Sweet Mulled Cider   **4 hours LOW**

1¼ litres (2½ pt) sweet cider, 1 cinnamon stick, 1 tsp whole cloves, 1 tsp whole allspice, 1 piece of whole mace, 120 g (4 oz) sugar, 10 crab-apples.

Place all the ingredients in the slow crock. Wrap spices in a muslin sachet. Replace lid and cook on LOW for 4 hours minimum until thoroughly heated. Remove spices before serving.

Mulled Dry Cider   4 hours LOW

1 litre (2 pt) dry cider, 60 g (2 oz) brown sugar, 8 whole
cloves, 1 cinnamon stick about 15 cm (6").

Heat all ingredients in slow crock on LOW for 4 hours.
Allow to cool. Remove spices and reheat on LOW.

Ale Punch   4 hours LOW

1 litre (2 pt) ale, $\frac{1}{2}$ litre (1 pt) water, 125 ml ($\frac{1}{4}$ pt) each of gin,
rum and whisky, small cinnamon stick, 5 cloves, 1 lemon,
sugar or honey to taste.

Slice the lemon, place spices in a muslin sachet. Place all
ingredients in the slow crock, replace lid and heat on LOW
for 4 hours minimum. To serve, remove spices and adjust
sweetening to taste.

Wenceslas Mull   4 hours LOW

1 litre (2 pt) red wine, 125 ml ($\frac{1}{4}$ pt) port, 2 tbs honey, $\frac{1}{2}$ tsp
Angostura bitters, juice of $\frac{1}{2}$ orange, $\frac{1}{2}$ glass each of brandy,
cherry brandy and orange flavoured liqueur (eg Cointreau,
Triple Sec, Curaçao), $\frac{1}{2}$ a lemon and $\frac{1}{2}$ an orange studded
with 2–3 cloves.

Heat all the ingredients in slow crock for 4 hours on LOW.
Then allow to stand and cool overnight. When required,
reheat on LOW for 2 hours or so. To serve, remove spices.

Wassail   4 hours LOW

1 litre (2 pt) sweet sherry, $\frac{1}{2}$ litre (1 pt) ale, $\frac{1}{4}$ litre ($\frac{1}{2}$ pt) water,
125 ml ($\frac{1}{4}$ pt) cognac, $\frac{1}{2}$ tsp nutmeg, 1 tsp ginger, 5 cm (2")
cinnamon stick, 6 whole allspice, 2 cardamom seeds, $\frac{1}{2}$ kg
(1 lb) sugar, 6 eggs, 3 dozen cloves, 12 crab-apples.

Stud each crab-apple with 3 cloves. Place all the ingredients except the eggs and the cognac in the slow crock.
Replace lid and heat on LOW for 4 hours. To serve, remove
spices, beat eggs lightly and stir into the slow crock. Add the
cognac.

Night Cap   4 hours LOW

1 large orange stuck with 10 cloves, 1 bottle of port, ¼ litre
(½ pt) water, juice of 1 lemon, pinch each of ginger, cinnamon and allspice, 200 g (6 oz) sugar, small glass of cherry
brandy (optional).

Place all ingredients in slow crock. Replace lid and cook
on LOW for 4 hours minimum until liquid is hot. To serve,
stir in a glass of cherry brandy.

Winter Grog   4 hours LOW

1 litre (2 pt) red wine, ¼ litre (½ pt) Jamaica rum, 1 glass
brandy, ½ litre (1 pt) water, juice and rind of 1 lemon, 1 stick
cinnamon.

Place all ingredients in slow crock and replace lid. Cook
on LOW for 4 hours minimum until thoroughly heated. To
serve, remove cinnamon stick and lemon rind.

MEAT AND VEGETABLE DRINKS

Mulled Tomato Juice   2–4 hours HIGH/LOW

1 litre (2 pt) tomato juice, 5 drops chilli sauce, ½ tbs Worcestershire sauce, 1 tsp each of salt and celery salt, ½ tsp
oregano, 90 g (3 oz) butter.

Place all ingredients in slow crock and stir. Replace lid and cook on HIGH or LOW until heated (2–4 hours). Stir before serving.

Tomato Bouillon   **2–4 hours HIGH/LOW**

1 litre (2 pt) tomato juice, ¼ litre (½ pt) rich beef stock *or* condensed beef broth diluted with water, 4 tbs sherry, 1 tbs lemon juice, dash of Worcestershire sauce, ½ tsp horse-radish.

Place all ingredients in the slow crock and stir well. Replace lid and cook on HIGH or LOW until thoroughly heated (2–4 hours).

Stock Tea   **2–4 hours HIGH/LOW**

1 litre (2 pt) vegetable, meat or chicken stock, salt to taste, 1 tbs each of tomato paste and yeast extract (Marmite or Bovril), 60 g (2 oz) rice or barley.

Rinse and drain the grain. Place all the ingredients in the slow crock. Replace lid and cook on HIGH for 2 hours or LOW for 4 hours. To serve, strain and adjust seasoning.

This recipe can be used for any stock you may just have made and don't know what to do with (see Chapter 4, page 34 for Stock recipes).

Beef Tea   **4–6 hours HIGH**

½ kg (1 lb) lean mince meat (beef, veal, mutton) to every ½ litre (1 pt) water, 1 minced onion, 1 grated carrot, 1 tbs yeast extract (Marmite or Bovril), salt to taste, pinch of mixed herbs, 1 bay leaf.
Optional: 1 tbs tomato paste.

Place meat and appropriate amount of water in slow crock and add remaining ingredients. Replace lid and cook on HIGH for 4–6 hours. To serve, strain the liquid and adjust seasoning.

Spicy Beef Bouillon   2–4 hours HIGH/LOW

1 litre (2 pt) rich beef stock *or* condensed beef broth diluted with water, 2 tsp horseradish, ½ tsp dill seed.

Place all the ingredients in the slow crock and stir well. Replace lid and cook on HIGH or LOW until thoroughly heated (2–4 hours).

12 FRUIT, JAM AND CHUTNEY

The slow crock with its low temperatures is suitable for softening both fresh and dried fruit. The quantities, in some cases such as jam or marmalade, may be rather small, but this is more than compensated for by the preservation of texture and taste.

Fresh fruit can be baked whole, stuffed with a variety of dried fruit, cooked in wine or a simple sugar syrup spiced with cinnamon or ginger, then served with cream custard, or some special sauce. Fruit is cooked in this way on a LOW setting for 3–4 hours. It will always keep its shape as long as it isn't overcooked.

Long cooking periods are meant for jams and chutneys, which can be prepared in a whole day or overnight. I have included a special chart (page 205) for small quantities of jam. Chutney is usually made in small quantities anyway, so the slow crock is particularly appropriate in this case.

I've also included some ideas for fruit soups, another example of using the slow crock to extract the maximum amount of flavour from its ingredients without loss of content.

Having laid down what I hope are useful guidelines, the rest is up to you to put your favourite ideas to work or think up some new ones. One thing I should stress is that fruit is not just something sweet at the end of a meal or in-between snack-food. Fruit can make a tremendous difference to a meat dish, whether cooked in with the meat or served separately as a side-dish. You will find in my meat chapter that I have added here and there ideas for ways in which fruit might be incorporated into the dish – one of the more traditional is prunes cooked with rabbit or hare, or fish served with a gooseberry sauce. The tradition of fruit cooked with meat is as old as the hills – and was popular in the

Tudor period. In this chapter are two recipes that are specifically meant as side-dishes for meat or fish.

FRESH FRUIT

Baked Apples   4–5 hours LOW

1–2 cooking apples per person depending on size, filling (see below), water, butter, molasses, or honey.

Wash and core the apples. Fill the core with mixture (see below) and place on a trivet or crumpled metal foil in the slow crock. Add water to depth of 1 cm ($\frac{1}{2}$″). Replace lid and cook on LOW 4–5 hours until soft but firm. To serve, remove apples and keep warm, add molasses or honey to the water and make a sweet syrup to pour over the apples. Serve with cream or custard.

Fillings for baked apples: Mincemeat; Currants, raisins, chopped nuts, honey; Chopped dates, bananas, molasses or treacle; Grated cheese, celery, raisins; Sultanas, lemon rind, jam or marmalade.

Apricot or Plum Bake   3 hours LOW

1 kg (2 lb) apricots or plums, 6 tbs sugar or honey, a few drops of vanilla essence, 6 tbs water.

Wash fruit and place in slow crock. Add sugar and moisten with water. Replace lid and cook on LOW until fruit is soft. Approximate time will be 3 hours but this depends on the ripeness of the fruit. Serve with cinnamon toast.

Cinnamon Toast: Steep slices of bread in 125 ml ($\frac{1}{4}$ pt) milk beaten with egg, then fry in butter. Sprinkle with Cinnamon and sugar to taste.

Stewed Rhubarb   2–3 hours LOW

1 kg (2 lb) rhubarb, 125 ml (¼ pt) water, 200 g (6 oz) sugar,
2 tsp each of grated lemon and orange peel, pinch of mixed
spice.

Wash and cut rhubarb and place in slow crock with water,
sugar and spice. Replace lid and cook on LOW 2–3 hours
until rhubarb is soft. Adjust seasoning, serve.
Variation: Add sliced bananas and segments of chopped
sweet orange.

Apples in Cider   3–4 hours LOW

1 kg (2 lb) apples, 200 g (6 oz) brown sugar, approx. 125 ml
(¼ pt) cider.

Peel, core and slice apples and place in slow crock with
sugar and cider to about ⅓ depth of the apples. Replace lid
and cook on LOW 3–4 hours until fruit is soft.

Pears in Red Wine   4–6 hours LOW

8 firm pears, 125 ml (¼ pt) each of red wine and water, 90 g
(3 oz) sugar per ½ kg (1 lb) pears.
Peel pears but leave their stalks on. Place them upright in
the slow crock. Sprinkle sugar over them and pour on liquid.
Replace lid and cook on LOW 4–6 hours until tender. If
wished, stand them on a trivet or crumpled metal foil during
cooking to help them keep their shape. Serve hot or cold
with custard or cream.

Ginger Pears   4–6 hours LOW

As above, except instead of red wine and water use ¼ litre
(½ pt) ginger ale, 2 tsp lemon juice, 2 cloves and a pinch of

cinnamon. To serve, stir 2 tbs redcurrant jelly into the cooking juice.

Savoury Bananas   4 hours LOW

6 bananas, 1 medium onion, 2 large tomatoes, 30 g (1 oz) butter, ½ tsp turmeric.

Peel and chop onion and *sauté* in butter until soft. Add onion, chopped tomatoes and peeled bananas to slow crock and stir in turmeric and any remaining butter. Replace lid and cook on LOW approx. 4 hours. Serve as a side-dish with gammon or as an hors d'oeuvre.

Curried Bananas   3–4 hours LOW

6 bananas, 2 tbs sultanas, 2 tbs mango chutney, 1 small onion, 2 tsp curry powder, 1 tbs each of flour and butter, 90 ml (3 fl oz) chicken stock, salt and pepper.

Peel and chop onion and *sauté* in butter until soft. Sprinkle on flour and curry powder and stir until cooked, about 1–2 minutes. Transfer to slow crock, add sliced bananas, and remaining ingredients. Stir well. Replace lid and cook on LOW 3–4 hours until ingredients are well blended and soft. Serve as a side-dish with pork or fish.

Curried Pears   4–5 hours LOW

3–4 medium pears, 3 tbs butter or margarine, 3 tbs brown sugar, 1 tbs curry powder, ½ tsp grated lemon peel, ¼ tsp salt, 125 ml (¼ pt) water.
Optional: 60 g (2 oz) raisins.

Wash, peel, core and halve pears. Blend together butter, sugar, lemon peel, curry and salt. Place this mixture in the centre of each pear and place them in a lightly greased slow crock. Pour on water. Replace lid and cook on LOW 4–5 hours until tender. Serve with ham, pork or poultry.

DRIED FRUIT

All dried fruit can be washed and placed in the slow crock with a small amount of liquid (about 125 ml ($\frac{1}{4}$ pt) depending on quantity) and without having been pre-soaked, cooked on LOW for 3–4 hours. Their taste will be rich and juicy and the concentrated taste of the sugar will not have boiled away as so often happens when cooking dried fruit in an open saucepan.

Basic Method for Dried Fruit Compote
1 kg (2 lb) mixed dried fruit (apples, figs, dates, prunes, apricots, raisins, etc), water, sugar, lemon rind.

Wash fruit and place in slow crock. Add water to almost cover, and sugar to taste, with a piece of lemon peel. Replace lid and cook on LOW until soft, about 3–4 hours.

FRUIT SOUPS

Method 1
A fruit soup can be easily made by sieving or blending cooked mixed fruit. It can be served hot or cold with cream and a garnish of chopped nuts.

Method 2
Fruit juice, heated in the slow crock for 3 hours with raisins or fresh fruit, can be served as a soup, thickened with a little arrowroot.

Rhubarb Soup   **3–4 hours LOW**

½ kg (1 lb) rhubarb, 1 litre (2 pt) water, ½ cinnamon stick, 2 slices lemon, 125 g (4 oz) sugar or honey, 1 egg yolk, 1 tbs each of cornflour and butter, 60 ml (2 fl oz) double cream.

Stew the rhubarb in water with cinnamon stick and lemon.

Elderberry Soup   **3–4 hours LOW**

½ kg (1 lb) ripe elderberries, 1 litre (2 pt) water, sugar to taste, pinch of cinnamon, 2 tsp grated lemon rind, 1 tbs each of butter and cornflour.

Stew the elderberries in water on LOW for 3–4 hours then *purée* them. Return to slow crock and add sugar to taste, cinnamon and lemon rind. Mix together the cornflour and butter and add bit by bit to soup. Stir until cooked and thick.

Fruit and Wine Soup   **3–4 hours LOW**

½ kg (1 lb) fruit (apple, rhubarb, strawberries), 1 bottle red wine or rosé, nutmeg, juice of 1 lemon, 1 tsp grated lemon rind, sugar to taste, sour cream.

Prepare fruit and stew in the wine for 3–4 hours on LOW. Blend and return mixture to slow crock, stir in sugar to taste, add lemon juice, a little rind, and a pinch of nutmeg. Serve with sour cream.

OTHER SUGGESTIONS FOR FRUIT SOUP INGREDIENTS

Cranberries and apples (plus water, sour cream, sugar,

thickening), redcurrants or blackcurrants with peaches; apples, pears, peaches, strawberries, orange juice, wine, fresh mint.

SOFTENING FRUIT FOR JAM AND MARMALADE

Although the slow crock cannot set the jam it can be used to soften the fruit beforehand and this is useful because it is during the softening process that the all-important chemical – pectin – is extracted which helps the jam to set. Every fruit has a different pectin-content and it is for this reason that a synthetic form of pectin is often used for fruits with a low pectin level. The slow crock will help to extract the maximum amount of pectin with the least loss through evaporation. Fruits rich in pectin include currants, gooseberries, apples, rhubarb and acid and stone fruit. Low in pectin are cherries, raspberries, strawberries, blackberries, marrow and pears and over-ripe fruit. The length of cooking depends on the quantity of pectin and acid the fruit contains. The higher the proportion of pectin the greater the amount of sugar added to the fruit, which is usually between 375 g–½ kg (¾–1 lb) of sugar per ½ kg (1 lb) of fruit.

	sugar	water
Apples: cooking	½ kg (1 lb)	125 ml (¼ pt)
Apples: dessert	375 g (¾ lb)	,,
Apricots	375 g (¾ lb)	,,
Currant, red or black	½ kg (1 lb)	,,
Damsons	½ kg (1 lb)	,,
Gooseberries: green	½ kg (1 lb)	,,
Gooseberries: red	450 g (14 oz)	,,
Greengages	475 g (15 oz)	,,
Lemon	475 g (15 oz)	,,
Marrow	375 g (¾ lb)	,,
Oranges	½ kg (1 lb)	,,
Peaches	375 g (¾ lb)	,,
Plum: egg	475 g (15 oz)	,,

	sugar	water
Plum: magnum bonum	375 g ($\frac{3}{4}$ lb)	125 ml ($\frac{1}{4}$ pt)
Raspberries	375 g ($\frac{3}{4}$ lb)	,,
Rhubarb	450 g (14 oz)	,,
Strawberries	450 g (14 oz)	,,

Basic Method for Making Jam

Prepare and wash fruit carefully. Place in slow crock and cook on LOW with very little liquid all night or all day (10–12 hours).

Then, transfer fruit to a saucepan, add the sugar and let it dissolve thoroughly in the fruit over a gentle heat before boiling.

Stir sugar, and when completely dissolved raise the heat and boil fruit rapidly for 2 minutes then test for gel. Stir regularly to prevent burning.

TESTS FOR GEL
1. plate.
2. methylated spirits.

MARMALADE

Use same method as for jam. Fruit need not be previously soaked. Hot water is added to a slow crock pre-heated on HIGH.

Add the fruit sliced as thinly as possible. The test for gel should be after 15 minutes rapid boiling, or even longer.

CHUTNEY

Chutneys play an important part in making dishes more interesting. They can be used with hot and cold food, often giving added zest to flat soups and sauces or providing a contrast to a rich or spicy meat dish. You will always find that chutneys are an automatic addition to an Indian meal as with other Asian and Middle or Far Eastern cuisine.

Chutneys which can be kept have to be cooked and bottled.

From a simple basic recipe it is quite easy to blend your own choice of ingredients, spices and flavourings. Usually it is best to use whatever vegetable or fruit is in season.

The aim in chutney cooking is to use a little liquid and reduce the ingredients to a soft pulp. In the slow crock the vegetable or fruit ingredients are first brought to the boil in a separate pan and transferred to a pre-heated slow crock and cooked on LOW for up to 8 hours.

Basic Recipe for Chutney   **8 hours LOW**

125 g (4 oz) sugar, $\frac{1}{4}$ litre ($\frac{1}{2}$ pt) vinegar, 15 g ($\frac{1}{2}$ oz) whole allspice, 30 g (1 oz) whole cloves, 1 bay leaf, 1 tbs salt, $\frac{1}{2}$ tsp pepper, 1 kg (2 lb) mixed vegetables or fruit and vegetables, water.

Pre-heat the slow crock on HIGH.

Peel and chop vegetables. Place root vegetables only in a saucepan with water to cover and parboil for 5 minutes. Transfer the ingredients to the slow crock, add vinegar, salt, sugar and spices in a bag. Replace lid and cook on LOW for 8 hours until the vegetables are pulpy. Then, lift off lid, switch to HIGH setting and reduce liquid by half. Bottle in hot jars or allow the chutney to cool first, then bottle.

Some suggestions for combinations:
Tomatoes with a dash of cinnamon and onions
Green tomatoes with ginger and apple
Green tomatoes with plums and apples, raisins, currants and
    ginger
Pumpkin with tomato and cinnamon
Chilli peppers with green figs and apple
Plums with beetroot, celery and apple
Apricots with apples and mixed spice
Cucumber with marrow, apples and plums
Celery with green tomatoes and beetroot
Blackberries with beetroot and apples
Damsons with green tomatoes, ginger, sprig of rosemary

Carrot Chutney   **8 hours LOW**

1 kg (2 lb) carrots, 1 tbs salt, 4 garlic cloves, 2 tbs mustard
seeds, 2 tsp cumin seeds, 2 tsp finely chopped ginger, 1 tbs
black peppercorns, $\frac{1}{4}$ litre ($\frac{1}{2}$ pt) vinegar, 200 g (6 oz) soft
brown sugar.

Peel and dice carrots very small. Place in a saucepan and
cover with water. Bring to boil and cook for 5 minutes.
Drain and transfer to slow crock. Add remaining ingredients
and vinegar. Replace lid and cook on LOW for 8 hours.
Follow method as in basic recipe (see page 207).

Tomato Chutney   **8 hours LOW**

$\frac{1}{2}$ kg (1 lb) cooking apples, 1 kg (2 lb) fresh or tinned tomatoes, 60 g (2 oz) root ginger, 30 g (1 oz) garlic, 1 tsp each of
salt and chilli powder, $\frac{1}{4}$ litre ($\frac{1}{2}$ pt) vinegar.

Peel and core apples. Dice apples and tomatoes small.
Pound ginger and garlic together. Mix all the ingredients
together in the slow crock and pour vinegar on. Replace lid
and follow method as in basic recipe (see page 207).

Sweet Apple Chutney   **8 hours LOW**

1 kg (2 lb) cooking apples, 1 tbs chopped ginger, 1 tbs
chopped garlic, $\frac{1}{2}$ kg (1 lb) raisins, 1 tbs dried red chillies,
1 tsp salt, $\frac{1}{2}$ kg (1 lb) soft brown sugar, $\frac{1}{4}$ litre ($\frac{1}{2}$ pt) vinegar.

Peel and core apples and cut into chunks. Pound the
ginger and garlic. Mix all ingredients together in the slow
crock and follow instructions as for basic chutney (see
recipe, page 207).

Rhubarb Chutney   **8 hours LOW**

¾ kg (1½ lb) rhubarb, 2 tsp chopped ginger, 4 garlic cloves, 1 tsp chilli powder, 2 tbs each of mustard seeds and ground almonds, ¼ kg (½ lb) soft brown sugar, ¼ litre (½ pt) vinegar.

Wash and dice the rhubarb small. Pound ginger and garlic. Mix all ingredients and place in slow crock. Follow method for basic chutney (see page 207).

Pineapple Chutney   **8 hours LOW**

¾ kg (1½ lb) tinned or fresh pineapple, 1 tbs salt, 8 garlic cloves or less, 2 tbs chopped ginger, ¼ kg (½ lb) raisins, 200 g (6 oz) soft brown sugar, ¼ litre (½ pt) vinegar.

Peel and trim pineapple, drain if tinned, and cut into small dice. Pound the ginger and garlic, and place all ingredients in slow crock. Follow method for basic chutney as above (see page 207).

Ginger and Garlic Chutney   **8 hours LOW**

½ kg (1 lb) root ginger, 375 g (¾ lb) garlic, 2 tbs mustard seeds, 2 tsp chilli powder, 2 tsp salt, 200 g (6 oz) soft brown sugar, ¼ litre (½ pt) vinegar.

Pound the ginger and garlic. Mix with other ingredients and place in the slow crock. Follow basic method for chutney. (See above, page 207.)

Mixed Fruit Chutney   **8 hours LOW**

¼ kg (½ lb) cooking apples, ¼ kg (½ lb) pears, 200 g (6 oz) dried apricots, 2 tbs sultanas, 400 g (¾ lb) soft brown sugar, ¼ litre (½ pt) vinegar, 1 tsp garam masala, 1 tsp caraway seeds or cumin seeds, 3 tsp salt, 1 tbs freshly chopped ginger, up to 12 garlic cloves.

Pre-heat the slow crock on HIGH.

Peel and core apples and pears. Cut all the fruit in small pieces and slice the garlic. Place all the ingredients in the slow crock and pour vinegar on. Replace lid and cook on LOW for 8 hours until the fruit is pulp. Then lift off lid, switch to HIGH setting and reduce liquid by half. Bottle in hot jars or allow the chutney to cool first, then bottle.

Remove cinnamon and lemon slices and *purée* rhubarb then return it to slow crock. Add sugar and stir until dissolved. Mix cornflour with butter and add bit by bit to slow crock, stir until thick and cooked. Serve with double cream mixed with egg yolk stirred in about 5 minutes before serving.

The basic method is as follows – stew fruit in liquid

purée fruit
add thickening
sweeten
serve

Proportions are $\frac{1}{2}$ kg (1 lb) fruit to 1 litre (2 pt) water, 1 tbs each of cornflour and butter, egg yolk (for a richer soup) cream (for a creamier texture), sugar or honey to taste.

13 CORDON BLEU MADE EASY IN THE SLOW CROCK

This chapter is not meant for specialists only. It demonstrates how easy it is for simple slow crock cooking to become advanced; how ingredients that are economical can be suitable for entertaining, with just a little extra time and trouble. You may find some of the ingredients unusual and more difficult to obtain in your local store and that you have to spend more time preparing the food at the beginning or adding to it at the end. But the cooking process itself is exactly the same – a HIGH or LOW setting with the lid on for a 6–8 hour, 10–12 hour, or overnight period.

I have also included recipes with an international flavour – Chinese, French or Indian, Caribbean and Danish. This is to give you an idea of how normally complicated dishes are easily cooked in the slow crock after you've done some initial groundwork on the ingredients. And I hope this will also give you some indication of how other recipes you might wish to use for slow crock cooking can be adjusted, adapted and modified.

I will explain where some of the dishes come from if it is important to convey an idea of what the finished dish will look and taste like. You might wonder why some of them are so special – perhaps it's a richer ingredient. Perhaps the method is not as straightforward as slow crock cooking usually is. Advance preparation may be necessary in some of the cold dishes so instead of thinking the normal one day ahead for slow crock cooking, you'll have to think two days ahead.

Beef Britannia   **10–12 hours LOW**

A piece of beef with layers of savoury stuffing cooked very slowly on LOW.

1½ kg (3 lb) rump steak or roll of silverside, 6 rashers of
streaky bacon, 60 g (2 oz) butter, 1 medium onion, 125 g
(4 oz) mushrooms, 90 ml (3 fl oz) each of white wine and
Madeira sherry. *Garnish* – lettuce leaves.
Stuffing: 170 g (5 oz) white breadcrumbs, 2 medium onions,
90 g (3 oz) chicken livers, 125 g (4 oz) mushrooms, 1 egg yolk,
60 g (2 oz) butter, ½ tsp allspice, milk, pinch of thyme, salt
and pepper.

Ask the butcher to cut the meat into about 12 slices joined
at the base. Try and choose a piece shaped like a cube.

To make the stuffing, soak the breadcrumbs in milk and
then squeeze them. Peel and mince onions, and slice the
mushrooms very small. Plunge the livers into hot water to
make them firm then mince or chop finely. Melt the butter
in a frying pan and heat the mushrooms until their moisture
has evaporated, then add the breadcrumbs, onion and liver.
Season with salt and pepper to taste, then add allspice and
thyme. Mix well and adjust seasoning. Set aside to cool, then
stir in the egg yolk and mix well.

Spread the stuffing evenly between the slices of meat,
reserving about 1–2 tablespoons. Tie the meat firmly but
not too tightly with a piece of string, at the same time
wrapping and securing the bacon to the joint.

Melt the other 60 g (2 oz) butter in a frying pan and brown
the chopped onion and sliced mushrooms, then transfer
them to the slow crock. Brown the joint well and place in
slow crock. Pour wine over the joint. Replace lid and cook
on LOW for 10–12 hours until the meat is tender. Half an
hour before serving stir in the reserved stuffing and the
Madeira sherry.

To serve, remove joint and keep warm. Serve the sauce
separately. Garnish the meat with lettuce leaves and accompany the dish with mashed potatoes or rice. The joint will be
easy to carve as the slices only have to be detached from each
other at the base.

Boeuf à la Mode   **10–12 hours LOW**

This famous French dish can be served hot or cold.

1½–2½ kg (3–5 lb) topside of beef, 1 calf's foot (chopped by butcher), 200 g (6 oz) chopped onion, 60 ml (2 fl oz) brandy, ¼ litre (½ pt) red wine, 2 tbs oil, 2 garlic cloves, 1–2 bay leaves, 2 sprigs of thyme, 2 sprigs of parsley, 125 ml (¼ pt) beef stock, *garnish* – chopped parsley.

Heat oil in a frying pan and brown the onion and beef. Transfer to slow crock. Warm the brandy, set it alight and pour it flaming over the beef. Then add the wine, cleaned calf's foot, crushed garlic and the herbs (tied with string). Add the beef stock. Replace lid and cook on LOW for 10–12 hours until the beef is tender. If you find that the beef is not tender enough at the end of the 10-hour cooking period and you want to speed up the final process, switch to HIGH.

Skim off as much fat as possible at the end of cooking; this can be easily done with a paper towel or two.

To serve hot: transfer beef to a warm serving dish and sprinkle with chopped parsley. A traditional accompaniment is boiled carrots which should be arranged around the beef. The carrots should be cooked separately in beef stock with a dessertspoon of sugar. Strain and skim some of the liquid and serve separately. Reserve the remaining liquid for soups, sauces, and other stews.

To serve cold: transfer the beef with its liquid to a large bowl and allow to cool for about 4 hours. Then, lift out the beef, cut away the string and place on a deep close-fitting dish. Place the separately cooked carrots around and underneath. Pour in some of the cooking liquid which should be strained, skimmed and reduced (boiled down) to a rich flavour. Let it set in the fridge before serving.

Beef Arrosto   **6–8 hours HIGH**

Italian stuffed roast beef, served hot or cold.

1–2 thick slices of beef from rump or shoulder each weighing
about ½ kg (1 lb).
Stuffing: 2 chicken livers or 60 g (2 oz) liver paste, 60 g (2 oz)
each of cooked ham and tongue, 30 g (1 oz) of grated
Parmesan cheese, 1 egg, 1 small onion, a thick slice of bread
– about 60 g (2 oz), small celery stalk, 1 small carrot, salt and
pepper, generous pinch of thyme and basil, 1 tbs chopped
parsley, 2 tbs oil.

Score beef on both sides to make it flexible to roll. To help
flatten it out, plunge in cold water for a minute and then lay
it out flat ready for the stuffing. To make the stuffing chop
the onion, carrot, celery, parsley and liver. Mix this with the
bread that has been soaked in water and squeezed dry. Stir
in ham and tongue cut in strips, cheese, herbs, seasoning and
beaten egg. Spread the stuffing onto the meat, roll up and
tie with string.

Heat oil in a frying pan and brown meat well all over.
Place in slow crock. Replace lid and cook on HIGH for 6–8
hours, or longer depending on the quality of the beef.

Method for a tough piece of stewing steak   **12 hours LOW**
With a tough piece of stewing steak the same recipe can be
used but on a LOW setting for 12 hours. Having browned and
stuffed the meat, add about 125 ml (¼ pt) water to the slow
crock before cooking.

Rolled Slices of Beef in Cream   **10–12 hours LOW**

¾ kg (1½ lb) fillet of beef cut in 4 slices, 125 g (4 oz) anchovy
fillets, 1 medium onion, 1 garlic clove, 3 parsley stalks, 4 tbs
butter, ½ tsp pepper, 1 tbs lemon juice, 1 carton of double
cream, ¼ litre (½ pt) veal stock.

Chop the anchovies. Chop the parsley and onion finely, crush the garlic. Mash these ingredients to a paste. Spread the paste evenly over the slices of beef, then roll them up and secure with string or a small stick.

Melt the butter in a frying pan and brown the rolls lightly all over. Transfer to slow crock and add stock and pepper. Replace lid and cook on LOW for 10–12 hours until meat is tender.

About ten minutes before serving stir the lemon juice and cream together and add to the liquid in the slow crock. To serve, remove the string from the beef rolls. Accompany with potatoes.

Beef or Mutton Vindaloo   **8–10 hours LOW**

1 kg (2 lb) lean beef or pork, 3–4 garlic cloves, 4 tbs each of butter and vinegar, 1–2 tsp chilli powder or madras curry powder, 2 bay leaves, 2–3 peppercorns, 1 medium onion, 1 tsp salt, pinch each of cinnamon and ground cloves, 2 tsp ground ginger, 1 tsp ground coriander, water to moisten.

Trim excess fat from meat and cut into cubes. Peel and chop onion. Grind the garlic with the vinegar and spices to make a paste. Melt the butter in a frying pan and lightly fry the onion, then add the spice and vinegar mixture and fry for a little longer. Place meat in the base of the slow crock and stir in the fried paste and onions. Add bay leaves and peppercorns, and a little water or lemon juice to moisten. Replace lid and cook on LOW for 8 hours until meat is tender. Serve with rice.

Biste Marti   **10 hours LOW**

This dish from Cuba is a seasoned casserole with individual steaks, Creole style.

4–6 beef steaks (rump, round or sirloin) weighing about ¼ kg (½ lb) each, 1 medium onion, 1 medium green pepper, 1 fresh chilli pepper, 6 medium tomatoes, 2 garlic cloves, 3 tbs lime or lemon juice, 3 tbs oil, 3 tbs red wine or red wine vinegar, salt and pepper to taste, 1 bay leaf, sprig of fresh coriander or 2 tsp coriander seeds or ground coriander.

Rub the steaks with a cut garlic clove and season with salt and pepper. Allow to stand for an hour or two in lime juice, turning once or twice if possible. Then, lift out, wipe dry and reserve any juice.

Melt oil in a frying pan and *sauté* the steaks one by one until brown all over. Set aside. Slice onion, de-seed and chop pepper and *sauté* in the remaining oil. Transfer to slow crock. Add the peeled and sieved tomatoes, chilli, bay leaf and coriander. Place meat on top and sprinkle on the reserved lime juice and wine.

Replace lid and cook on LOW for 10 hours until the steaks are tender. To serve, transfer steaks to a warm dish and reduce sauce if necessary. Adjust seasoning. Accompany with a vegetable *purée*.

Sheikh's Delight   6–8 hours HIGH

An Egyptian speciality with beef, chick peas and eggs cooked in their shells.

1 kg (2 lb) lean stewing beef, 6 small potatoes, 6 eggs in their shells, 2 large onions, 200–250 g (6–8 oz) chick peas, 2 garlic cloves, 1 tsp allspice, salt and pepper, oil, water, bicarbonate of soda.
Optional: 1 calf's foot.
Modified ingredients for a smaller slow crock: ¾ kg (1½ lb) lean stewing beef, 4 small potatoes, 4 eggs in their shells, 2 medium onions, 200 g (6 oz) chick peas, 2 garlic cloves, 1 tsp allspice, salt and pepper, oil, water, bicarbonate of soda.

Soak chick peas overnight in cold water. Rinse, drain and place in base of slow crock. Cut meat into cubes. Peel the potatoes and scrub the egg shells thoroughly. Blanch the potatoes and the calf's foot in boiling water. Fry the chopped onions in oil until soft and golden. Place all these ingredients in the slow crock.

Cover two-thirds of the ingredients with cold water. Add crushed garlic, a pinch of bicarbonate of soda and pepper (*no* salt at this stage as it prevents the peas from softening). Replace lid and cook on HIGH for 6–8 hours until the peas and beef are tender. The meat should be falling apart and the peas rich and impregnated with the calf's foot stock. The eggs will be creamier than the normal hard-boiled egg. Serve in shells accompanied with rice. Adjust seasoning with salt after cooking.

Sauerbraten   10–12 hours LOW

This is a classic German dish that is marinated for 2 to 10 days!

1½–2½ kg (3–5 lb) shoulder, rump or top round of beef. *Marinade*: ¼ litre (½ pt) each of water and vinegar, 1 medium onion, 2 bay leaves, 1 tsp peppercorns, 60 g (2 oz) sugar, 2 tbs flour, 2 tbs cooking oil, 1 large garlic clove. *Optional*: 60 g (2 oz) of gingerbread, 1 tsp salt and pepper.

Rub the meat with a cut garlic clove and pepper and place in a large bowl. Heat to boiling the water and vinegar with the sliced onion, bay leaves, peppercorns and sugar. Pour over beef. Cover the bowl and put it into the refrigerator. Turn the meat once a day and let it marinate at least two days, or up to ten days – the longer the better.

Drain the meat and wipe dry. Reserve the marinade. Heat the oil fiercely and sear the meat till crisp on all sides. Add the flour and cook well. Transfer meat to slow crock and pour half the marinade over it, about ¼ litre (½ pt). Salt the meat and place the gingerbread in the liquid. Replace lid and cook on LOW for 10–12 hours, turning the meat perhaps once, if possible, during the last two hours.

To serve, lift meat from slow crock and slice it, then return it to the slow crock or serve the gravy separately. Accompany with dumplings or buttered noodles.

Bei Jing Casserole   **8–10 hours LOW**

A simple, straightforward beef stew, Chinese style.

1½ kg (3 lb) stewing beef, 4 tbs each of soy sauce and sherry, 2 medium onions, 2 tsp sugar, 1 tbs dried tangerine peel*, oil for deep-frying, 2 slices root ginger, ½ litre (1 pt) cold water.

Cut beef into cubes and deep-fry for about 3 minutes. Drain and transfer to a large saucepan then cover with boiling water and boil for 2 minutes. Drain and transfer to slow crock. Add sugar, soy sauce, sherry, ginger, sliced onion and tangerine peel. Pour on cold water. Replace lid and cook on LOW for 8 hours at least, and turn once in a while after the initial 6 hours. When ready, the beef should be so tender that it almost disintegrates. Serve with rice.

Veal Roll   **8 hours LOW**

¾ kg (1½ lb) lean veal in a piece, 2 eggs, 60 g (2 oz) Parmesan cheese, 2 tbs chopped parsley, 60 g (2 oz) smoked salami or sausage, butter and oil, salt and pepper, 1 medium onion, 50 ml (2 fl oz) each water and milk.

* Tangerine peel can be bought at any Chinese supermarket although you can make it yourself simply by drying tangerine peels in an oven at 120°C (250°F), Gas Mark 2, for ½ an hour. Double the quantity if using home-made, instead of bought, peel.

Make an omelette with the eggs, water, cheese, chopped salami and parsley, and a little seasoning.

Beat the meat as flat as possible and spread the omelette over it. Roll the meat up and tie with string. Mix equal parts of oil and butter in a pan and fry the chopped onion. Then add the meat and brown all over. Transfer to slow crock. Pour on milk to cover the base of slow crock. Replace lid and cook on LOW for 8–10 hours. This dish can be served hot or cold.

Stuffed Veal   **8–10 hours LOW**

1 kg (2 lb) boned leg of veal, 4 anchovy fillets, 2 bay leaves, 1 onion stuck with 2 cloves, 2 carrots, 2 celery stalks, 2 sprigs of parsley, salt and black pepper, $\frac{1}{4}$ litre ($\frac{1}{2}$ pt) dry white wine.
Sauce: 125 ml ($\frac{1}{4}$ pt) mayonnaise, 125 g (4 oz) tuna fish, 4 anchovy fillets, 2 tbs lemon juice, 1 tsp capers, a few lemon slices.

Make small incisions in the meat and stuff them with small pieces of anchovy fillet. Then roll and tie meat. Place it in the slow crock. Add sliced onion, carrot and celery, seasoning, herbs and dry white wine. Replace lid and cook on LOW for 8 hours until the meat is tender.

When cooked, transfer it to a large bowl, remove string and allow it to cool. Then slice it thinly, cover with sauce (see method below) and marinate overnight. Serve garnished with lemon slices.

To make sauce: Pound the tuna fish and anchovies, add the mayonnaise gradually, stirring continuously. Squeeze on the lemon juice and add the strained capers. The sauce should be fairly liquid.

Veal Marengo   8–10 hours LOW

About ¼ kg (½ lb) breast of veal per person, 1 onion, 1 garlic clove, 2 tbs oil, ½ kg (1 lb) tomatoes, ¼ litre (½ pt) white wine, salt and black pepper, *bouquet garni*. *Garnish* – chopped parsley, lemon slices, and garlic *or* glazed mushrooms and onions with *croûtons* of bread.

Heat oil in a frying pan and cook sliced onion and chopped garlic until transparent. Drain and set aside, then brown meat well on each side. Transfer meat, onion and garlic to slow crock. Add washed and chopped tomatoes, wine, seasoning, and *bouquet garni* and replace lid. Cook on LOW for 8–10 hours until meat is very tender.

When cooked, remove meat and keep warm. Switch slow crock to HIGH setting. Remove *bouquet garni* and sieve the remaining ingredients. Reheat in slow crock with lid off and allow liquid to reduce, then pour around the meat.

Garnish the dish with the traditional mushroom, onion and *croûtons* or with parsley, lemon slices and minced garlic or garlic powder.

Veal Marseilles   10–12 hours LOW

1 kg (2 lb) veal fillet in a piece, 1 carrot and onion, *bouquet garni*, 1 clove, 1 garlic clove, salt and pepper, butter.
Sauce: 2–3 aubergines, ¼ kg (½ lb) tomatoes, ½ tbs each of chopped tarragon and parsley, glass of sherry or stock, seasoning, olive oil.

To prepare sauce, peel and slice aubergines, salt and allow to stand for an hour to allow bitter juices to run out. Then, rinse, drain and squeeze dry. Heat olive oil in frying pan and *sauté* aubergines until brown, then add them to slow crock with the tomatoes, peeled, quartered and with seeds scooped out. Sprinkle on herbs.

Trim veal and tie it in a roll. Brown on all sides in butter and transfer to slow crock. Add chopped and blanched carrot and onion, *bouquet garni*, clove, garlic and seasoning. Replace lid and cook on LOW for 10–12 hours until tender.

When veal is cooked, remove and slice it thinly, and place on a serving dish surrounded by the vegetables. Add the sherry to the slow crock, switch to HIGH setting and allow liquid to reduce with the lid off. Then adjust seasoning and strain sauce over the dish. This dish can also be served cold.

Marbled Veal   **6 hours HIGH**

375 g (¾ lb) each of boned leg of veal and fat loin of pork, ¼ kg (½ lb) cooked tongue, 2 eggs, 3 tsp chopped chives or green stalks from spring onions, 3 tsp chopped parsley, 2 tsp grated lemon rind, 3 tbs cold water, salt and pepper, pinch of thyme, hot water, tin or bowl to fit slow crock, metal foil.

Switch slow crock to HIGH during preparations.

Trim any skin and gristle from the meat and mince it very finely. Add the herbs and seasoning and bind with the eggs. Add 3 tbs cold water to give a soft texture. Grease a container that will fit your slow crock and fill it with the mixture. Then cover the container with metal foil.

Place the container in the slow crock. Pour boiling water around the side until it reaches half-way up the side. Replace lid and cook on HIGH for 6 hours until cooked. Then, remove container from slow crock, press it down with weights and let it stand and mature until cool. When cool, transfer to refrigerator and let it set. To serve, turn it out onto a dish garnished with salad.

Breast of Lamb Braised and Fried   **8–10 hours LOW**

A two-stage recipe, that takes quite a bit of work, but is cheap, different and tasty.

1 breast of lamb cut in 2 pieces, 1 large onion, *bouquet garni*, 2 carrots. For second stage – mustard, 1 large egg, about 200 g (6 oz) fine breadcrumbs, melted butter, salt and pepper to taste, ½ litre (1 pt) water.
Optional: 90 g (3 oz) boiling bacon.

Stage one: Place sliced vegetables and bacon with *bouquet garni* in base of slow crock. Lay breast of lamb on top, season it and pour on water. Replace lid and cook on LOW for 8–10 hours.

When cooked, remove meat and allow to cool. Strain stock into a bowl. Remove bones from meat using a sharp knife. Place meat on a flat dish, cover with greaseproof paper and a weighted board.

Stage two: When cold, slice meat into thin strips about 2 cm (1″) wide, cut on the bias. Spread them with mustard. Coat them with beaten egg and then with breadcrumbs. Leave them on a rack to dry and set.

The final cooking stage involves grilling or frying them until they are brown and crisp. First place them in a grill pan or dish, pour melted butter over and then heat them in the oven until hot. Then place them under a grill or in a frying pan and cook until dry, crisp and even a little scorched. Serve hot with *sauce tartare* or *vinaigrette*, and accompany with lemon wedges and watercress.

Lamb and Aubergine Stew   8 hours LOW

1 kg (2 lb) boned lamb from shoulder or neck, 2 aubergines, 1 large onion, ¼ kg (½ lb) tomatoes, salt and pepper, 1 garlic clove, 2 tsp ground cumin or whole cumin seeds, fresh or dried mint or basil, 4 tbs oil, 4 tbs water or stock.

Cut aubergines into cubes, salt and let stand for an hour to let bitter juices run out. Before cooking, rinse and squeeze dry.

Cut the lamb into cubes and sprinkle with seasoning and herbs. Peel and slice onion. Heat oil in a frying pan and *sauté* the onion. Then add the meat and brown well all over. Drain and place in slow crock. If necessary add more oil to pan to fry aubergine for 5 minutes or so. Drain and mix with ingredients in slow crock. Add chopped tomatoes and garlic, cumin and water to moisten. Replace lid and cook on LOW for 8 hours until the meat is tender. Before serving, adjust seasoning and sprinkle a few more herbs over dish. Serve with rice.

Lamb Shoulder Stuffed with Olives   8–10 hours LOW

This dish is also very good cold.

1 kg (2 lb) boned shoulder of lamb or mutton, 4 tomatoes, 2 garlic cloves, salt and pepper, 1 bay leaf, 90 ml (3 fl oz) white wine or stock, 1 tbs fat; *for stuffing* – 2 slices of bread, 1 tbs white wine, 8 pitted black olives, 125 g (4 oz) streaky bacon, 1 egg, ¼ kg (½ lb) minced veal, 2 garlic cloves, 1 tbs each of chopped chervil and parsley, salt and pepper, pinch of nutmeg.

To make stuffing: Soak the bread in wine, squeeze it dry and crumble into a bowl. Chop the olives and bacon and mix them with the bread. Add the remaining stuffing ingredients and mix thoroughly.

Spread the stuffing evenly over the meat, roll and tie it. Heat fat in a frying pan and brown the joint well all over. Place in slow crock. Chop tomatoes and garlic and place around the meat. Add wine and seasoning. Replace lid and cook on LOW about 8–10 hours turning the meat twice in the last few hours. To serve, adjust seasoning, remove bay leaf.

Spring Navarin of Lamb   8–10 hours LOW

This recipe is meant to be used when the first spring vegetables are available in the shops. The quantities I have given are small enough for a small slow crock but ideally should be doubled for the large ones.

½ kg (1 lb) boned shoulder of lamb or 6–8 neck cutlets, 5 new potatoes, 4 small new carrots, 5 small onions, 2 young turnips, 1 garlic clove, *bouquet garni*, 2 tbs each of flour and butter, 2 tbs tomato paste, 2 tbs parsley, salt and pepper, 1 tsp sugar, ½ litre (1 pt) beef stock, ¼ kg (½ lb) shelled peas, chopped parsley.

Trim excess fat from meat and cut into pieces if using shoulder. Melt butter in pan and brown lamb. Drain and transfer to slow crock. Stir flour into the butter and make a *roux*. Then mix in the tomato paste and stock. Stir until smooth then add to slow crock with seasoning, herbs and minced garlic.

Peel the vegetables and dice the turnip. Parboil them (except the peas) for 5 minutes and add to slow crock. Mix the ingredients together in the slow crock. Replace lid and cook on LOW for 8–10 hours until meat and vegetables are tender. Cook the peas separately. To serve, adjust seasoning and remove *bouquet garni*. Garnish with chopped parsley.

Desert Lamb   8–10 hours LOW

Lamb in yoghurt. A favourite dish in the Middle East.

1 kg (2 lb) lean lamb, 2 medium onions, salt and black pepper, ½ litre (1 pt) yoghurt, 1 tbs cornflour, 2 garlic cloves, 1 tsp ground coriander, 2 tbs butter, 1 tsp salt, water, a slice of lemon.

Cube the lamb, peel and slice the onions. Place the lamb

in a saucepan with a slice of lemon and cover with fresh *cold* water. Add a little salt. Bring the liquid slowly to the boil then drain and refresh in cold water to wash away the scum.

Add drained meat and onion to slow crock and pour in 125 ml ($\frac{1}{4}$ pt) fresh water. Add salt and pepper to taste. Replace lid and cook on LOW for 8–10 hours until meat is soft and tender. Reduce the liquid if necessary by switching to HIGH and cooking with the lid off for $\frac{1}{2}$ an hour or so.

To prepare yoghurt sauce – beat yoghurt in a large bowl until liquid. Add the cornflour mixed to a light paste with water, and a little salt. Stir with a wooden spoon. Pour this mixture carefully into the slow crock and stir the yoghurt into the liquid. Keep the lid off and use the HIGH setting. Keep stirring in one direction and allow the yoghurt to bubble. Then let the yoghurt cook uncovered for about 10 minutes until the sauce has thickened.

Meanwhile, fry the crushed garlic and coriander in butter until the garlic turns golden. Pour this mixture over the meat and yoghurt. Serve with plain or saffron rice.

Hong Kong Lamb   **8–10 hours LOW**

A very simple Chinese style dish – red-cooked lamb.

$1\frac{1}{2}$ kg (3 lb) leg of mutton or lamb or best end of neck, 2 scallions cut in 5 cm (2″) long sections, 6 tbs soy sauce, 1 tsp salt, water.

Chop mutton or lamb into pieces. Wash and place in slow crock. Add water to cover about $\frac{2}{3}$ of the meat. Add remaining ingredients. Replace lid and cook on LOW 8–10 hours until meat is tender.

Sagh Lamb   **8–10 hours LOW**

Indian casserole of lamb and spinach.

T–H

1 kg (2 lb) spinach, ¾ kg (1½ lb) boned lamb, 6 spring onions or shallots, 5 cm (2″) fresh ginger, 60 g (2 oz) clarified butter or ghee, 3 cardamom pods, 1 tbs ground coriander, 2 tsp turmeric, 1 green chilli, ¼ tsp paprika, 1 tbs mustard seed, 4 garlic cloves, 4 tbs warm water, ¼ tsp salt, 90 ml (3 fl oz) yoghurt.

Pre-heat slow crock on LOW during preparations.

Wash the spinach thoroughly and steep in cold water for several hours. Then, drain, chop finely, cover and set aside. Make an infusion with the crushed garlic cloves and warm water and steep for ½ an hour.

Cube the lamb and fry it in butter with the crushed cardamom and ¾ of the coriander until brown all over. Add the grated onions and stir-fry until golden. Mix in the ginger cut in thin strips (*julienne*), and cook for a minute. Sprinkle on the turmeric, remaining coriander and the green chilli cut in thin slivers. Stir-fry for another minute without burning. Then add paprika, stir-fry for a few seconds, scraping the bottom of the pan.

In another little pan, melt some more butter, just enough to grease the base and fry the mustard seeds until they begin to make a popping sound. Then add them to the meat. Add the garlic infusion and cook for a minute on a high heat. Stir in spinach, season with salt, moisten with yoghurt and cook covered for a minute. Shake pan several times, then mix well.

Then transfer ingredients to slow crock. Replace lid and cook for 8 hours on LOW until meat is tender and spinach soft.

An hour before serving switch to HIGH and add a cup of water, stir and allow it to cook with lid off. This helps in the process of blending flavours and absorbing the excess fat and juices. When a lot of moisture has dried off, replace the lid and switch to LOW and leave for about 20 minutes – this is the second stage of blending flavours.

Serve with rice.

Lamb Korma   **6–8 hours LOW**

1 kg (2 lb) boneless lamb, 1 large onion, 2 tbs tomato paste,
2 garlic cloves, 2 tbs butter, 125 ml (¼ pt) yoghurt, 60 ml (2
fl oz) stock or water, 1–2 tbs mild curry powder *or* 1 tsp each
of turmeric and cumin, 3 tsp ground coriander, 2 cloves, 2
cardamom seeds, ¼ tsp each of cinnamon and ginger, 1–3 tsp
chilli powder, 2 tbs flour. *Garnish* – blanched almonds.

Trim excess fat from meat and cut into small cubes. Peel
and chop onion and garlic. Melt butter and *sauté* first vegetables then meat lightly, and transfer to slow crock. Mix
spices together and stir with the flour into the hot butter.
Cook over a gentle heat for a minute or two, add tomato
paste and a little stock, and stir. Add remaining stock, stir
and transfer to slow crock. Mix all the ingredients together
well. Add salt and pepper.

Replace lid and cook on LOW for 6–8 hours until meat is
tender. To serve, stir in yoghurt and adjust seasoning.
Garnish with blanched almonds. Accompany with rice.

Lamb's Head Special   **12 hours/overnight LOW**

1 lamb's head with brain, 1 onion stuck with 3 cloves, 2
carrots, 1 parsnip, 1 small turnip, 1 leek, 125 g (4 oz) pearl
barley, water, 30 g (1 oz) each of butter and flour, 125 ml
(¼ pt) milk. *Garnish* – grilled bacon rolls, lemon chunks,
parsley.

Ask butcher to clean and split head, remove and reserve
brain. Before cooking, soak the head in cold salted water for
an hour or so. Then rinse it and place it in the slow crock.
Add seasoning and vegetables, with barley on the bottom.
Add water until ⅔ full. Replace lid and cook on LOW 12
hours until the meat comes away from the bones.

The brains should be soaked in cold salted water for half
an hour and then a little of the thin membrane removed. Tie

brain in small cloth and cook in the slow crock for half an hour at the end of the cooking period.

Remove brain, drain and chop it. Then make a sauce by the basic *roux* method, then add brains. Adjust seasoning and add a drop or two of lemon juice if wished. Stir in a little chopped parsley.

Remove lamb's head and discard bones. Chop up meat and arrange on a serving dish garnished with bacon rolls, vegetables and lemon chunks. Lift out barley with a perforated spoon and place around lamb. Serve sauce separately.

The remaining stock can be served as a soup on another occasion after being strained and cooled.

Eastern Risotto   **6–8 hours HIGH**

1 kg (2 lb) minced lamb, $\frac{1}{4}$ kg ($\frac{1}{2}$ lb) chick peas, 1 small onion, 375 ml ($\frac{3}{4}$ pt) chicken or veal stock, $\frac{3}{4}$ kg (1$\frac{1}{2}$ lb) cooked (or frozen) chopped spinach, 1 tsp each of turmeric and cumin, salt and pepper to taste, 2 tsp ground coriander, 2–4 cardamom pods, 1 carton of yoghurt, 2 tbs oil.

Soak chick peas overnight in cold water. Rinse, drain and place in base of slow crock. Add chicken stock to cover. Allow the frozen spinach to thaw.

Season minced lamb with salt, pepper, spices and minced garlic. Heat oil in a frying pan and *sauté* chopped onion until transparent then add seasoned meat and brown lightly. Transfer ingredients to slow crock. Replace lid and cook on HIGH 6–8 hours until peas are tender.

Half an hour before serving, mix the spinach and yoghurt into the slow crock. To serve, adjust seasoning.

Summer Chicken   **10 hours LOW**

1 boiling or roasting fowl (1$\frac{1}{2}$–2$\frac{1}{2}$ kg, 3–5 lb), giblets, 2 rashers of bacon, 1 medium onion stuck with 3 cloves, 1

garlic clove, 1 carrot, 1 small celery stalk, ¼ tsp each of marjoram and thyme, 1 bay leaf, salt and pepper, 1 litre (2 pt) chicken stock or water.

Place rashers of bacon in base of slow crock. Place chicken, giblets, chopped vegetables and herbs on top. Season. Pour in enough stock to cover ⅔ of chicken. Replace lid and cook on LOW for 10 hours until the chicken is very tender.

Transfer chicken to a large bowl and pour the contents of the slow crock over it. Cover and let stand for about 4 hours.

Remove chicken from stock, cover with foil and leave until next day.

Strain liquid into a saucepan and boil until reduced by half. Adjust seasoning then refrigerate for a day. Scrape off fat when jelly has formed.

To serve, cut chicken in slices and pile onto a serving dish. Spread chicken cream over (see page 231) and refrigerate until set. Then pour the sauce over and serve.

Chicken Pudding de Luxe   6 hours HIGH

375 g (¾ lb) boned chicken, 125 g (4 oz) ham in a piece, 125 g (4 oz) mushrooms, 2 tbs chopped parsley, salt and pepper, ½ tsp each of rosemary and tarragon, 1 tsp grated lemon peel, 60 ml (2 fl oz) chicken stock.
For pastry: ¼ kg (½ lb) flour, 90 g (3 oz) butter, 2 egg yolks, water to moisten. Metal foil, container, boiling water.

Switch slow crock to HIGH during preparations.

Grease a container that will fit inside your slow crock. Make a pastry lining and line the container. (See method, Chapter 8, page 172.) Reserve some for lid.

Cut chicken into bite-size chunks and ham into thin strips then place in layers in the bowl with other dry ingredients and seasoning. Pour on chicken stock then put a pastry lid

on top. Cover with metal foil. Place in slow crock. Surround
with boiling water. Replace lid and cook on HIGH for 6 hours
until chicken is tender.

Chicken in a Crock   10 hours LOW

1 chicken, 1½–2½ kg (3–5 lb).
Stuffing: 125 g (4 oz) each of bacon and fresh pork, 90 g
(3 oz) dry breadcrumbs, chicken liver, 2–3 garlic cloves, 2–3
tbs chopped parsley, ½ tsp of tarragon or chervil, pinch of
mixed spice, 2 eggs, salt and pepper, milk or water.
For stock: chicken giblets, neck and feet, 1 veal knuckle, 2
carrots, 2 leeks, 1 turnip, 1 potato, 1 onion stuck with 2
cloves, *bouquet garni*, a few greens if available, pepper, 1–1½
litres (2–3 pt) water.

Stage one: Make the stock overnight. Combine all the
stock ingredients in the slow crock and add water to cover.
Replace lid and cook on LOW for 10–12 hours. Then strain
off liquid. Discard vegetables and giblets. Rinse out slow
crock.

Stage two: Make the stuffing (this can be done the night
before and refrigerated if wished) and stuff the bird. Mince
the bacon and pork, chicken liver and garlic. Moisten the
breadcrumbs with a drop of milk and combine with the
minced meats. Add remaining seasoning and herbs and stir
in the beaten eggs. Adjust seasoning. Stuff bird and secure
with string.

Stage three: Place chicken in slow crock and add reserved
stock to cover ⅔ of chicken. Replace lid and cook on LOW for
10 hours until chicken is tender and stuffing is cooked.

To serve, heat up stock and serve as a soup course. Serve
chicken hot or cold.

Chicken Cream

2–3 tbs jellied stock, 2–3 tbs double cream, about 90 g (3 oz) chicken fragments from carcass, 1 tsp grated orange peel.

Blend or mix all these ingredients together and spread over the dish of sliced chicken before refrigerating (see page 229).

Sauce: 30 g (1 oz) each of flour and butter, ½ litre (1 pt) jellied stock, 125 ml (¼ pt) cream, 2 egg yolks, 2–3 tbs brown sherry or orange liqueur, salt and pepper, squeeze of lemon juice, 1 tsp grated orange peel.

Melt butter, add flour, cook for 2 minutes. Add jellied stock, then cream. Add orange peel. Let sauce boil and thicken gently. Beat egg yolks and add a ladle of sauce to them, mix and return to the pan. Stir alcohol and lemon juice. When cool and thick pour over chicken and mousse.

Basic Method for Chicken Galantine

1½ kg (3 lb) boiling fowl.

Stock: 1 chicken carcass, 1 calf's foot or pig's trotters, ¼ kg (½ lb) veal or ham bones, 1 onion stuck with 2 cloves, 1 carrot, *bouquet garni*, ¼ litre (½ pt) white wine, ½ litre (1 pt) water, 4 chicken stock cubes, 1 bay leaf, 6 peppercorns.

Stuffing: 375 g (¾ lb) each of pork fat and lean meat (pork, veal, ham or a combination), 125 g (¼ lb) streaky bacon, 1 egg, salt and pepper, 1 tsp each of thyme and parsley, dash of Worcestershire sauce, generous pinch of nutmeg or ground mace.

Optional ingredients (*for a salpicon – additional ingredients cut up small and bound with a sauce*): 125 g (4 oz) each of cooked tongue and ham (or pork), fat, 1 chicken liver, 90 ml (2 fl oz) sherry or brandy, small tin of truffles, 30 g (1 oz) blanched pistachio nuts.

Stage 1: boning the chicken – choose a boiling fowl as

flavour is very important in this dish. Battery chickens are often so disappointing and are just not suitable.

You will need a very sharp knife for scraping the flesh from the bone.

Cut flesh from neck to tail down the backbone and loosen the flesh away from the ribs, being careful not to tear the skin. You'll be able to push some of the flesh away with the fingers. Then do each wing as follows: cut off the wing at the 2nd point and remove the flesh by pulling it off like a glove. The legs are more difficult although the principle is the same as that of the wings. Pull the muscle and skin off gradually and turn inside out – again like a glove. Use a knife to help loosen the flesh. Then separate the membrane under the body without breaking it and you should have the flesh and skin in one piece and a skeleton.

Lay the meat skin side down on a cloth and sprinkle with salt and pepper. Any extra bits of flesh from the carcass should be laid over areas where there is just skin or only a thin layer of flesh. Store the meat in a cool place, or refrigerate, covered, until needed.

Make the stock. Dissolve stock cubes in hot water and add to slow crock with other ingredients for stock. Replace lid and cook on LOW for 10–12 hours or overnight. Strain and reserve for next stage of recipe.

Stage 2: stuffing, rolling and cooking the chicken. Make the stuffing. With equal parts of lean and fat meats – $\frac{1}{4}$ kg ($\frac{1}{2}$ lb) of stuffing per $\frac{1}{2}$ kg (1 lb) of chicken. Chop or mince all the ingredients finely, bind with the egg and season to taste with salt and pepper. Add herbs and spices.

The optional *salpicon* should also be chopped or minced (separately) but then marinated in the brandy or sherry which can therefore be done overnight.

These two separate lots of stuffing can then either remain separate or be mixed together. Lay the chicken flat out on a board and spread the stuffing over in alternate layers or as one single mixture.

Then fold over the edges of the chicken and sew it up into a chicken-like shape. Wrap this in muslin or cheesecloth and tie securely. Place in slow crock and pour strained stock over until it nearly covers the bundle. Replace lid and cook on LOW 10 hours. Then transfer chicken and stock to a large bowl and allow to cool. When cool, squeeze out most of the liquid and leave it overnight pressed down with weights on a board. Neither squeeze out too much liquid nor use too heavy a weight as the dish is meant to be succulent.

Strain the stock and adjust the seasoning with a little lemon juice or sherry. Let it set, if need be with the help of gelatine dissolved in a little warm water. Skim off the fat when set. If the stock needs clarifying do so before adding gelatine and leaving to set (see method, Chapter 4, page 36).

Stage 3: Next day, unwrap the chicken and set it on a rack over a dish. Melt some of the stock jelly and brush the chicken liberally with it. Allow this layer to set and then decorate the chicken if wished with small pieces of colourful salad ingredients or chopped herbs (carrot slivers, mint, parsley, chives, celery curls) and 'glue' these on with another layer of melted jelly. After this has set, transfer the whole chicken to a serving dish and surround with chopped jelly and jelly mixed with mayonnaise in the proportion of 3 tbs jelly to 4 tbs mayonnaise.

Galantine of Poultry and Game (or Veal)   10 hours LOW

This is a cold dish of chicken, turkey, game or veal which has been boned, stuffed and then tied in muslin or cheesecloth and simmered in a stock until cooked. It is not a difficult dish although it takes a long time to prepare and has to be done a day or so in advance, so the ingredients can mature together. The dish is served with its own jelly.

The timetable is as follows:
Day 1   Bone the meat and make the stock, using carcass.
Day 2   Stuff and roll the meat and cook in stock.

Let stock gel, press meat and allow to mature.
Day 3   Glaze the meat with some of the stock, decorate the
dish, serve with chopped jelly and mayonnaise.

Chicken Mousse   **10 hours LOW**

1½ kg (3 lb) boiling fowl, 1 calf's foot or pig's trotters, 1
carrot, 1 onion, 2 garlic cloves, a strip of lemon peel, 6 bacon
rinds, ¼ litre (½ pt) thick cream, 2 egg whites, 2 tbs brandy,
1 bay leaf, pinch of thyme, chopped parsley, salt and pepper,
water, chicken giblets, 1 tbs butter, gelatine, mayonnaise,
fennel, celery.

Place the boiling fowl in the slow crock with the calf's
foot or pig's trotters, vegetables, lemon rind, bacon, seasoning, herbs and giblets (except chicken liver) and pour in
water until it covers about ⅔ of the bird. Replace lid and
cook on LOW for 10 hours until tender.

When the chicken is ready remove it from the slow crock,
replace the lid and let the other ingredients go on cooking.
Skin the chicken and remove all flesh from the bones. Chop
then pound flesh in a mortar with garlic and seasoning to
taste, add a teaspoon or so of chopped parsley. Cook chicken
liver in a little butter and then add brandy to it and set
alight. Add this to the chicken mixture and pound again
until smooth. Stir in 125 ml (¼ pt) strained stock and the
whipped cream. Let this stand for an hour before adding the
stiffly beaten egg whites. Store overnight in refrigerator.

Meanwhile, strain stock and allow it to cool and set. Skim
the fat off and if necessary add gelatine to help stock set.

To serve, pile the chicken mixture onto a shallow dish and
place chunks of jellied stock around the edge. Serve with
mayonnaise that has been seasoned with bits of celery and
fennel.

Duck in Jelly   **10 hours LOW**

1 duckling, a dozen each of button mushrooms and onions,
4 young turnips, *bouquet garni* (bay leaf, parsley, thyme,
celery), ¼ litre (½ pt) veal or chicken stock, 6 tbs butter, 8 tbs
white wine, salt and pepper, 2 tbs gelatine, 12 bacon rinds.
Garnish – green salad.

Clean bird and then brown in butter until golden on all
sides. Season generously and place in slow crock. Pour on
wine and stock and add *bouquet garni*.

Chop bacon rinds into small pieces and heat in pan until
fat melts. Add parboiled turnips and *sauté* until golden
brown. Combine bacon, turnips, mushrooms and onions
and add to slow crock. Replace lid and cook on LOW for 10
hours until duck and vegetables are tender.

Transfer duck to a flat-bottomed bowl and surround it
with the vegetables and bacon rinds. Strain stock into a
separate bowl and skim fat off with absorbent paper towels.
Dissolve gelatine in a little cold water and stir it into stock
then pour it over duck. Cover and allow to set for about half
a day. Serve with a green salad.

Danish Roast Pork   **6–8 hours HIGH**

A Danish way of cooking marinated pork.

1½–2½ kg (3–5 lb) loin of pork, 2 large onions, 2 carrots, 2
celery stalks, 5 bay leaves, 8 peppercorns, dry red wine, 90 g
(3 oz) butter, salt. *For gravy* – sliced mushrooms and cream.

Trim excess fat from meat. Place in a large earthenware
bowl. Place sliced vegetables, herbs and seasoning around.
Pour on red wine to cover. Refrigerate for a day. Then,
drain meat and wipe dry. Strain marinade and reserve.

Melt butter and brown pork all over. Drain meat and
transfer to slow crock, then add enough of the marinade to

cover the base of the slow crock in 2½ cm (1″) of liquid.
Replace lid and cook on HIGH for 6–8 hours until meat is
very tender. When cooked, transfer to a serving dish, slice
and keep warm. Make a gravy from the liquid in the slow
crock by adding sliced *sautéed* mushrooms and cream.

Danish Braised Pork   **8–10 hours LOW**

A Danish version of braised pork with apples and prunes.

2 pork fillets each weighing approx. ¾ kg (1½ lb), 1 large
cooking apple, 125 g (4 oz) pitted prunes, 90 g (3 oz) butter,
15 g (½ oz) flour, 60 ml (2½ fl oz) water, milk or cream, approx.
125 ml (¼ pt) water, salt and pepper.

Trim fat and sinews from meat. Cut a long pocket in
each for stuffing. Mince apple and chop prunes and fill the
pockets with the mixture. Secure with string or skewer.

Dredge meat in lightly seasoned flour. Melt butter in a
pan and brown meat on all sides. Transfer to slow crock and
add water. Replace lid and cook on LOW for 8–10 hours until
meat is tender.

To serve, remove meat and keep warm. Add water, milk
or cream depending on how rich and thick you want the
gravy. Switch to HIGH setting and allow gravy to become
smooth and thick. Then pour gravy over meat. Accompany
dish with boiled potatoes and green vegetables.

Pork au Lait   **10 hours LOW**

¾ kg (1½ lb) loin of pork or boned leg, ¼ litre (½ pt) milk, 40 g
(1½ oz) butter, 60 g (2 oz) ham, salt and pepper, 1 onion, 1
garlic clove, pinch of fennel or marjoram, 3–4 coriander
seeds.

Remove the rind from pork. Roll and tie with the garlic,

coriander and a pinch of herbs inside. Chop the onion and ham. Melt the butter in a frying pan and brown the onion and ham, then add the meat seasoned with salt and pepper.

Transfer these ingredients to the slow crock with the onion and ham on the base. Heat the milk to boiling in a saucepan and pour over the meat. Replace lid and cook on LOW for 10 hours until tender.

Take lid off and switch to HIGH, allowing the liquid to reduce until fairly thick. To serve, transfer meat to a serving dish and pour the sauce over it with all the chopped ingredients.

This dish can be eaten hot or cold.

Cold Pork with Jelly   10–12 hours LOW

1½–2½ kg (3–5 lb) boned loin of pork with skin removed, small tin of truffles, salt and pepper, 2 garlic cloves, 125 ml (¼ pt) each of wine and water.

Ask the butcher to give you the skin and bones he removes from the loin as these will be used in the stock for the dish.

Lay the meat on a board, boned side up, and season generously with salt and pepper, spike with garlic and truffles. Roll and tie the meat so that it fits into your slow crock. Place in slow crock. Surround it with the bones and rind. Add juice from truffle tin, wine and water, or stock. Replace lid and cook on LOW for 10–12 hours until meat is tender.

When cooked, remove meat and place it in a deep bowl then strain the liquid over it. Allow to cool and set. Next day, remove fat from surface and reserve it to use as a delicious spread for bread. Serve the pork sliced surrounded with the chopped jelly.

Canadian Glazed Bacon   **10–12 hours LOW**

1½–2½ kg (3–5 lb) sweet pickled back bacon piece, ½–¾ litre
(1–1½ pt) apple juice.

Place bacon in slow crock and pour apple juice onto it.
Replace lid and cook on LOW until tender, 10–12 hours.
Then remove bacon from slow crock and bake in the oven
at 204°C (400°F), Gas Mark 6, for half an hour in a ham
glaze (see page 241). Remove from oven and baste bacon
as the glaze cools and hardens.

Slice and serve either hot or cold.

Parsley Ham   **10–12 hours LOW**

1½–2½ kg (3–5 lb) piece of gammon, 1 calf's foot or 2 pig's
trotters, veal knuckle, 8 peppercorns, *bouquet garni*, salt and
pepper, ½ litre (1 pt) dry white wine, 6 tbs chopped parsley,
1 tbs wine vinegar.

Cut gammon into chunks and place in slow crock with
calf's foot or pig's trotters, veal knuckle, peppercorns and
herbs. Pour on white wine. Replace lid and cook 10–12
hours on LOW until gammon is cooked.

Then, strain off liquid into a bowl and adjust seasoning.
Add vinegar and allow to cool.

Use calf's foot or pig's trotters and knuckle to make a
brawn (see page 239).

Pound the ham in a large bowl. Add the parsley to the
liquid and then pour it over the ham and mix well. Leave to
set and serve in slices.

Chinese Braised Pork   **8–10 hours LOW**

1 kg (2 lb) boned cubed pork, 2–4 tbs fat, 6 tbs soy sauce,
3 tbs sake (rice wine) or dry sherry, 6 tbs water, 1 tsp

chopped ginger, 1 garlic clove, generous pinch of brown sugar, black pepper, a little salt.

Heat fat in frying pan and *sauté* pork until brown. Transfer to slow crock. Combine soy sauce, sake (or sherry), water, ginger, crushed garlic, sugar and pepper to taste and pour over meat. Replace lid and cook on LOW for 8–10 hours until tender.

This dish is best served with spinach cooked in oil.

Cold Hong Kong Sui   8–10 hours LOW

Cold, red-cooked pork.
1½ kg (3 lb) leg of pork, 2 pig's trotters, 4 tbs soy sauce, 2 tbs sugar, 1 cinnamon stick, 1 tsp salt, 1 chicken stock cube, 4 tbs sherry, 1½ tbs gelatine powder, 1 tbs chopped chives, ½ litre (1 pt) water.

Blanch pork and trotters by placing in a saucepan of cold water and bringing to boil, then drain and transfer to slow crock. Add sugar, soy sauce, cinnamon, fresh water and salt. Replace lid and cook on LOW for 8–10 hours until tender.

Then, half an hour before end of cooking time add sherry, crumbled chicken stock cube and gelatine dissolved in a little cold water. When cooked, remove pork and trotters to a large bowl and pour this liquid over them. Allow to cool and then refrigerate for a few hours until the jelly has set. Remove fat from the surface. Slice the meat thinly and place on a serving dish around the trotters. Spread the jelly over the trotters and garnish with chopped chives.

Brawn   10–12 hours LOW

½ or 1 pig's head, calf's foot or pig's trotter, veal knuckle, *bouquet garni*, 2 carrots, 2 onions stuck with 2 cloves, blade of mace, 6 peppercorns, 12 allspice, 2 hard-boiled eggs. *Brine*: ¼ kg (½ lb) salt to 2 litres (4 pt) water.

Wash and clean head thoroughly and steep in brine overnight.

Next day, rinse head and place in slow crock with ingredients (except eggs). Fill slow crock ⅔ with cold water. Replace lid and cook on LOW for 10–12 hours, until the meat leaves the bones easily.

Then, remove head and cut out tongue and remove bones. Return bones to slow crock, switch to HIGH setting and leave the lid off. Allow the liquid to reduce by a third.

Meanwhile, skin the tongue and slice or dice it. Chop meat from head and cut into large dice, season with salt and pepper. Cut meat from calf's foot or pig's trotter, and knuckle.

Line a large bowl with hard-boiled egg slices and lay tongue pieces on top. Then add chopped meat. Season to taste. Strain the liquid from the slow crock into the bowl until it has covered the meat. Allow to cool and set. To serve, garnish with fresh bay leaves and rosemary.

Pork and Herb Pâté   4 hours HIGH

½ kg (1 lb) pork throat meat, 125 g (4 oz) pig's liver, 90 g (3 oz) each of streaky bacon and gammon, 375 g (¾ lb) cooked chopped spinach, 1 medium onion, 1 large garlic clove, 1 egg. *Options* for seasoning – rosemary, thyme, basil, marjoram, nutmeg, salt and pepper. Metal foil, container, boiling water.

Switch slow crock to HIGH during preparations.

Mince or chop meat and bacon, onion, garlic and spinach. Mix everything together with seasoning to taste. Put mixture into a greased bowl or tin that will fit into your slow crock. Cover with foil. Place container in slow crock and pour boiling water around. Replace lid and cook on HIGH for 4 hours until *pâté* is firm.

Then, remove container from slow crock and press down with weights to give pâté a good shape.

Glaze for Ham

¼ kg (½ lb) brown sugar, 1 tsp dry mustard, 1 tbs corn syrup, 1 tbs flour, 90 ml (3 fl oz) vinegar.

Mix ingredients together and spread over top of ham. Bake in the oven (see page 238) and then baste while the glaze cools and hardens.

GLOSSARY OF COOKING
TERMS USED

Bain-marie   a container of hot water in which dishes of food (eg sauces) can be placed to keep them hot. The *bain-marie* is kept at an even temperature usually by electricity, but any dish placed inside another containing water which is kept hot (for example, in an oven) can be used as a *bain-marie*.

Blanch   There are two methods of blanching. To remove skins from tomatoes, fruit or nuts for instance, food is dipped into boiling water for a minute or so and then plunged into cold water. In the second method the food is placed in cold water which is then brought to the boil and poured away. The food is then drained and put into cold water again. This method is most often used for offal.

Bouquet garni   a small bunch of herbs tied together with string and used for flavouring soups, stews, stocks and other savoury dishes. It is usually made up of a bay leaf, a sprig of parsley and a sprig of thyme, and is removed at the end of the cooking period. Alternatively, dried herbs may be used tied in a muslin bag.

Braise   Food is first browned in fat then cooked in a covered casserole in a small amount of liquid.

Degrease   to remove accumulated fat or oil from the surface of liquids.

Marinade   a liquid mixture, often containing wine or other alcohol, in which food is steeped before cooking in order to tenderize or give flavour.

Mirepoix   a mixture of chopped vegetables, herbs and bacon used to flavour meat and poultry during cooking.

Parboil   to boil an ingredient for part of the cooking time only, then finish cooking it by some other method.

Purée   to render solid food to a pulp by mincing, sieving or liquidizing, eg for a soup, sauce or mash.

Reduce   to boil down a liquid, reducing it in quantity and concentrating its taste.

Roux   a mixture of melted fat in which flour is cooked, and which forms the basis of most sauces.

Sauté   to cook or brown food in hot shallow fat.

INTERNATIONAL CONVERSION TABLES

The weights and measures used throughout this book are based on British Imperial standards and metric. However, the following tables show you how to convert the various weights and measures simply.

International Measures

Measure	U.K.	Australia	New Zealand	Canada	U.S.A.
1 pint	20 *fl oz*	20 *fl oz*	20 *fl oz*	20 *fl oz*	16 *fl oz*
1 cup	10 *fl oz*	8 *fl oz*	8 *fl oz*	8 *fl oz*	8 *fl oz*
1 tablespoon	$\frac{5}{8}$ *fl oz*	$\frac{1}{2}$ *fl oz*	$\frac{1}{2}$ *fl oz*	$\frac{1}{2}$ *fl oz*	$\frac{1}{2}$ *fl oz*
1 dessertspoon	$\frac{2}{5}$ *fl oz*	no official measure			
1 teaspoon	$\frac{1}{6}$ *fl oz*	$\frac{1}{8}$ *fl oz*	$\frac{1}{6}$ *fl oz*	$\frac{1}{6}$ *fl oz*	$\frac{1}{8}$ *fl oz*
1 gill	5 *fl oz*	—	—	—	—

Conversion of fluid ounces to metric

1 *fl oz*	= 2·84 *ml*
35 *fl oz* (approx 1$\frac{3}{4}$ Imperial pints)	= 1 litre (1000 *ml* or 10 *decilitres*)
1 Imperial pint (20 *fl oz*)	= approx 600 *ml* (6 *dl*)
$\frac{1}{2}$ Imperial pint (10 *fl oz*)	= 300 *ml* (3 *dl*)
$\frac{1}{4}$ Imperial pint (5 *fl oz*)	= 150 *ml* (1$\frac{1}{2}$ *dl*)
4 tablespoons (2$\frac{1}{2}$ *fl oz*)	= 70 *ml* (7 *cl*)
2 tablespoons (1$\frac{1}{4}$ *fl oz*)	= 35 *ml* (3$\frac{1}{2}$ *cl*)
1 tablespoon ($\frac{5}{8}$ *fl oz*)	= 18 *ml* (2 *cl*)
1 dessertspoon ($\frac{2}{5}$ *fl oz*)	= 12 *ml*
1 teaspoon ($\frac{1}{6}$ *fl oz*)	= 6 *ml*

(All the above metric equivalents are approximate)

Conversion of solid weights to metric

2 *lb* 3 *oz* = 1 *kg* (*kilogramme*)
1 *lb*   = 453 *g* (*grammes*)
12 *oz*   = 339 *g*
8 *oz*   = 225 *g*
4 *oz*   = 113 *g*
2 *oz*   = 56 *g*
1 *oz*   = 28 *g*

U.S. Equivalents

In converting American recipes for metric or Imperial use, note that the U.S. pint is 16 *fl oz* (454·6 *ml*) against the Imperial pint of 20 *fl oz* (568·3 *ml*). Americans tend to use cups (8 *fl oz*) for measuring quantities of solids, like flour, beans, raisins, even chopped vegetables. If you own a number of American recipe books, invest in a U.S. cup measure as well.

Oven temperatures

Description	Electric Setting	Gas Mark
Very cool	225°F (110°C)	$\frac{1}{4}$
	250°F (130°C)	$\frac{1}{2}$
Cool	275°F (140°C)	1
	300°F (150°C)	2
Very moderate	325°F (170°C)	3
Moderate	350°F (180°C)	4
Moderately or	375°F (190°C)	5
fairly hot	400°F (200°C)	6
Hot	425°F (220°C)	7
	450°F (230°C)	8
Very hot	475°F (240°C)	9

These temperatures are only an approximate guide as all ovens vary slightly, according to the make and country of manufacture.

INDEX